Contents

About Island Press

Island Press is the only nonprofit organization in the United States whose principal purpose is the publication of books on environmental issues and natural resource management. We provide solutions-oriented information to professionals, public officials, business and community leaders, and concerned citizens who are shaping responses to environmental problems.

In 1994, Island Press celebrated its tenth anniversary as the leading provider of timely and practical books that take a multidisciplinary approach to critical environmental concerns. Our growing list of titles reflects our commitment to bringing the best of an expanding body of literature to the environmental community throughout North America and the world.

Support for Island Press is provided by Apple Computer, Inc., The Bullitt Foundation, The Geraldine R. Dodge Foundation, The Energy Foundation, The Ford Foundation, The W. Alton Jones Foundation, The Lyndhurst Foundation, The John D. and Catherine T. MacArthur Foundation, The Andrew W. Mellon Foundation, The Joyce Mertz-Gilmore Foundation, The National Fish and Wildlife Foundation, The Pew Charitable Trusts, The Pew Global Stewardship Initiative, The Rockefeller Philanthropic Collaborative, Inc., and individual donors.

The Corps and the Shore

To Orrin H. Pilkey, Sr. (1905-1994)
Engineer, Father, and Friend

Orrin H. Pilkey and
Katharine L. Dixon

The
Corps
and the
Shore

ISLAND PRESS
Washington, D.C. / Covelo, California

ISLAND PRESS is a trademark of The Center for Resource Economics.

Library of Congress Cataloging in Publication Data

Pilkey, Orrin H., 1934–
 The Corps and the shore / by Orrin H. Pilkey and Katharine L. Dixon.
  p.   cm.
 Includes bibliographical references and index.
 ISBN 1-55963-438-3 (cloth)
  1. Coastal engineering—United States—Case studies.   2. United
States. Army. Corps of Engineers—Public relations—Case studies.
3. Fallacies (Logic)—Case studies.   4. Errors, Scientific—Case
studies.   I. Title.
TC223.P55   1996
353.0086—dc20
                                                            96-803
                                                            CIP

Printed on recycled, acid-free paper ∞

Manufactured in the United States of America

10 9 8 7 6 5 4 3 2

Acknowledgments

Our heartfelt thanks to the featured "heroes" of our book: Joe Kelley of Maine, Robert Morton of Texas, Gered Lennon of South Carolina, Paul Knuth of Pennsylvania, and Stan Riggs of North Carolina. They are all true heroes in their devotion to the health of their respective state coasts and to furthering our scientific knowledge of coastal processes. Behind the scenes, Evelyn Anderson, devoted naturalist of Presque Isle, was a more than generous source of information, fact checking, and encouragement. Vicki Zick of Folly Beach, South Carolina, has earned not only our gratitude, but also our admiration for her outspoken devotion to her community. Thanks to A.W. Sam Smith, Australian coastal engineer, and Victor Baker, riverine geomorphologist, for their inspiration and their work at the forefront of sensible "science of sand movement."

U.S. Army Corps of Engineers personnel from the national to the district level tirelessly answered many questions. Marty Reuss, Corps historian and invaluable source of insight, reviewed several chapters and helped us focus our criticisms (even though it meant agreeing to disagree on several occasions). U.S. Fish and Wildlife refuge manager B.D. King filled in the gaps at Sargent Beach. We have been especially impressed by the enthusiastic willingness to assist from both the Corps and the National Park Service public affairs personnel; on more than one occasion, they went out of their way to track down information promptly. Sadly, we cannot thank by name a number of individuals within state and federal agencies who have asked to remain anonymous for political reasons.

There are also many, many other individuals to whom we are grateful, including: Brent Blackwelder, long-time Tombigbee activist; Cory Dean, outstanding journalist and editorial advisor; Buford Mabry, South Carolina attorney; Theresa Woody, guardian of the waters of south Florida; Kathleen Van Velsor, Pacific Coast activist; and Beth Millemann and Melissa Sagun of the Coast Alliance, Dery Bennett of the American Littoral Society, and Cindy Zipf of Clean Ocean Action, who devote themselves professionally and personally to protecting beaches for future generations. Jane Bullock and Lafe Myers offered thoughtful editorial support.

We'd especially like to thank our colleagues at Duke University: Amber Taylor, our tireless draftsperson; and geologists David Bush, Rob

Thieler, Rob Young, and Bill Neal, who edited, encouraged, discussed, and helped keep the peace in tense moments. Special thanks to our editors, Monte Basgall of Duke University News Service and Barbara Dean and Barbara Youngblood of Island Press, who transformed scientific jargon and convoluted phrases into respectable prose.

Finally, our gratitude to our respective spouses, Sharlene Pilkey and Walter Wheeler, for their patience and enlivening support. Sharlene, who was instrumental in background research and text composition, was the original co-author with Orrin. Katharine became co-author to save the Pilkey marriage.

The Beach: Resilient, Dynamic, Threatened

The beach is so solidly a part of American culture that the connotation overwhelms definition. Each one of us carries a different mental image of "the beach." To some, it is an unending strip of white sand, with waves gently lapping and breezes stirring the moisture-laden air. To many, it is colorful umbrellas, volleyball games, and surfing. To others, it is miniature golf, water slides, dancing, drinking, and loud beach music. To a very few, it is a front yard.

Whatever the viewpoint, all agree that beaches are worth preserving. But how and for what purpose? To beachfront dwellers, the beach is what protects their buildings, and when it no longer adequately serves that purpose, it should be replaced with a wall or a new beach. The coastal dweller dreads erosion, watching fearfully and resentfully as the beach "washes away" and waves lap closer and closer to the front stoop. Many well-meaning beachfront property owners have rushed to put up sand fencing and plant dune grasses in an effort to "save" the beach.

But to a coastal scientist, buildings, not beaches, are ephemeral in the shoreline environment. The coastal scientist understands that a beach needs saving only when something, like a house, stands in the way of its natural movements in response to a rising sea level and the forces of weather (Photo A).

Standing at the forefront of the struggle between people and the sea is the U.S. Army Corps of Engineers. With thirteen divisions and thirty-eight districts, the Corps is virtually everyone's neighbor (Figures A and B). This organization of engineers builds seawalls, pumps up beaches, dredges inlets, stabilizes inlets with long rock jetties, gives permission to others to do any of these activities, and more. Individual states retain some control over the destiny of their beaches, but the Corps controls federal moneys. Strange but true, the future of the American shoreline is not in the hands of a natural resource agency but in the hands of an agency run by the U.S. Army.

This book presents a concerned scientist's view of the impacts of the Corps' activities on American open-ocean beaches. We are concerned

Photo A. The Morris Island Lighthouse stands 400 yards offshore as a symbol of the U.S. shoreline erosion dilemma. The lighthouse was on the beach in World War II. A wide and healthy beach remains on Morris Island behind the lighthouse illustrating that shoreline retreat doesn't change the beach, only its position in space. (Photo by Dinesh Sharma)

with the scientific quality of the Corps of Engineers' design efforts, how this agency interacts with scientists and environmentalists, and how its various divisions and districts present their projects on a local level.

A generalized difference between scientists and engineers, at least in coastal studies, is that scientists are trained to observe natural systems and engineers are trained to manipulate them. Victor Baker, geologist at the University of Arizona, compares the disparate approaches of engineering and science as "the practical problem-solving approach of engineering to the academic puzzle-solving of science." In many cases, including those discussed in the pages to come, a society in search of solutions chooses the seemingly straightforward "can do" nature of engineering over the questioning, theoretical approach of science. Scientific criticism is often dismissed as nit-picking. But science, which studies the way nature works, is the necessary underpinning of engineering. It is geology that determines where and how bridges, dams, and other great works of engineering should be located. In coastal engineering, time and time again, however, scientific uncertainty about

Figure A. The U.S. Army Corps of Engineers is divided into thirteen divisions and thirty eight districts for administrative purposes.

Figure B. Corps Atlantic and Gulf of Mexico divisions and districts. Also shown are the locations of the major projects discussed in the book.

nature, which is perhaps at its height at the coast, is ignored. And, time and again, it is natural events about which there can be no certainty that undo even exemplary feats of engineering.

Coastal engineering is different from most other forms of civil engineering. It is easier to discern the failure of a bridge, a water tank, or a high-rise building than the failure of a beach project. The general public may not make the connection between a sudden increase in the erosion rate of a beach and construction of a nearby jetty. In some cases, the effects of human intervention take a long time to become apparent; at the ocean entrance to Charleston Harbor, South Carolina, and at Camp Ellis, Maine, beach erosion caused by jetties took two decades or more to ensue. Artificially replenished beaches that disappear more rapidly than anticipated by the design engineers are frequently said to have been damaged by an unusually strong or unexpected storm. The public would not accept the "unusually strong storm" excuse for a failed bridge, fallen water tank, or crumbled high-rise building, but it seems to work for beaches.

In the following chapters, we tell the story of the Corps at the beach on the local level. Through a series of case studies from the U.S. Atlantic, Great Lakes, and Gulf of Mexico coasts, we examine several Corps districts' interactions with local citizens and scientists. We also discuss beach replenishment and the mathematical models that increasingly serve as underpinning for replenishment design. In each case, we criticize the Corps' use of science but do not attempt an exhaustive scientific critique of their work. Rather, we are interested in revealing the scientific and engineering fallacies that pervade the statements the districts make to the public and through the media. We also describe the dismissive way that district engineers treat local scientists.

Many of our arguments are controversial. If past experience is a good guide, they may unfortunately be taken by the Corps as attacks rather than criticism, but our goal is to spur public debate toward improved coastal management. To this end, the final chapter discusses several recommendations that we believe would help the Corps in its current role as steward of the nation's beaches.

ONE

America and the Beach

The American shoreline has a long history of development. New Jersey's was the first U.S. ocean beach to be developed extensively. The first advertisement for beachfront tourist accommodations appeared in 1802 in the *Philadelphia Aurora*, proclaiming the beauty of the shore and quality of the lodging in Cape May, New Jersey. The elaborate ad, foreshadowing those for modern beach resorts, claimed "extensive house room," though the lodging actually consisted of a single multiple-occupancy room; a curtain down the center separated men on one side from women on the other.

Many of the affluent of Philadelphia and New York promenaded the boardwalks of Atlantic City and Ocean City, New Jersey. The train from New York City unloaded happy swimmers directly onto the beach at Seabright; seven presidents visited Long Branch, New Jersey.

But time and tide quickly caught up with the houses and hotels along the Jersey Shore, and people began to build seawalls and groins (walls perpendicular to the beach) to protect them. Soon shoreline erosion became serious enough that whole communities had to pitch in to build ever larger and grander walls. Groins got larger too, and eventually one could spot the boundaries of individual New Jersey towns by the presence of extra large groins designed to capture the last grain of sand before it flowed down the beach to the next town. These became known as "spite groins."

What became apparent after a century of shoreline armoring was that those hard stabilization structures worked modestly well to save buildings but, sooner or later, destroyed the beach—the very reason the buildings were there to begin with. "Newjerseyization" eventually became the term used for the process of stemming erosion at the price of the beach.

The problem of threatened buildings and beaches became even more

1

critical after World War II as the American rush to the beach began in earnest. Houses of the wealthy began to crowd the shores of Malibu, Miami, and other now-famous seaside resorts. A greater number of deep inlets was needed to allow passage of the boats belonging to the home-owners; extensive jettying and dredging of inlets commenced. As a result, the flow of sand along these shoreline reaches was interrupted. Houses and motels became fixed points by which to measure the changes in the shoreline caused by the inlets held in place by engineering structures.

The federal government became involved in coastal management incrementally. As Rutherford Platt and his co-authors point out in *Coastal Erosion: Has Retreat Sounded?*, new policies and programs governing coastal management have been, primarily, disaster driven. Hurricanes, severe winter storms, and chronic erosion problems in popular, heavily populated coastal communities have caught national, particularly congressional, attention. Unfortunately, the response has been a piecemeal approach to coastal management. According to Platt, "Over the past 60 years the federal government has lurched from one approach to another, according to the conventional wisdom of the moment and the whims of the congressional appropriation process." At the federal level alone, various departments and their agencies, including the Corps (Department of the Army); the National Oceanic and Atmospheric Administration (NOAA) within the Department of Commerce; the National Park Service and the U.S. Fish and Wildlife Service, both within the Department of the Interior; the Federal Highway Administration (Department of Transportation); to name only several, along with the Federal Emergency Management Agency and numerous international, national, and regional commissions, have degrees of coastal jurisdiction. There are more at the state and local levels. Without a comprehensive approach to provide guidance, these departments, agencies, commissions, and other governing bodies apply conflicting philosophies to coastal management that often run afoul of one another.

The Corps initially resisted involvement in the coastal engineering activities for which it is known today. Development and beach erosion in New Jersey, particularly in Cape May and Long Branch, brought the agency to the shore in a broader role than it had been willing to take before. Involved it became, and it has arguably been one of the most influential federal managers of the coast ever since.

In the early days of coastal management, erosion was assumed to mean that beaches and barrier islands were washing away. To combat a perceived land-loss problem on North Carolina's Outer Banks, the federal government started construction in the 1930s of a long dune extending from the Virginia–North Carolina line south to Ocracoke, North Carolina. By 1940, the Civilian Conservation Corps (CCC) had constructed 115 miles of high dune planted with nearly 142 million square feet of dune grasses and over 600 miles of sand fencing. It was a major construction project that happily employed hundreds of young Depression-era workers. Unhappily, the dune was not only not needed, it actually increased the rate of the shoreline erosion it was intended to halt.

In addition to battling erosion, federal involvement at the coast included setting aside parks and wildlife refuges. Within the national park system, the first "national seashore" was authorized by Congress in the 1930s to be established at Cape Hatteras, North Carolina. The system expanded with the addition of Cape Cod, Massachusetts, in 1961, and Padre Island, Texas, in 1962; by 1993 it included ten areas and 592,000 on the Atlantic, Gulf of Mexico, and Pacific coasts. By the late 1960s the National Park Service (NPS), steward of the national seashores, was confronted with the problem of retreating shorelines. Should national seashores be lined with seawalls? The NPS decided no. In 1972 it made a landmark decision with far-reaching consequences. Rather than try and halt shoreline erosion, the Park Service took a brave step outside the bounds of accepted coastal management practice and instituted a policy that, as one official put it, "let nature rip at the shoreline."

The decision to retreat was based on the research discovery by botanist Paul Godfrey and geographer Bob Dolan that barrier islands move shoreward in response to rising sea level. Their findings dispelled the notion that beaches and islands would be lost to natural erosion. Once natural beach erosion was recognized as island movement, fear of land loss evaporated.

When the decision to "let nature rip" was revealed to the public, it was greeted with a storm of protest. Even Walter Cronkite noted the decision with barely contained contempt for the National Park Service on the *CBS Evening News*. But with time, the wisdom of the decision became apparent. Why would anyone come to a national seashore without beaches? Where would the money come from to build hundreds of miles of seawalls?

The Park Service has made exceptions to its no-shoreline-engineering policy. A large sheet-iron seawall was constructed on the Gateway National Recreation Area at the point at which Sandy Hook, New Jersey, joins the mainland, to prevent an ocean breakthrough that would turn the hook into an island. Perdido Key, Alabama, has been artificially replenished since its sand supply was cut off at an updrift channel dredged for access to the port of Pensacola, Florida.

In 1983, about ten years after the National Park Service decision, the state of Maine, to preserve its few sandy beaches, declared that hard stabilization would not be allowed on its shoreline. North Carolina followed suit in 1985. With allowance for variances, the rules in both states have so far held firm. At the time of this writing, the principal threat to North Carolina's regulations comes from influential oilman Walter Davis, who wants to build a wall in front of his erosion-threatened beach house on Bald Head Island. Under pressure from a lawsuit from Davis and under the guise of an "innovative structure" provision in the regulations, the state allowed, through permitting, emplacement of groins made of plastic sandbags. South Carolina prohibited structures in 1988 with more stringent regulations than North Carolina's. The South Carolina approach requires existing seawalls to be removed in 40 years and prohibits reconstruction of walls destroyed by storms.

When South Carolina implemented its rules, 27 percent of its developed shoreline was lined with structures. North Carolina instituted its provisions when only 5 percent of its developed shoreline was armored. Most coastal states began discussion in the 1980s of adopting a policy of retreat from eroding shorelines; these three states instituted it.

Ironically, Florida, with the most miles of open-ocean beach in the United States (excepting Alaska), remains essentially detached from the societal dialogue about armoring and the preservation of beaches for future generations. Although it has been bureaucratically complex to get permits seawall construction has continued along both sides of the Florida peninsula. In 1995 the state turned over to local communities the decision of whether to permit seawall construction. The state has chosen to preserve its few remaining pristine beaches through the purchase of coastal lands and by limiting the availability of state funds for development on undeveloped barrier islands.

Throughout the evolution of national coastal philosophy, the Corps of Engineers, especially on the local level, has remained steadfastly rooted in the engineering approach to shoreline management, both in navigation channel maintenance and in its response to beach erosion. The Corps' first published recognition of the passive role of seawalls in beach destruction came in a 1991 technical report, twenty years after the National Park Service had learned the lesson of Newjerseyization. Some

Corps district coastal engineers continue to insist that there is no evidence that seawalls harm beaches.

How the Corps Got to the Shore

The beginnings of the U.S. Army Corps of Engineers date to the early days of the Revolutionary War, when, in June 1775, Commander George Washington and the Second Continental Congress appointed Colonel Richard Gridley as "chief engineer for the grand army." Gridley and his fellow engineers were charged with design and construction of wartime fortifications. Rufus Putnam took Gridley's place as chief engineer of the Continental Army in August of 1776, resigning later that year after a dispute with Congress.

Putnam urged Congress to establish a separate engineer corps of specially trained men, but Congress did not take his advice until March 1779. The new corps of engineers, commanded by Louis LeBègue Du-Portail, was composed mostly of volunteers from the French Royal Corps of Engineers. Congress disbanded the Continental Army, including the Corps, in November 1783, as the war ended.

When the English and French went to war in 1793, both sides sought help from the new United States, sometimes quite forcefully. In response, Congress authorized President Washington to fortify the coasts in what became the "first system" of fortifications. To do that, Washington recruited former Corps engineers, mostly French émigrés. In May 1794, Congress officially authorized the engineers as a new army unit, the Corps of Artillerists and Engineers. This iteration of the Corps was organized in February 1795 and was commanded until 1798 by Stephen Rochefontaine.

On March 16, 1802, as war was ending between the English and the French, Congress enacted legislation that officially created the U.S. Army Corps of Engineers. The size of the Corps was limited to sixteen officers. They were charged primarily with running a military academy at West Point, which, until 1835, was the only school in the nation to award an engineering degree. This charge lasted until 1866, when management of West Point was placed directly in the War Department.

Under the financially austere Jefferson administration, no expansion of coastal fortifications was made until war broke out again, in 1803, between England and France. Both the French and the English disrupted shipping and forcibly recruited American sailors to serve in the war.

Congress appropriated $1 million for the "second system" of coastal harbor fortifications and divided the Atlantic Coast into administrative sections.

The Corps was not involved in internal improvements, now known as public works, until 1824, when the U.S. Supreme Court ruled (in *Gibbons v. Ogden*) that the federal government had authority over interstate navigation under its regulation of commerce. With the General Survey Act of 1824, the Corps' responsibilities were expanded to include roads and canals of national importance. In May 1824, the Corps became permanently involved in civil works construction with congressional direction to clear the Mississippi and Ohio rivers of navigation obstacles.

Along the coasts, from the 1830s until the 1930s, the Corps' primary domestic activities consisted of channel dredging, jetty construction, and other activities associated with coastal and inland waterway commerce and defense. Erosion control, such as the construction of breakwaters and some jetties, was built solely for the protection of coastal fortifications and the improvement of harbors. In 1829, Lieutenant Robert E. Lee supervised the construction of jetties at Fort Moultrie in South Carolina. Lee later oversaw construction of jetties at Fort Macon in North Carolina. After the devastating hurricane of 1900 in Galveston, Texas, the Corps built the massive seventeen-foot-high seawall that still fronts the city. As we will discuss, the long-lasting effects of Corps activities at Presque Isle, Pennsylvania (chapter 7) and Camp Ellis, Maine (chapter 8) influence present-day circumstances and decision making.

The Corps initially resisted broader involvement in what they viewed as a state responsibility, agreeing with Congress that public funds should not be used to protect private shoreline property. Two studies and the formation in 1926 of the American Shore and Beach Preservation Association (ASBPA), a private organization, changed the nature of federal involvement on the coasts. The New Jersey Board of Commerce and Navigation conducted a state-commissioned study, consisting of two reports released in 1922 and 1924, on protecting New Jersey's eroding beaches. At about the same time, a similar study was conducted by the National Research Council's new Committee on Shoreline Studies. The ASBPA, which formed as an outcome of the studies, advocated greater federal (i.e., Corps) participation, arguing the importance of recreational beaches.

In 1929, Senator Walter E. Edge of New Jersey introduced a bill authorizing the Corps to conduct studies of coastal erosion and shoreline protection. Introduction was followed by two years of hearings. As a result of the ASBPA's lobbying, the 1930 Rivers and Harbors Act authorized cooperative federal and state studies of communities with beach erosion problems and created a Beach Erosion Board within the Corps. The purpose of the Beach Erosion Board was to conduct shoreline studies, but only on federal property, and to give advice to coastal states, which were financially responsible for their own erosion control. Full state responsibility ended with the budget crunches of the Great Depression.

The Flood Control Act of 1936 gave the federal government responsibility for protecting public and private property from flooding. Congress enacted a similar act that same year, the Act for the Improvement and Protection of Beaches Along the Shores of the United States, to define for coastal areas the federal responsibility in the battle against coastal erosion. The coastal law, however, did not define the federal role well and limited any federal action to construction, not maintenance. It was under the coastal legislation that the Civil Works Administration, the Federal Emergency Relief Administration, and the Works Progress Administration undertook the construction of the massive dunes along the Outer Banks of North Carolina. The Army Corps of Engineers took a more conservative view of the act and confined its limited shoreline activities to federally held lands.

Under the 1936 beaches and shores "improvement and restoration" act, the Beach Erosion Board was directed to continue its shoreline studies, publish results, and advise states, local governments, and individuals as to the best location for recreation facilities. As part of its studies and reports, the board was to comment on the expediency of a proposed erosion-control project, whether federal involvement was warranted, and, if so, to recommend an appropriate federal share in the construction cost.

After World War II, the Beach Erosion Board urged greater Corps of Engineers involvement but encouraged nonstructural solutions, presumably to restrict federal expenditures that would directly benefit private property. Corps erosion-control projects remained relatively limited along ocean shorelines until the Great New England Hurricane of 1938 and a 1944 Atlantic Coast hurricane after which federal involvement increased rapidly. In 1945, the responsibilities of the Beach Erosion Board were expanded to include the support and publication of basic scientific studies of beach processes. In 1946, the federal government, for the first time, set its share to up to one-third of the cost of erosion-control projects on public property. Then, in the mid-1950s, six hurricanes struck the Atlantic Coast within thirteen months, killing hundreds of people and doing extensive property damage. Congress subsequently directed the Corps to study hurricane hazards.

The first federal beach-replenishment project was authorized in 1956. Previously, the Corps considered beach replenishment as maintenance rather than construction and, therefore, ineligible for federal funding under the improvement and restoration of beaches act. After the 1956 project, a series of complex federal-nonfederal cost-share arrangements were tried.

In 1962 the devastating Ash Wednesday storm destroyed hundreds of shorefront buildings, many huddled behind seawalls, most in New Jersey (Photos 1–1 and 1–2). The loss of New Jersey beaches in that storm precipitated the nation's first widespread beach-replenishment program, bringing the Corps of Engineers squarely into the people-versus-nature fray at the shoreline. The federal cost share of coastal erosion-control projects increased to 50 percent, 70 percent for public lands vacant of private structures.

In 1963, the Beach Erosion Board was replaced by the Coastal Engineering Research Center (CERC), based at Fort Belvoir, Virginia, near

Photo 1–1. A view of Harvey Cedars, New Jersey, after the 1962 Ash Wednesday storm. Water rushing seaward from the bay apparently was funneled across the island by the bulkhead on the lagoon side of the island, forming a new inlet. The Ash Wednesday storm is the event that propelled the Corps into the national replenishment scene. (Photo courtesy of the Philadelphia District of the U.S Army Corps of Engineers)

Washington, D.C. At about the same time, the Coastal Engineering Research Board was established as an advisory board that brings together leading coastal engineers from within and outside the Corps and works very closely with CERC. In 1983, CERC moved to Vicksburg, Mississippi, where it became one of six research arms of the Corps' Waterways Experiment Station (WES). CERC now has an annual budget of over $25 million and a staff of over one hundred coastal engineers and scientists, of which twenty-six have a Ph.D.

During the 1970s, the Corps released the National Shoreline Study, the first coastal study done on a national scale. The study concluded that 20,500 of over 40,000 miles on the continental U.S. coast were eroding. The 1970s also saw Congress pass several pieces of legislation that further increased the Corps' involvement at and near the nation's ocean shores. In 1972, Section 404 of the Clean Water Act put the Corps in charge of granting permits for dredge and fill activities. The 1972 Marine Protection Research and Sanctuaries Act gave the Corps responsibility to issue permits for offshore dumping. The Water Resources Development Act of 1974 also contained an explicit coastal-zone planning

Photo 1–2. Long Beach, New Jersey. A U.S. Navy destroyer being towed to port for repairs was washed ashore by the 1962 Ash Wednesday storm after its towing cable broke. Notice the particularly catastrophic destruction of the trailer park. The Ash Wednesday storm was the most damaging northeaster storm of this century. (Photo courtesy of the Philadelphia District of the U.S Army Corps of Engineers)

component. But Corps' shore protection activities were restrained on some barrier island coasts with the establishment of the Coastal Barrier Resources System in 1982, which limits federal expenditures on certain undeveloped coastal barriers.

In 1995, President Clinton proposed a budget that would essentially roll back the Corps responsibilities to those it had before the 1962 Ash Wednesday storm. He told Congress that Corps activities should be limited to those in the "national interest." At the time of this writing, replenishment proponents in coastal states and communities have successfully fought off this attempt at reducing the Corps' responsibilities. Current federal budget restraints have, nonetheless, cast a shadow on the national beach replenishment scene.

From the Drawing Board to the Beach

A Corps of Engineers project entails much more than construction. It includes economic justification, a political funding process, an appraisal of the environmental impact, design, construction, and maintenance, along with politics, politics, and more politics. Of course, the process should be political; citizens must decide whether a project is worth the expenditure of their tax money. Problems arise, as we will demonstrate, when politics determines scientific and engineering findings and practice.

Over the years, a complex process has evolved for approval and funding of Corps projects. The current procedure was established in the Water Resources Development Act of 1986. The following is a simplified list of steps in this process, which takes ten to fifteen years to accomplish (in the absence of major opposition) for most major coastal projects.

1. A member of Congress sponsors legislation to study a problem, such as shoreline erosion.

2. Congress authorizes, either by committee resolution or by legislation, and funds a "reconnaissance study" by the local Corps district.

3. A "two-part study process" begins. The district spends about a year and a half doing a reconnaissance study, during which it assesses the federal financial interest, examines several solutions to the problem, and performs a preliminary cost-benefit analysis. If the analysis is positive, it is on to the next phase.

4. The feasibility report is next prepared, which usually takes about three years. Public comment is sought and an environmental impact statement drafted. The state and community agree to participate financially in the recommended plan of action by signing a draft Local Cooperative Agreement. Alternative approaches to the problem—including the cost-benefit analysis that determines which alternative will be taken—are analyzed.

5. Once the district's report has been approved at the division level, a Division Engineer's Notice is issued calling for more public comment on the proposed project. The district continues "preconstruction engineering and design" of the project (funded through annual congressional appropriations). The feasibility report goes through a process of interagency and state review. A final environmental impact statement is submitted to the Environmental Protection Agency. And the final report goes to the chief of engineers, who submits it to the secretary of the army, who transmits it to Congress, where the project is proposed for authorization.

6. A bill authorizing the project is considered by Congress, usually the Water Resources Development Act for that year. This is a crucial step because, once authorized, a project, no matter how controversial, never dies until it is officially deauthorized by Congress.

7. A separate bill, usually the Energy and Water Development Appropriations Act, funds engineering and design. Once Congress has appropriated funds to implement the project, a formal Local Cooperative Agreement is signed by state and local project "sponsors" and the Corps.

8. Congress appropriates funds for project construction.

9. After project construction, the Corps is responsible for a designated period of operation and maintenance.

TWO

Coastal Processes
and What To Do about Them

If sea level had been standing still for a few hundred thousand years or if it were dropping, our coastlines would be relatively straight, with no estuaries or lagoons and few sea cliffs or islands. Instead, the shores of the world are a fascinating and highly irregular hodgepodge of coastal features, typical of land recently flooded.

The sea reached its present level only four to five thousand years ago. The ultimate cause of sea level change can be found in the world's high latitudes, where, over the last few million years, glaciers have grown and melted many times. When glaciers grow, the volume of the sea is reduced, sea level falls, and shorelines move seaward. When glaciers melt, the water is returned to the sea, sea levels rise, and shorelines move landward.

About eighteen thousand years ago the glaciers began to melt, and sea level began its latest rise from a low of perhaps 300 feet below its present level. The shoreline moved landward across the continental shelves, the portion of the sea floor between the beach and the continental slope that, while sea level was low, was high and dry, covered by vast forests, jungles, or deserts, depending on the climate. The rising sea flooded river valleys, turning them into estuaries with clear retention of the shape of the old valleys, as well as tributary valleys, whose shape derives from the erosive action of rivers. The shape of the Chesapeake Bay, for example, is that of the Susquehanna River valley with all of its tributaries.

On many shelves of the world, the valleys that once contained rivers coursing their way to the sea are still visible. Off the eastern United States, the most prominent drowned river valley, extending across the entire shelf, is that of the Hudson River off New York City. On the California continental shelf, the submarine canyons that extend to the

13

nearshore zone were also once occupied by rivers. The presence of shallow-water oyster shells, tree stumps, mastodon teeth, and, very rarely, the artifacts of human beings, all under water and miles from shore, further attest to this history of sea level fluctuation. In more northerly places, such as the coast of northern Maine, glaciers made scours that the sea later filled.

A lot of water is still held by the world's glaciers. If all the glaciers in Greenland and Antarctica were to melt, sea level would be at least 400 feet higher, most of the major cities of North America would be under water, and mile-high Denver would be in the running for U.S. capital. The worst-case scenario for sea level rise in coming decades is not quite that drastic. It requires the detachment of the West Antarctic Ice Sheet (the part that is currently floating or grounded on the Antarctic continental shelf). If that were to occur, a faint possibility at best, sea level could rise between 5 and 20 feet in a few decades. Current estimates indicate that sea level is rising about 1 foot per century. But the rate of sea level rise varies considerably from location to location. In Galveston, Texas, sea level rise may be on the order of 2 feet per century because the land is sinking from groundwater removal by the city of Houston and its industries. In Juneau, Alaska, sea level is dropping because the land is rising, rebounding from the release of the weight of recently melted glaciers. Thus, sea level change is a product of the adjustment of both the land and the sea.

The Coast

The coast can be defined biologically as the zone where land, ocean, and air interact, extending inland to the limit of tidal or sea spray influence. Politically, however, the inland limit of the coastal zone varies by state, sometimes defined as the band of counties that border the sea.

There are two basic types of coasts in the widely used classification of coasts by a Scripps Institution oceanographer, the late Francis Shepard. One, called a primary coast, owes its shape and general character to geologic processes that occurred on land, such as the river-formed Chesapeake Bay. Basically, these are coasts whose shape reflects recent flooding by rising sea level. The other coast type, called a secondary coast, is one heavily influenced by marine processes, such as the cliffed coasts of California, Oregon, and Washington.

The glacially scoured coast of northern Maine affords a good example of a primary coast, one shaped by land processes. This highly irregular coast consists of long, narrow embayments carved into the bedrock. The embayments are unaltered grooves left behind a few thousand years ago by the scouring action of seaward-moving glaciers.

Many coasts have a combined marine and land origin. The Outer Banks of North Carolina are barrier islands formed by the sea. The Pamlico and Albemarle sounds behind them, on the other hand, are simply a series of river valleys flooded in the last sea level rise. The Mississippi Delta comprises sediment that pours from the Mississippi River into the Gulf of Mexico where it is sculpted by waves into long fingers of land that protrude into the sea.

Secondary coasts formed by marine processes include much of the U.S. Pacific Coast, with its cliffs formed by wave erosion. Outer Cape Cod, Massachusetts, is another secondary coast, formed by the wave erosion of a deposit of glacial sands and gravel. The predominant marine-formed coast in North America is the barrier island coast that extends from the south shore of Long Island to Mexico's Yucatán, with only a few interruptions. These islands occupy more shoreline distance in the United States than any other open-ocean shoreline type.

Barrier Islands

Barrier islands, the most dynamic real estate in the United States, are also the most sought after, treasured, and costly. Barrier islands are the site of the most extensive beachfront development in the nation. As a result, the beaches on the ocean side of the barrier islands are probably the most endangered in the United States. Burgeoning development and retreating beaches have made barrier islands and their beaches sites for much of the Corps of Engineers' coastal engineering efforts.

Unto themselves, barrier islands are unique and fascinating ribbons of sand. Four conditions are needed for their formation. First, they are a product of a rising sea level; no rising sea level, no barrier islands. Second, they form exclusively on coastal plain coasts, low flat surfaces extending to the sea's edge, such as those of the U.S. Gulf of Mexico and Atlantic coastal plains. Also necessary are a sand supply large enough to be piled up in the shape of an island and waves large enough to move the sand about.

The Florida shoreline along the northwest Gulf of Mexico (from Wakulla to Pasco County and all the counties in between) has three of the four ingredients for barrier island formation. The missing link and the explanation for the lack of barriers there is the wave energy. Waves are so small that sand transport toward land is insufficient to form the big bars of sand that are barrier islands.

As sea level began to rise about eighteen thousand years ago, when the last major ice advance began its retreat, the river valleys of the coastal plains were flooded and tidal waters extended for miles into the continents. What were once ridges between the valleys were left exposed to the sea as headlands, vulnerable to wave attack. The headland erosion formed spits of sand extending into and across the mouths of the newly formed estuaries. In effect, a highly irregular shoreline was smoothed. Storms probably cut through the sandy spits, isolating them as islands that then began to evolve independently of the mainland. As sea level continued to rise, the islands moved apace toward the retreating mainland through a process known as "island migration."

Migration occurs as the barrier island rolls over itself like the tread on a bulldozer. The ocean side of the island retreats as storms push sand across the island to form sand overwash fans (Photos 2–1 and 2–2). Overwash fans, which often extend into the lagoon behind the island, may cause the island to widen in a landward direction. Simultaneous shoreline retreat of the open-ocean side of the island results in island migration (Photo 2–3).

A second mechanism of island widening is the incorporation into the island of flood tidal deltas. Tidal deltas are bodies of sand formed at

Photo 2–1. Overwash occurring during the 1991 Halloween Northeaster on the Outer Banks of North Carolina. (Photo by Carl Miller)

Photo 2–2. The North Carolina Department of Transportation trying to keep Highway 12 open during a storm. The sand pile (on the left) is overwash material that was deposited on the road and has been pushed back to the sea. The white areas on the seaward side of the dune are waves topping over the pile of bulldozed overwash sand. A better way to manage barrier islands is to allow the overwash sand to remain on the island. (Photo courtesy of the Duke University Program for the Study of Developed Shorelines)

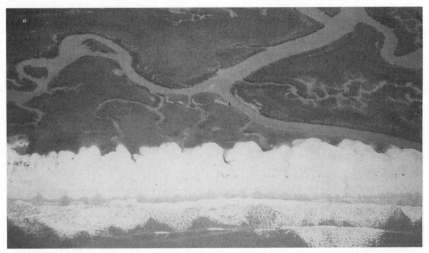

Photo 2–3. A barrier island at Cape Romain, South Carolina, immediately after Hurricane Hugo. This island is actively and rapidly migrating toward the mainland. Lobes of sand were pushed into the marsh by the hurricane, and at the same time the beach retreated. If Shackleford Banks, a barrier island in North Carolina, continues to narrow (Photo 2–4), this is what it will look like within a hundred years or so. (Photo by Rob Thieler)

inlets by tidal currents (Figure 2–1). Flood tidal deltas extend into the
lagoon and are formed by sand forced into the lagoon by incoming or
flood tides. The ebb tidal delta is the body of sand pushed seaward by
the ebbing tide. Flood tidal deltas, once the inlet migrates or opens
somewhere else, are colonized by salt marshes or mangroves and eventually add to an island's width just as overwash fans do.

On Padre Island, Texas, a third mechanism of island widening takes
place. There, wind-propelled sand from the island blows across broad
sand flats on the shores of Laguna Madre, gradually building the flats out
into the lagoon.

Most barrier islands are not migrating at this instant in geologic time.
Narrow islands like Assateague Island, Maryland; Masonboro Island,
North Carolina; and the Timbalier Islands of Louisiana, however, are ac-
tively migrating, often at rates exceeding 10 feet per year.

As migration occurs, sand and mud that once lay landward of the island in the lagoon and marsh appear on the ocean side. Lagoonal oyster

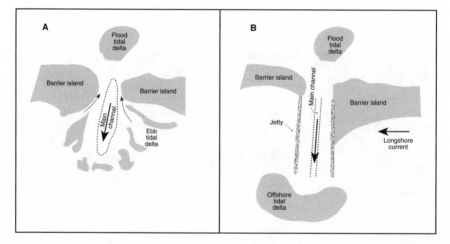

Figure 2–1. Barrier island inlets are complex features. The tidal deltas of these
inlets, which are formed by tidal currents, may contain huge volumes of sand.
The body of sand in the lagoon is called the flood tidal delta because it is formed
by the flood tides. The body of sand on the open-ocean side is called the ebb
tidal delta. When an inlet is jettied to stabilize a navigation channel (B), the ebb
tidal delta is broken up, and for a few years or decades after jetty construction,
the sand from the ebb tidal delta accretes on adjacent shorelines. Eventually, a
new and completely submerged tidal delta forms far off shore at the end of the
jetties, taking sand "permanently" away from the beach.

shells are commonly picked up by shell collectors strolling along the open-ocean beaches of barrier islands, especially along mid-Atlantic and southern U.S. beaches. There is no better proof of island migration than the presence of black oyster shells on the beach. Where the beach shells are found, a lagoon once existed and the barrier island was well to seaward. When the island migrated to avoid drowning by the rising sea level, the black shells were overrun and released to the sea floor by erosion and then washed up on the beach by the waves (Figure 2–2).

Superimposed on this process of island migration is the formation of dunes and inlets. Dunes are formed by the wind carrying sand to the island from the beach. These windblown piles of sand raise the elevation of the islands and can, if large enough, temporarily halt island migration. Larger dunes block overwash of storm waves and prevent island widening. Inlets form during storms, usually when storm waters that were forced into the estuaries behind the island rush across the island on their return to sea, cutting a channel through the island.

Something fundamental is happening globally to barrier islands right now. Over the last four thousand years or so, sea level has remained more or less the same. During this time, evidence indicates that many islands grew seaward and widened to the point that overwash rarely, if ever, crossed the island during a storm. Galveston Island, Texas, and Bogue Banks, North Carolina, are examples of islands that have widened

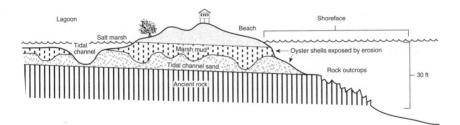

Figure 2–2. Cross-section of a barrier island showing the geologic components of a typical island along the U.S. Atlantic or Gulf of Mexico coast. This diagram shows why oyster shells are an abundant component of open-ocean beaches on U.S. barrier islands even though oysters live and grow in the lagoon. As the shoreface moves landward in response to rising sea level, channel sands and marsh mud release oyster shells, which are then pushed up to the beach by waves. Rock outcrops are a common component of shorefaces and sometimes an important influence on their shape.

seaward a half mile or more over the last few thousand years. Starting in the last century or two, these islands and many others began narrowing in response to erosion on all sides (Photo 2–4). Such erosion is probably a response to sea level rise.

This fundamental change from accretion (building seaward) to erosion leads to requests for help from the U.S. Army Corps of Engineers to protect buildings that were built in what has turned out to be the wrong place at the wrong moment in geologic time.

What Is a Beach?

A beach is the strip of unconsolidated material found at the seaward margin of the coast. The shoreline, which marks the wet-dry boundary of the beach, moves up and down with the tide, of course; but, for mapping purposes, its location is determined by some mean position such as the mid-tide line or mean sea level. A beach on a barrier island or spit is often referred to as a barrier beach. Beaches tucked between rocky headlands are called pocket beaches.

With almost incredible tenacity, a beach, a mere strip of easily moved sand, withstands the constant pounding of waves, the tug of tide-driven currents, and the tear of wind. Storms slice through the beach and its dunes. The beach should be retreating at a rapid clip, taking a big landward jump every time a storm comes by; the continents should be getting smaller and smaller as the sea eats away at their fringes.

The beach is a perfect buffer, however. It retreats when things get tough during a storm and returns when the weather is calm (Figure 2–3). It shapes itself to best absorb the pounding storm waves and forms a different shape when the waves are small. It's a unique and amazingly flexible natural environment. It is so dynamic that patterns in the changes of the shape and position of a beach are described as beach "behavior," and a major goal of coastal engineering and coastal geology is to predict how beaches will behave.

A beach is perhaps the most effective national boundary possible. Those intending harm to a coastal nation must first cross the land-sea boundary. Often this has proven to be an expensive and even impossible task for invaders. The beaches of the world are lined with forts and fortifications of many ages designed to repel unwanted interlopers. Among the reasons noted in chapter 1 for the establishment of the U.S. Army Corps of Engineers was the fortification of the U.S. shoreline following the Revolutionary War. Along the shorelines of all the combatant coastal

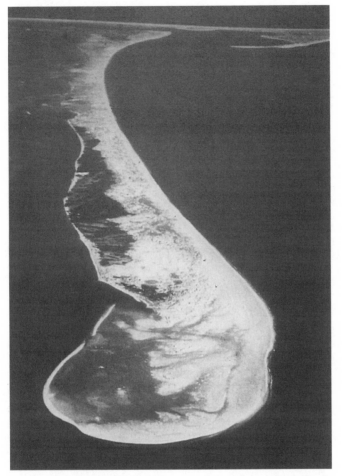

Photo 2–4. Photo of Shackleford Banks, North Carolina. This island is part of the Cape Lookout National Seashore and is a good example of an island that is narrowing, probably in response to sea level rise. Both the ocean side (to the right) and the lagoon side (to the left) are eroding. At the top of the photo is Core Banks and Cape Lookout. (Photo courtesy of Duke University Program for the Study of Developed Shorelines)

nations in World War II are concrete pillboxes, now more often than not tumbled onto the beach or inner continental shelf, victims of relentless shoreline retreat.

The beach can be a major source of materials for the land. Sand blown inland from the beach piles up as sand dunes, sometimes forming

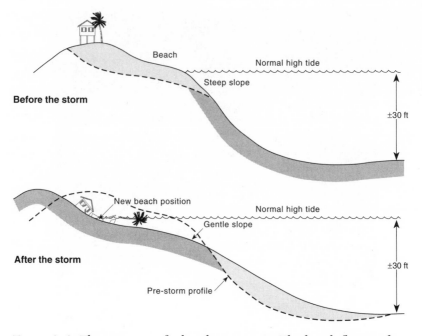

Figure 2–3. The response of a beach to a storm. The beach flattens during a storm by moving sand from the upper beach to the lower beach. Flattening allows the wave energy of the breaking storm waves to be dissipated over a broadened surface relative to the beach before the storm. After the storm passes, much of the sand will return over ensuing months and years. Sometimes this process of beach flattening takes out beachfront houses.

huge dunes such as Jockeys Ridge in North Carolina or large fields of dunes such as those at Coos Bay, Oregon. All the sand that makes up the volume of barrier islands, large and small, once resided on a beach before being blown or washed ashore.

Most scientists describe beaches according to the grain size of the materials that make them up. Thus beaches are referred to as sandy, gravel, or boulder beaches. Beaches are also frequently described by the composition of their sand—volcanic beaches in Hawaii, coral beaches in Bermuda, and quartz sand beaches in Cape Cod, for example. Armstrong Price, Texas A&M professor and the first coastal geologist to study Gulf of Mexico beaches, devised a simple and widely used wave-energy classification scheme for beaches. Beaches are referred to as high energy, moderate energy, or low energy, according to some average measure of regional wave height. Price distinguished himself in other ways too; in 1989, just before he died, Price presented his last paper to a scientific audience. He was 99 years old at the time!

Along some coasts, such as those off major river mouths (for example, the Amazon), beaches may be nonexistent because of the predominance of mud coming from the river. Instead of beaches, broad, gentle mud flats may form at the land-sea boundary.

The Equilibrium That Is the Beach

When it comes to describing beaches, variety is the key word. No two beaches have the same set of sand sources; type, size, or quantity of sediment; orientation; continental shelf width; or wave and climate conditions. All beaches, however, exist in a dynamic equilibrium (Figure 2–4) involving four major controls: (1) wave and tidal energy; (2) quality and quantity of the sediment supply; (3) beach shape and location; and (4) the level of the sea. As any of these four factors change, the others adjust accordingly.

A storm provides a good example of how this dynamic equilibrium works. A storm will cause a dramatic increase in wave energy, which is proportional to wave height, as well as a temporary rise in sea level. In response, the shape of the beach will change to accommodate the higher-energy environment. Sand will be moved around; offshore bars may form, or the beach may flatten out. The storm-related rise in sea level helps waves reach dunes or bluffs to wash sand back to the beach, which then uses the influx of sediment to further buffer wave and wind attack. The amount of sand movement and the ultimate shape taken by the beach depend, in part, on this sediment supply and the grain size of the beach sand.

The rapid retreat of the beaches on the Timbalier Islands off the Mississippi Delta in Louisiana demonstrates the dynamic equilibrium in a different and spectacular way. The rapid sea level rise there of 4 feet per century is four times that of most of the U.S. Atlantic and Gulf coasts. Compaction of the Mississippi Delta muds that underlie the Timbalier Islands is causing the land to subside, which translates into an accelerated rate of local sea level rise. This, combined with a very low sand supply (the Mississippi Delta contains relatively small amounts of sand), leads to a Timbalier beach retreat rate measured in tens of feet per year.

A large sand supply may cause a shoreline to accrete or grow seaward, depending on the rate at which sea level rise removes the new sediment. For example, infusion of a large sediment supply (from sources that aren't understood) is allowing a small barrier island in North Carolina, Sunset Beach, to widen by building seaward. Onshore coastal winds

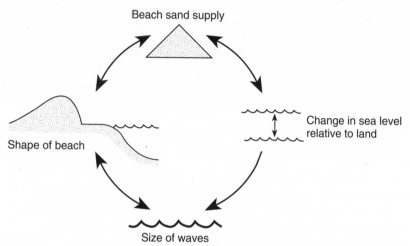

Figure 2–4. The beach exists in a dynamic equilibrium among the four factors shown in this diagram. When one factor changes, the others adjust accordingly.

have pushed sand into four rows of sand dunes since a beachfront row of buildings was constructed in the 1940s and 1950s. The accretion is particularly puzzling because adjacent beaches for many miles in either direction are retreating landward.

High-latitude beaches are a special case of the dynamic equilibrium. During the long winter of storms, these beaches are unaffected because they remain solidly encased in ice. Along Alaska's Bering Sea shoreline, icing of the sea usually begins in October and breaks up in May. For a month or so at either end of the winter, chunks of ice may gouge the beach and push sand ashore and even drag it out to sea. Most of the movement of sand on these beaches must occur mainly during the four months without ice. Barrier island dwellers along the Bering shores have a special problem during October. The resident Eskimos are sometimes endangered (in this already very harsh environment) by their inability to escape the island during the stormiest month because the surrounding waters are too ice clogged to use boats but not solid enough to use snowmobiles or dog sleds.

Where Beach Sand Comes From

Each beach obtains sand from a unique combination of sources. Primary sand sources—the continental shelf, rivers, and eroding cliffs—provide new sand to the beach, sand not previously within the surf zone. Secondary sand sources supply material to a beach from adjacent beaches by the surf-zone currents moving parallel to the shoreline, called long-shore currents.

The continental shelf is perhaps the most important source of sand for most U.S. beaches, particularly for the barrier island coast. As soon as the sea floor is within reach of fair-weather ocean waves, a point thought to be at about a 20- to 40-foot water depth (depending on typical wave size), sediment is caught by the lowermost wave orbitals and moved, grain by grain, toward shore. During storms, waves excavate the upper beach and, combining with bottom currents, can move large volumes of sediment in an offshore direction. Sand that is carried back out to sea by storms to depths exceeding the point of shoreward transport is "permanently" lost from the beach. The mechanics of shoreward sand movement are not well understood; hence, it is impossible to pinpoint the exact water depth of no return of sand under given wave conditions.

Continental shelf sands are also contributed from erosion of the shoreface, as the whole shoreface retreats in response to sea level rise. The shoreface is the surface extending from the beach to the offshore point of slope change from relatively steep to relatively gentle. Usually, the shoreface extends anywhere from a few hundred yards to a few miles offshore, reaching water depths of 25 to 40 feet. As the shoreline retreats, the entire shoreface is believed to move landward, more or less in step with the retreat of the shoreline, all the while furnishing newly eroded material to the beach. Along the Atlantic and Gulf of Mexico coasts, the shorefaces of migrating beaches and islands march over ancient barrier islands and overrun old marsh and lagoonal sediments. In Virginia and South Carolina, some barriers are retreating so rapidly that the outline of old tidal creek meanders can be seen in the surf zone.

John Wehmiller, a University of Delaware geologist, found that the contributions of ancient lagoons, channels, and marshes to the eroding shoreface of barrier islands make fossil shells, pried loose by waves and deposited on the beach, a dominant component of some beaches. As previously discussed, mid-Atlantic and southern U.S. beaches owe their abundant (lagoon-dwelling) oyster shell content to this phenomenon of erosion of the shoreface followed by onshore transport. This is all part of the aforementioned barrier island migration process. Radiocarbon dates of such shells have revealed ages that are commonly greater than ten thousand years. In addition to displaced oyster shells, beach sands often contain fossil shark teeth and shells millions of years old from the erosion of rocks outcropping on the shoreface or inner continental shelf. On Topsail Beach, North Carolina, giant oyster shells of a species that lived more than thirty million years ago are a common component of beach sands. These oysters, some of which are more than 18 inches long, could have made a meal for two!

Seashells in beach sediment usually arrive from offshore and are considered part of the continental shelf contribution. Calcareous marine organisms can provide a major source of beach sediment. Most common are the shells of mollusks and barnacle plates, plus a host of other components including corals, sea urchins, and calcareous algae fragments. Sometimes, on rocky coasts, storm waves rip shells from the cliffs and deposit them on the beach. In tropical waters the skeletal material of calcareous marine organisms can make up the entire beach, providing the sparkling white or pink color characteristic of some Caribbean beaches. Along the north coast of Puerto Rico, the beaches are black within a few hundred yards of river mouths (due to the mineral species in the river sands) but are light brown to white along the rest of the shore, where seashells and coral make up the beach sediment.

Often the shell material on a beach is responsible for the overall beach coloration. For example, most southeastern U.S. beaches have a light brown color derived from the formation of iron oxide (in the form of the mineral limonite) in the microscopic interstices of the shells. The stain is apparently imparted to the shells while they reside on the beach. The black color of oyster shell and other shells, comes from the incorporation of very fine and widely dispersed iron sulphide (pyrite) within the shells. The black color is formed when the shell is buried in oxygen-poor lagoonal mud. The requisite mud for black coloration of shells is absent from the vigorous wave environment of much of the U.S. Atlantic continental shelf.

Shell coloration is often a clue to the origin of sand on engineered beaches. A gray beach with black shells and very few brown shells is almost certainly a replenished beach. The extent to which a replenished beach is furnishing sand to adjacent beaches can sometimes also be estimated by shell color. The all-important coastal engineering question of where sand from a replenished beach goes may someday be answered by tracing the paths of shells contained within the replenishment sand.

Along the Pacific Coast and in the western Gulf of Mexico, rivers are important sources of sediment. Dams built even hundreds of miles from shorelines along these coasts can cause beach erosion in a few years or decades by preventing naturally replenishing sand from reaching the beach. Dramatic examples of the effects of damming can be seen along coastal Southern California, where river damming is so extensive that virtually no new sediment reaches the ocean shore. Along most of the

Atlantic Coast, damming rivers will have little impact on the beaches; coastal plain rivers generally dump their sand loads when they reach the quiet water at the head of an estuary, sometimes more than 50 miles from the nearest open-ocean beach. This is not true along portions of the Gulf of Mexico coast, however. The damming of the Rio Grande River, for example, may be responsible for part of the erosion problem of South Padre Island, Texas.

Beaches often receive sediment from the erosion of cliffs, bluffs, or dunes that line their landward edge. This became painfully apparent along the south shore of Massachusetts when homeowners began to build seawalls on the eroding faces of drumlins in order to save their houses. Drumlins are loose piles of sand, gravel, and boulders left behind by the glaciers; their erosion provides a steady source of material for the beaches. As seawalls were built, erosion rates accelerated on shorelines adjacent to the seawalled drumlins. Massachusetts now forbids locking up the beach sediment supply provided by eroding drumlins.

Dunes can also furnish sand to the beaches. Robert Morton, a geologist with the University of Texas, in a study of storm recovery of beaches in Texas, observed that a significant volume of windblown sand was contributed to the storm-recovering beach from the dunes. This sand was voluminous enough to be an important part of the storm-recovery process of natural beaches. In turn, the beach is an important source of sand for adjacent land areas. Most coastal dunes are built by windblown sand from the beach.

The Beach As a Shock Absorber

As wind strength and wave height fluctuate between storm and fair weather and between winter and summer, the beach maintains its dynamic equilibrium. As previously described, during a storm, the beach responds by changing shape to a profile that will best absorb the shock of breaking waves (Figure 2–3). The beach resumes a steeper calm-weather shape after the storm passes, much like the recovery of a car's shock absorber after a bump. Every beach will react slightly differently to a storm. But all beaches with a reasonably healthy sand supply and no seawall will respond to strong storm waves by either flattening or forming offshore bars. Why different beaches respond in these different fashions to storms is not understood, but the end effect of dissipating storm-wave energy is the same.

Beaches that flatten in response to large waves cause breaking waves to spread their energy over a broad surface. Picture a breaking wave striking a vertical surface, such as a seawall, where the immense energy of the wave is concentrated within a small area. The same amount of energy is released by a wave breaking over a gently sloping beach, but the energy is spread out rather than concentrated.

Offshore bars, small ridges of sand parallel to the shore, are to be found at one time or another on most beaches and can also spread the energy of breaking storm waves. Their presence can easily be recognized by watching the surf zone for two or sometimes three distinct rows of breaking waves. The shoaling depths atop the bars virtually trips incoming waves, forcing them to break.

In the 1960s, John Zeigler, then a Woods Hole Oceanographic Institute coastal geologist, first observed the role of offshore bars when he studied seasonal changes in beaches along the outer shore of Cape Cod. Although he did not see offshore bars during the summer, he observed that after the first storm waves of winter, three offshore bars appeared parallel to shore and remained there until the next summer. The largest waves broke on the outer bar, intermediate-size waves broke on the middle bar, and so on. Zeigler noted that the waves that reached the shoreline were quite small compared to the waves breaking on the outer bar.

The beach, whether it has responded by flattening or forming offshore bars, usually "recovers" after each storm or after the winter storm season. The sand that moved offshore under the influence of the big waves moves onshore under the influence of the smaller fair-weather waves. Offshore bars flatten or gradually move onshore, and the beach between the low- and high-tide lines tends to steepen over a time frame ranging from days to years, depending on the size of the storm or severity of the winter and the subsequent amount of adjustment made by the beach within the constraints of its dynamic equilibrium.

Storm conditions cause large-scale changes of slope, extending from the dune line hundreds of yards into the surf zone. The grain size of beach sand is also responsible for the slope of the beach on a smaller scale, between the high- and low-tide lines. The effect of grain size on beach slope is related to the permeability of the beach sand: its ability to allow water to pass through it. On a coarse beach—for instance, one consisting of gravel—as the breaking wave rushes landward, a lot of the water is absorbed into the gravel and little water remains for wave backwash. In other words, the forces pushing beach material up on to the beach are stronger than those moving material seaward, and the beach steepens in response.

On beaches composed of fine sand, permeability of the fine material is much less than for gravel, so little water from breaking waves is absorbed; the upwash and backwash of the wave have essentially equal volumes of water. Backwash tends to move sand in a seaward direction, with the net result of a flattened beach.

The Beach As a River of Sand

Winds, waves, and storms keep sand in constant motion in every direction on the beach. Sand is moved offshore to deeper water by bottom currents, usually storm related. Wind blows sand from the beach into nearby dunes to be trapped by dune vegetation. But by far the largest volume of sand is carried by longshore currents. Longshore currents are formed as waves strike the shoreline at an oblique angle, forcing some of the surf-zone water to move laterally (Figure 2–5); the strongest current is formed when the waves strike the shoreline at a thirty-degree angle. Large volumes of sediment are carried by longshore currents because the current acts in concert with breaking waves. Breaking waves suspend sand, and currents move it. By this wave-current interaction, even large particles, such as seashells, can be carried at very low current velocities.

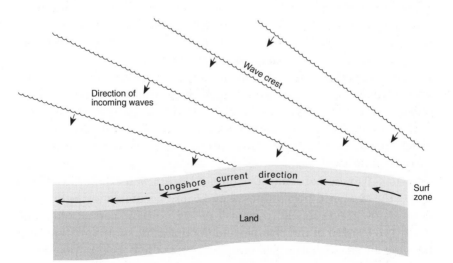

Figure 2–5. Breaking waves approach the shoreline at an angle and direct a part of their energy parallel to the shoreline. This produces the longshore current responsible for transporting beach sand laterally.

The longshore current, sometimes called littoral drift, is very much like a river. In a river, direction is referred to as upstream and downstream. Along a beach, directions of sand movement are referred to as updrift and downdrift. On a given beach, the direction of flow changes from time to time. For example, at Nags Head, North Carolina, beach sand is carried along shore to the north in the summer. During the winter, under the influence of storm waves from the north, sand is transported in large part to the south. The dominant or net direction of longshore transport is the one toward which the longshore current carries more sand. This is also called the downdrift direction. At Nags Head, as along most of the U.S. Atlantic Coast, the net direction of transport is south, which is thus called downdrift.

In California, net longshore drift is usually to the south, although significant reaches of the shoreline are dominated by northerly transport. Along the coast of Southern California, the river of sand is sometimes interrupted by submarine canyons, the heads of which extend practically into the surf zone. These features, such as the Scripps and Monterey canyons, capture beach sand that is eventually swept down canyon to the deep ocean floor.

Large volumes of sand may travel long distances in the longshore transport system. A study of the minerals contained within beach sands by Robert Giles of the University of Georgia concluded that sand along Florida's east coast may have traveled hundreds of miles in a southerly direction from Georgia to Miami Beach. Possibly such transport took thousands of years to accomplish. But movement of large volumes of sand can take place within a much shorter time.

The net amount of sand transported by longshore currents varies widely from place to place. Contrast the large volume of sand, perhaps one million cubic yards per year, transported from north to south on the Santa Barbara, California, shoreline with the 10,000 cubic yards per year along Atlantic Beach, North Carolina. (For reference, a dump truck may carry 10 cubic yards.)

As in a river, human-built structures interrupt water flow. A dam built across the river will trap sediment and cause accumulation behind the dam. Below the dam, the river will pick up a new load of sediment, leading to erosion of the channel and floodplain downstream. Similarly, building a wall, such as a groin or jetty, across the beach perpendicular to the shoreline will interrupt the longshore current and cause sand to deposit updrift and erode downdrift. Along the shoreline, a good maxim is that any device that traps sand is robbing some beach somewhere else of that sand.

Why Shoreline Erosion?

Saving buildings from beach erosion is the main reason the Corps of Engineers is involved on the shoreline. However, as we shall see, because of fundamental geologic forces, the primary environmental impact of their various activities is, ironically, usually more erosion.

Most estimates indicate that 80 percent or more of the U.S. shoreline is eroding. The other 20 percent is either stable or accreting, but these are probably temporary states. For all practical purposes, the American shoreline is eroding everywhere.

The causes of shoreline erosion are numerous but often difficult to pinpoint in any quantitative way. Fundamentally, erosion is occurring because the forces of the ocean are nibbling away at the edges of the continent (Photo 2–5). Storms, the primary "nibbling" agent, "permanently" remove a certain amount of sediment every year to the adjacent continental shelf. A certain amount of shoreline change—how much is difficult to say—is attributable to that simple fact. However, a number of other factors are involved.

Sea level rise is commonly called on to explain a lot of shoreline retreat, bringing forth the specter of ever-increasing erosion rates as sea

Photo 2–5. A World War II German pillbox, originally built 75 yards inland, rests at sea along the coast of France. World War II fortifications along both sides of the Atlantic have succumbed to erosion. (Photo by A. Miossec)

level rise accelerates apace with global warming (Figure 2–6). Global warming, or the "greenhouse effect," occurs with an atmospheric increase in carbon dioxide, which causes heat to be trapped near the earth's surface, just like in a greenhouse. The increased atmospheric temperature should melt portions of the ice caps, raising the sea level.

In 1994 the Topex/Poseidon satellite, a joint French-American project, reported a tenth of an inch per year sea level rise worldwide—a one inch per decade rate. The satellite measurements are the most accurate measurements of sea level rise yet made, and that rate was the highest yet observed globally. But since the observed rate of sea level rise is based on only two years of observations, its meaning is not yet certain.

The effects of sea level rise can be seen with absolute certainty on rapidly subsiding coasts such as the Mississippi Delta, where the relative sea level rise, as mentioned previously, is extreme (four feet per century). Unfortunately, it is impossible to quantify the exact contribution of sea level rise to coastal erosion. Some idea of its likely importance can be gained by considering the slope of the mainland adjacent to the shoreline. Along most of the U.S. Pacific Coast the slope is steep, so sea level rise must be an insignificant factor. Along the Gulf and Atlantic Barrier Island coasts the slopes are 1:2,000 or much less; in theory, therefore, a

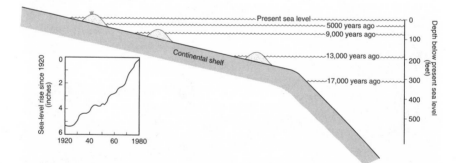

Figure 2–6. Since eighteen thousand or so years ago, sea level has been rising as a result of melting glacial ice. Barrier islands probably formed at the edge of the continental shelf and migrated into their present locations during that time span. The graph shows the current rate of sea level rise along most of the U.S. Atlantic and Gulf of Mexico coasts. This rise is about one foot a century but varies considerably from location to location depending on whether the land is sinking or rising.

one-foot rise in sea level could push the shoreline back 2,000 feet or more (Photo 2–6). Along some estuarine shorelines backed by marshes and other wetlands, a one-foot sea level rise could push the shoreline back a mile or two.

Anything that affects the supply of sediment to beaches could create or reduce erosion. Reducing sand supply to beaches by the damming of rivers is a major problem discussed earlier. Other events that affect sediment supply to rivers can play a role. These include agricultural practices, urbanization, and forest and brush fires. Closer to the beach, sand lost to the flood tidal deltas associated with inlets can be a major but temporary loss of beach sand, leading to erosion. Sooner or later, however, the rising sea level will cause the spit or barrier island to migrate over and gobble up the sand trapped in deltas.

Often, perhaps more often than not, the local erosion villain is human activity. Seawalls, jetties, groins, breakwaters, navigation channel

Photo 2–6. Sea level rise in the extreme. In Baytown, Texas, groundwater has been extracted for years to furnish water to petroleum refineries. Removal of the water has resulted in compaction of some of the sedimentary layers, resulting in sinking of the land and rising of the sea level from Galveston Bay. An entire subdivision of Baytown, a suburb to the south of Houston, was inundated and destroyed by a sea level rise of more than three feet over a large area. This is an example of sea level rise caused by behavior of the land rather than of the sea. (Photo by Robert Morton)

deepening, inlet formation, and sand removal by mining have all contributed to increasing shoreline retreat rates (Photos 2–7, 2–8, and 2–9). Some engineers and geologists argue that this may be the principal cause of erosion along developed shorelines today. Through their interruption of the sediment supply to beaches, all effective shoreline engineering procedures create erosion.

Beaches or Buildings?

The real threat to America's beaches is neither storms nor sea level rise, no matter how severe or rapid. In natural shoreline retreat, often called shoreline erosion, the beach simply changes its location but retains its shape. For most of the world's beaches it is fair to say: no people, no problem (Photos 2–10 and 2–11). But as humans place obstacles, such as houses, highways, and seawalls along a beach, shoreline retreat is blocked. The beach jams up against these objects, which causes it to narrow and leads to a reduction in the supply of sand to adjacent beaches (Photo 2–12).

Photo 2–7. One of the major causes of beach erosion worldwide is mining of sand. In this scene from Portugal huge amounts of beach sand are being removed by front-end loader. The sand will be used for construction purposes. (Photo courtesy of Duke University Program for the Study of Developed Shorelines)

Photo 2–8. Sand mining occurs on all scales. A young man in the Marshall Islands gathers sand to help build the foundation of his new house. (Photo courtesy of Duke University Program for the Study of Developed Shorelines)

Photo 2–9. A snowy scene on September 9, 1991, in Barrow, Alaska. Removal of huge volumes of sand for the purpose of constructing the community's international airport caused the beach to narrow. Although few people swim here, the beach is very important to the community for social (strolling on the beach) and practical reasons (storing whaling boats). (Photo courtesy of Duke University Program for the Study of Developed Shorelines)

Photo 2–10. A log-strewn beach on Ossabaw Island, Georgia. These trees did not grow on the beach but in what was once an inland portion of the island; the island is subject to rapid shoreline retreat. However, no buildings are threatened, no highways about to fall in, no telephone lines about to topple. Thus, erosion is not considered a problem. (Photo courtesy of Duke University Program for the Study of Developed Shorelines)

Photo 2–11. Long Beach, North Carolina, immediately after Hurricane Hazel in 1954. Most of the houses were destroyed or moved off their foundation, and the beach moved back a few tens of feet in a few hours. Note that shoreline retreat does not harm the beach, which remains wide and healthy. (Photo by Hank Gaynor)

Photo 2–12. On the day of completion of this condominium in Garden City, South Carolina, the construction workers celebrate by fishing in the surf zone from the condominium balconies. No better illustration exists of what is responsible for the American erosion problem: the seawall in front of the building has already taken away the recreational beach. The seawall shown here was destroyed in a January 1, 1987, northeaster, rebuilt, and destroyed again by Hurricane Hugo in 1989. We recommend that you should not be able to fish from your condominium window. (Photo from the *Coastal Observer*)

Compounding the American erosion problem is an axiom of our times: the number of people owning and occupying beachfront buildings is small relative to the number who would like to use the beach for recreation. The beaches belonging to all and enjoyed by thousands are being threatened with destruction in order to save the properties belonging to hundreds.

Solutions

Overall, there are three available responses to a local shoreline erosion problem: (1) hard stabilization, such as seawalls, groins, and the like; (2) soft stabilization, such as beach replenishment; and (3) relocation of threatened buildings. Each of these approaches has advantages and disadvantages. For example, hard stabilization may be the best way to save buildings, but retreating from the problem by removing buildings is the best way to save beaches.

The *hard stabilization* alternative involves armoring the shoreline with structures designed to hold it in place, that is, to stabilize it. The most common and widespread of these are seawalls, coastal engineering structures built on the beach, parallel to the shoreline. Seawalls can be large or small, high or low, and constructed of a range of materials including wood, plastic, concrete, rock, construction rubble, steel, old cars, aluminum, rubber tires, and sandbags. Seawalls, properly constructed for the particular situation, are the best way to save beachfront property, provided the severe disadvantages they impose are acceptable. If a community's only priority is the preservation of its beachfront buildings, seawalls are the way to go (Photo 2–13).

There are several members of the seawall family. *Bulkheads* are relatively low and small walls designed to hold land. They are built not to protect buildings from waves, but to keep land from eroding out from underneath them. *Revetments* are a common type of seawall built directly on a surface such as the seaward slope of a dune or an eroding bluff. Usually revetments are constructed of boulders. These large rocks have the advantage of providing ample interstitial cavities that collect some of the water from a breaking wave, reducing sand-removing wave reflection and backwash.

Seawalls, if built to the appropriate strength and maintained properly, can be very effective in protecting shorefront property from a retreating shoreline. Sometimes, if high and strong enough, seawalls can even protect against the onslaught of storm waves (Photo 2–14). In most cases along the American shore though, seawalls are low enough

Photo 2–13. A gabion seawall retains the community's landfill on Majuro Atoll on the Marshall Islands. Gabions consist of wire baskets filled with rocks. Unfortunately, the wire baskets will eventually corrode and the seawall fall apart. In this case, when the wall disappears, the landfill will be exposed to the waves. (Photo courtesy of the Duke University Program for the Study of Developed Shorelines)

Photo 2–14. The seawall at Seabright, New Jersey, during a minor storm. The beach has long since disappeared, and the shoreface in front of the seawall has steepened. As a result, there is less friction to slow incoming waves, allowing large waves to strike the seawall. (Photo by Mary Jo Hall)

to be overstepped by major storms. In South Carolina, numerous low seawalls prevented shoreline retreat during Hurricane Hugo in 1989 but allowed storm waves to crash through beachfront buildings.

A heavy price is exacted for using engineering structures, however (Photos 2–15 and 2–16). Hard stabilization has proven to be irreversible. No one ever seems to yank out seawalls; instead, they always get larger, higher, and longer. In the view of most beach users, seawalls are ugly, or at least they are ugly contradictions to the unobstructed beach shown in the real estate advertisements. Some of the long seawalled beaches of New Jersey, covered by the clutter of previously destroyed walls, are arguably the most unsightly beaches in the world (Photo 2–17). Seawalls restrict beach access and can be dangerous to pedestrians. Before the beach there was replenished in an effort to replace what had been lost to erosion, the walls at Folly Beach, South Carolina, caused injury to more than one unwary surfer, abruptly ending their rides with a crash landing in the rocks. Innumerable minor injuries have been reported of people clambering down boulder revetments or jumping to the beach from the top of a high seawall. In several places at Sandbridge, Virginia (Photo 2–18), public access paths lead to the edge of the vertical seawall and a 12-foot leap to the beach!

Seawalls also destroy beaches (Figure 2–7). Some seawalls take away part of a beach on the day they are constructed by being built well out on the beach, beyond the high tide line. This happened in Miami Beach, Florida, and is referred to as *placement loss*. The lack of beaches in the 1960s and 1970s in Miami Beach was the result of the conscious choice of hotel owners who vied to have the most seaward seawall. Seawalls also cause loss simply by providing a stationary object against which a retreating beach narrows and eventually disappears (Photo 2–19). Generally, this beach loss, referred to as *passive loss*, occurs over several decades.

It is widely believed that under the right circumstances, seawalls may intensify surf-zone processes during storms, also leading to beach loss (Photo 2–20). Wave energy is intensified rather than dissipated, so even more sand is swept offshore to the continental shelf. This direct participation of a seawall in the degradation of a beach is called *active loss*. As the beach narrows in front of the wall, reducing the available beach area, the amount of sand transported past the wall in both directions is reduced because of the smaller surface area of the surf zone. The reduction leads to erosion on adjacent shoreline reaches.

The January 1994 newsletter of the Florida Shore and Beach Preservation Association provided a clear statement of the political predicament posed by combined active and passive loss in front of seawalls: "It

Photo 2–15. On the beach of a short, unseawalled segment of Sandbridge, Virginia, a couple rests their beach chairs up against an exposed septic tank. Here the erosion rate accelerated considerably when seawalls were built to protect adjacent properties. (Photo courtesy of the Duke University Program for the Sutdy of Developed Shorelines)

Photo 2–16. A seawall on a recreational beach along the south coast of Puerto Rico near Ponce. The seawall was constructed to protect three small concrete-block buildings. Are these buildings worth the destruction of this important recreational beach and the hazards posed to young swimmers? (Photo by Eric Wright)

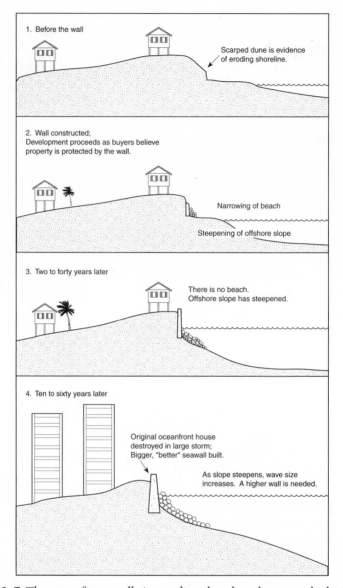

1. Before the wall

Scarped dune is evidence of eroding shoreline.

2. Wall constructed;
Development proceeds as buyers believe property is protected by the wall.

Narrowing of beach

Steepening of offshore slope

3. Two to forty years later

There is no beach.
Offshore slope has steepened.

4. Ten to sixty years later

Original oceanfront house destroyed in large storm;
Bigger, "better" seawall built.

As slope steepens, wave size increases. A higher wall is needed.

Figure 2–7. The saga of a seawall: An eroding shoreline threatens the buildings. Understandably disturbed, homeowners build a small wall to stop the shoreline retreat. A decade or three later, the wall has grown, the beach has disappeared, and the building is still endangered. Fifty years later, the seawall is very large, the beach is long gone, the entire shoreface has been steepened, and the house is gone. In front of the massive seawall is a large pile of rubble made up of the past generations of seawalls and groins that have been destroyed by storms. Condominiums have replaced the beach cottages, but no beach remains for the residents or visitors to play on. This is Newjerseyization.

Photo 2–17. Here is Newjerseyization at its worst. The New Jersey shoreline near Asbury Park has a long history of stabilization using seawalls and groins made of wood, stone, steel, and concrete. If the shoreline had not been armored, the first and possibly the second row of buildings would have disappeared, but because of shoreline armoring, the beach is no longer usable for recreation. (Photo by William Neal)

is imperative that [armoring] regulations balance the need to protect both our beach and animal resources as well as lives and property."

Clearly the association wants the proverbial eaten cake. But their wish that the regulations balance the need to preserve beaches and preserve buildings at the same time fails to recognize the uncompromising nature of shoreline armoring. Build a wall, and you lose the beach. Do not build a wall, and you lose the building. You either save buildings or save beaches, but, over the long term, unless you move the building, you will not save them both. In 1995 the association won. The Florida legislature passed a bill placing the decision to armor or not to armor in the hands of local communities. The Newjerseyization of Florida has begun in earnest.

A long-standing controversy has existed over the role of seawalls in the destruction of beaches. Initially, before the environmental revolution of recent decades, the coastal engineering community and the Corps of Engineers simply ignored the environmental impact of walls under the assumption that protection of buildings was worth any price. By the 1980s the destructive role of seawalls was recognized by most coastal scientists and residents but not by the engineering community.

Photo 2–18. The seawall at Sandbridge, Virginia, in January 1989, as it was under construction. The wall took away the recreational beach in order to preserve two hundred houses. At present, no beach exists even at low tide along much of Sandbridge. A large portion of this wall was destroyed during Hurricane Gordon in 1994. (Photo courtesy of National Oceanographic and Atmospheric Administration)

Photo 2–19. A television crew at high tide at North Myrtle Beach, South Carolina. The seawall has saved the buildings, but as a result there is no dry beach in front of this community for about half of the tidal cycle. A beach replenishment project is planned here for 1996. (Photo courtesy of the Duke University Program for the Study of Developed Shorelines)

Driven by their faith in the engineering solution and the instinct to side with their customers, consulting, academic, and Corps coastal engineers alike stonewalled on the seawall issue. The evidence "wasn't in yet" was the word that was spread. And the few locations where walled beaches had yet to disappear were cited again and again as proof that a problem did not exist. This, in spite of the profound evidence of seawall effects along the long walled, and long beachless, Jersey Shore.

Although most coastal engineers now agree that seawalls degrade beaches, a few, for whatever reason, refuse to abandon their pro-wall stance. David Basco, a coastal engineer from Old Dominion University in Norfolk, Virginia, is one of the best-known holdouts. Basco states in a 1990 publication: "It is apparent that on coastlines with a demonstrated long term erosion trend, a new seawall provides a convenient reference point for the average beach visitor to judge beach widths over time. Before construction it was not as convenient. Shrinking beach widths fronting the seawall are innocently but naively blamed on the seawall by the general public. What is unfortunate is that some who know better, fan the flames of misconception by stating categorically that seawalls destroy the beach." We believe Basco is wrong. Were it not for the wall, the beach, although it would change location through shoreline retreat, would maintain its width. The beach narrows because it is, literally, backed up against a wall.

Another type of coastal engineering structure built parallel to the shore is the *offshore breakwater*, a wall built offshore to reduce wave energy and, particularly, the longshore transport of sand along a beach. The "wave shadow" formed in the lee of a breakwater reduces and usually stops transport of sand. This results in the formation of a seaward-extending bulge of the beach, protecting beachfront buildings and providing a wider recreational beach. These are becoming increasingly popular along eroding shorelines, principally because seawalls have gained such a bad reputation among coastal managers and engineers whose interest is in beach preservation. But these too cause erosion along adjacent and immediate shores by taking sand out of the longshore current and probably also by preventing offshore sand from returning to the beach after storms.

Downdrift erosion is not the only problem; breakwaters give rise to a safety problem. Offshore breakwaters alter water currents in their vicinity, creating a hazard for swimmers. Breakwaters also become a dangerous attraction, as people swim out (or walk out if enough sand has collected in the shadow of the structure) to climb on the rocks. Sand and swimmers are not the only things drawn to breakwaters; breakwaters are

Photo 2–20. Myrtle Beach, South Carolina, after Hurricane Hugo. A wide beach remains where there was no seawall (to the right), but there is no beach where a seawall was present (to the left). Buildings were protected by the seawall, but the public beach was lost. (Photo by Rob Thieler)

magnets for floating trash, and large volumes of debris have been known to accumulate in their lee.

A breakwater built off Redington Shores in southwest Florida in 1986 (Photo 2–21) has had safety problems to the extent that within the first two years following construction, five deaths were attributed to it. The exact causes of the deaths are uncertain, but the most likely scenario is that swimmers were caught in breakwater-induced currents and thrown against the rocks. Today, the Redington Shores breakwater lies buried beneath replenishment sand emplaced in 1989. We discuss these structures in greater detail in the chapter on Presque Isle, Pennsylvania, where fifty-five offshore breakwaters were recently constructed to "protect" a state park.

Other kinds of hard stabilization include groins and jetties. *Groins* are walls built perpendicular to the shoreline to trap sand traveling laterally in the surf zone. These engineering structures, which like seawalls can be built of almost anything, are generally successful in building up a beach in one place but, in so doing, cause a sand deficit and erosion downdrift (Photo 2–22).

Jetties, similar to groins but generally much larger, are built at inlets

Photo 2–21. The offshore breakwater at Redington Shores, Florida. Note the shoreline bulge in the wave shadow behind the breakwater. Erosion is thinning the beach to the north (upper part of the photo) because of the loss of the sand trapped behind the structure. (Photo courtesy of the Florida Division of Beaches and Shores)

to stabilize navigation channels (Figure 2–1). A dramatic example of the shoreline changes caused by jetties can be seen at Ocean City Inlet, Maryland. The inlet, opened by a storm in 1933, was immediately stabilized (by the Corps) with jetties. The dominant direction of longshore transport is to the south, so the resort city of Ocean City gained a wide beach at its southern end as the north jetty trapped sand on its updrift side. Downdrift, Assateague Island, the next island to the south, has eroded so rapidly that it has moved landward its own width. At the island's northern end, the surf zone is landward of the location of Assateague's former lagoonal shoreline. There has been little public outcry about this erosion problem because Assateague is an undeveloped

Photo 2–22. The groins at Cape May, New Jersey, have caused more than a half mile of retreat on the shoreline to the south (downdrift). Except for brief periods of time right after the beach has been replenished, there is no high-tide beach here; promenading on top of the seawall is a popular form of recreation.

national seashore. The much-widened beach next to the north jetty at Ocean City is now a municipal parking lot. Perhaps this is a better use of the so-called jetty sand fillet than the construction of a twenty-seven-story condominium on the jetty-formed beach at the south end of Fort Lauderdale, Florida. This building on the "artificial" sand body, updrift of the jetty, is one of the tallest beachfront buildings in America.

Because of its detrimental and irreversible impacts on beaches, hard stabilization has fallen out of favor as an open-ocean shoreline erosion management tool. As discussed in chapter 1, North Carolina, South Carolina, and Maine prohibit the construction of hard stabilization structures on open-ocean shorelines. Several other coastal states restrict, but do not prohibit, their use. Structures are still used to protect buildings in many locations, however, and, occasionally, large-scale seawalls are constructed, as in the case of Sargent Beach, Texas.

The prevailing view among geologists is expressed by Jim Tait and Gary Griggs of the University of California at Santa Cruz: "Where long term erosion is taking place, as is the case on many Atlantic and Gulf coast barrier islands, and the process cannot be mitigated [by beach replenishment], then the beaches in front of seawalls in these locations will eventually disappear."

Photo 2–23. A beautiful salt marsh on the lagoon side of Bogue Banks, North Carolina. This salt marsh started out in the early 1970s as a four-foot-wide strip of marsh grass sprigs on an eroding shoreline adjacent to the Pine Knoll Shores Country Club golf course. Its spectacular growth since then attests to the viability of using "natural" methods to mitigate shoreline erosion as opposed to shoreline armoring or beach replenishment.

Replacing hard stabilization along open-ocean shores as the erosion response of choice is soft stablization, such as *beach replenishment*. We have devoted chapter 3 to this seeming panacea. Beach replenishment involves the placement of new sand on a shore in an attempt to restore an eroded beach. The practice, always expensive and always temporary, has met with mixed success and is of questionable merit as a long-term coastal management strategy. But it is far better for the beach than seawalls and other engineering structures. On lagoon shorelines, some communities are employing another form of soft stabilization by planting vegetation instead of seawalls to halt erosion (Photo 2–23).

The third option, *relocation*, moving buildings back from retreating shores, is the old way of keeping both buildings and beaches (Photos 2–24 and 2–25). In the early days of coastal dwelling, relocation was the only option. Until about the turn of the century the choice was "move it or lose it!" The town of South Seaside, New Jersey, originally built all of its houses on wooden runners, so that they could be moved back with the beach. In 1888, the Brighton Beach Hotel of Coney Island, New York, was drawn landward by a team of six steam locomotives (Photo 2–26). As

Photo 2–24. A small cottage being moved back from the shoreline after Hurricane Hugo struck Ocean Isle, North Carolina. (Photo courtesy of the Duke University Program for the Study of Developed Shorelines)

Photo 2–25. The Outlaw family house on the beach at Nag's Head, North Carolina, is famous in the annals of coastal management. In the past one hundred years, it has been moved back three times, a total distance of 600 feet, in response to an eroding shoreline. In 1995, it was perched close to the sea again. (Photo courtesy of the Duke University Program for the Study of Developed Shorelines)

Photo 2–26. The relocation of the Brighton Beach Hotel on Coney Island, New York, in 1888 was a momentous event. This large building was moved back 2,000 feet from a rapidly eroding shoreline by six steam locomotives. Perhaps not surprisingly the hotel was owned by a railroad company. (From *Scientific American*, April 14, 1888)

discussed in chapter 10, in 1989, the National Academy of Science advised the National Park Service that the best way to save the 208-foot Cape Hatteras lighthouse was to move it landward.

Today, coastal communities and beachfront property owners often scoff at the notion of relocation. But the day is likely to come when taxpayers refuse to continue paying the millions of dollars needed to maintain artificial beaches. Then the ocean will reclaim its shores.

The Ten Truths of Shoreline Armoring

1. *Armoring destroys the beach, it's ugly, and it reduces beach walkability.* On an eroding shoreline, the use of engineering structures leads to loss of the beach. Armoring is a choice that benefits beachfront property owners but few others.

2. *There is no need for hard stabilization unless someone builds too close to the shoreline.* Without buildings, there is no need for

stabilization. This point is a critical one in determining if there really is a justification for shoreline armoring (or beach replenishment), and, if so, who should pay for it.

3. *A relatively small number of people create the need for shoreline armoring.* In a typical beachfront community, a few hundred property owners line the beaches used by thousands. If threatened shorefront buildings were relocated, demolished, or allowed to fall in, erosion problems would disappear, and the community would still have a beach.

4. *Once you start, you cannot stop.* Hard stabilization is irreversible. Removal of groins, jetties, seawalls, and the like almost never occurs. Coastal engineering structures are often altered or replaced but seldom taken away. Once while examining the coast of northern Portugal we discovered a stone groin in the process of being dismantled, its rocks being removed by dump trucks. After extensively photographing this most unusual event, we followed the dump trucks around a shoreline bend to discover that the rocks were being used to construct a much longer groin. Once buildings have that protection, it is a near political impossibility to remove it. The state of Texas did once require the removal of an illegally constructed groin on its shoreline near the Louisiana border. But even in states with strong regulations prohibiting all kinds of hard structures, the existing walls are virtually always "grandfathered" and allowed to remain.

5. *It costs more to save the property than it is worth.* When viewed over a period of decades, the cost of most efforts to stabilize an eroding shoreline with hard structures exceeds the value of the property to be saved. When the cost of the eventual degradation of the public beach is thrown in, the expense of holding the shoreline in place with armor is orders of magnitude greater than the value of the property.

6. *Shoreline armoring begets more shoreline armoring.* All structures eventually cause sand supply deficits on adjacent beaches, resulting in a need for armoring. Seawalls get longer, single groins become groin fields, and offshore breakwaters are extended. Some thought is being given by the Louisiana legislature to continuing the segmented offshore rock breakwaters already begun off Holly Beach for more than 100 miles to the Texas line. This would be the

ultimate in lengthening of shoreline armoring in all of North America.

7. ***Shoreline armoring grows bigger.*** Shoreline engineering structures are inevitably damaged or destroyed and are then replaced by grander ones. Often the reason a structure is damaged is because the waves have removed the protective beach. This loss of a beach's wave-buffering effect can be seen clearly along the long seawalled portions of the Jersey Shore. Here, waves from minor storms smash directly against the walls, producing spectacular displays of spray. As the protective beach is diminished, walls must be increased in size.

8. ***Shoreline armoring is a politically difficult issue because of its long-term environmental impact.*** Surely it is a rare politician who can withstand the complaints of beachfront homeowners and developers seeking seawalls and think ahead three to four decades to the beach destruction the walls will cause.

9. ***Shoreline armoring is a politically difficult issue because no compromise is possible.*** Shoreline armoring allows no compromise; it is irreversible and leads to longer and higher structures. It is not possible to armor a short stretch of beach and walk away. The impacts on adjacent shorelines inevitably lead to demands for more armoring.

10. ***You can have buildings or you can have beaches; you cannot have both.*** Long stretches of the Atlantic shoreline are walled and beachless. The good news is that many buildings have been saved from falling into the sea; the bad news is that a steep price has been exacted: the beach.

In order to survive, eroding beaches must be continually replenished artificially or allowed to erode naturally. To keep a beach on an eroding shoreline, you have to sacrifice the buildings.

THREE

Beaches by the Numbers

Assigned to duty in Cairo during the 1930s, young British army officer Ralph Bagnold set out across the desert regions of Egypt in his dependable (and easily repairable) Model-T Ford. Bagnold spent every available hour learning to navigate and survive harsh desert conditions, later recounting his experiences in his book *Libyan Sands: Travel in a Dead World*. In World War II, Bagnold put his knowledge to work by envisioning equipment and tactics for the British army in North Africa. It was his idea to harass General Rommel's supply lines with the Long Range Desert Groups, units with vehicles, that raced hundreds of trackless miles in the desert (assumed unnavigable) behind the front lines.

In all of his desert adventures, Bagnold had a lot more on his mind than travel. His engineer's mind was intrigued by the formation of sand dunes by wind and awed by the sandstorms he experienced. In later years, he devised the first basic mathematical equations describing sand movement by wind. Simple and ingenious, these equations still form the basis of much of our thinking about how wind moves sand. Still later, Bagnold worked on the problem of sand transport by water. His equations of sand movement by currents in water also remain an important tool for describing sand movement in the surf zone.

Like Bagnold before them, today's engineers are quantitative people. Modern engineering students learn to use equations at every design occasion. Many such occasions involve mathematical expressions of relatively straightforward and measurable phenomena, such as the strength of steel or concrete or the resistance of a circuit. To rely simply on intuition or on qualitative or "eyeball" observations as even a partial basis of the design of a project has become unthinkable for many modern engineers.

Coastal engineers are no different from other engineers in their reliance on equations and computers. There is, however, a great deal of difference between the engineering of beaches and the engineering of steel beams. The characteristics of steel beams are known, and their response to various stresses is predictable. Beaches do not behave so predictably. The basic equations of sand movement in the surf zone are all derived from studies of one-way flow in river channels. We are still early in the development of basic equations describing the two-way, back-and-forth movement of sand by waves. No equation describes the exact response of a beach to a particular set of waves. Although we now know that waves work in conjunction with bottom currents in the surf zone, less is known about currents than about waves and less still about the interactions of waves and currents.

Driven by their quantitative engineering heritage, coastal engineers, specialists within the field of civil engineering, continuously struggle to devise sophisticated equations to describe and predict beach behavior. The resulting mathematical models are used in the design of replenished beaches and prediction of their durability; prediction of the impact of groins, jetties, and breakwaters on adjacent shorelines; and improvement of channels and harbors. Mathematical equations are combined into complex computer models to describe beach behavior in the future. Unfortunately, where beaches are concerned, that approach does not work. As we will discuss in this chapter, experience has taught us that we cannot predict the behavior of beaches within any useful time frame.

Models, the Modern Way

From Bagnold's observation of sand-wind and sand-water interactions, the modern world of coastal engineering models has become remarkably sophisticated. For example, the mathematical model GENESIS, the Generalized Model for Simulating Shoreline Change, is used by coastal engineers to predict how shoreline position will change as a result of coastal engineering structures' effects on longshore sediment transport. Such structures could include groins, jetties, seawalls, and offshore breakwaters. GENESIS is called a generalized model because it is assumed to be applicable to any stretch of shoreline.

Basically, the GENESIS model consists of two parts. The first is an equation calculating the volume of sand transported by longshore currents that move parallel to the shore in the surf zone. The second is an equation describing change in shoreline position. This equation is based on the assumption that as the shoreline moves, the shape of its offshore underwater profile remains unchanged (known as the concept of conservation of sand volume).

While relatively simple mathematically, the GENESIS model equations are used to describe a very complex natural system. The first equation, the longshore sand transport equation, is:

$$Q = \left(H^2 C_g\right)_b \left[a_1 \sin 2\theta_{bs} a_2 \cos \theta_{bs} \frac{\delta H}{\delta x} \right]_b$$

where:

Q is the longshore sand transport rate on the beach

H is wave height

C_g is the wave group speed characteristic for a given beach

b is a subscript describing breaking wave conditions

θ_{bs} is the angle of breaking waves with the shoreline

$$a_1 = \frac{K_1}{16\left(\rho_s / \rho - 1\right)\left(1 - p\right)\left(1.416\right)^{5/2}}$$

$$a_2 = \frac{K_2}{8\left(\rho_s / \rho\right)\left(1 - p\right)\tan\beta\left(1.416\right)^{7/2}}$$

where:

K_1 and K_2 are empirical coefficients, otherwise known as "fudge factors"

ρ_s is the density of beach sand

ρ is the density of sea water

p is the porosity of sand on the beach

$\tan\beta$ is the average nearshore bottom slope

Once the modeler has obtained Q, it is then possible to calculate the rate of shoreline change, or in a common application, the rate of loss of a replenished beach. To do that, the second equation, the shoreline change equation, is used:

$$\frac{\delta y}{\delta t} + \frac{1}{\left(D_b + D_c\right)} \left[\frac{\delta Q}{\delta x} - q \right] = 0$$

where:

y is the change in shoreline position

t is time

D_b is the height of the berm on the beach

D_c is the closure depth or the water depth beyond which, it is assumed, very little beach sand will be transported in a seaward direction

x is the length of the shoreline under consideration

Q is the longshore sand transport rate on the beach

q is the volume of a discrete addition or subtraction of sand, for example, in a beach replenishment project

What does all this mean? For real beaches, it means very little. Fundamentally, the assumptions behind the equations concerning natural processes on the beaches are wrong: for example, the assumption in GENESIS, as in most models, that bottom currents moving in an offshore direction do not exist. Even if the assumptions were not wrong, there is no meaningful way to obtain real numbers for the unknowns (such as wave height) in the equations. That is especially the case for the characteristics of waves on a storm-tossed beach. In addition, the equations require some mathematical sleight of hand. In the first GENESIS equation, the values of a_1 and a_2 are uncertain, because K is a number arbitrarily chosen to come up with a "reasonable" Q.

Nevertheless, this model enjoys widespread use by the U.S. Army Corps of Engineers and by private consultants. Major financial decisions are made based on its results. Increasingly, engineering reports to state coastal zone management offices include GENESIS to "prove" that a coastal construction permit should be granted. Part of the site selection and construction design for a Mexican nuclear power plant involved the use of GENESIS.

For GENESIS and the other shoreline engineering models, a basic understanding is required of the shape of the nearshore sea floor, the nature of the waves and currents that form under given weather conditions, the amount of sand being supplied to the beach, and the amount of sand that waves and currents can be expected to transport, to where, and at what rate. For lack of understanding, assumptions are made and integrated along a given length of shoreline for a given time period.

A mathematical modeler of natural phenomena must make a large number of assumptions, good, bad, and indifferent, and mathematically integrate their effects over long time spans and large areas to come up with an answer to a specific question. Shoreline change models have been used to answer very specific short-term questions such as a replenished beach's durability (as at Folly Beach, South Carolina), jetty impact on the downdrift beach (as at Oregon Inlet, North Carolina), and offshore breakwater effects on adjacent and downdrift beaches (as at Presque Isle, Pennsylvania).

Some questions are more amenable to modeling than others. It is reasonable to ask of mathematical models the direction of a long-term trend (e.g., will sea level rise or fall in the next century?). But as the questions become more and more specific (e.g., what will the absolute rate of sea level rise be at New York City or in Boston Harbor?), the minor weaknesses and unknowns in a model's assumptions loom larger, and model results become more and more uncertain.

Models are an integral part of weather prediction, and sophisticated though they are, everyone knows that the weather forecast is sometimes completely wrong. Who hasn't gone out toting an umbrella on prediction of rain, only to find a beautiful sunny day? Bob Sheets, former director of the Hurricane Center in Miami, Florida, demonstrated the uncertainties of mathematical models to millions of anxious viewers waiting for news about Hurricane Gordon in November of 1994. Tropical Storm Gordon had just passed across Florida from the Gulf of Mexico to the Atlantic, where it had become Hurricane Gordon. Then the storm stalled somewhere off South Carolina. Sheets told his anxious audience that, at the moment, he didn't know where the storm would head next. One model, he said, predicted a southerly course, while another suggested that the storm would move north. (The precarious nature of weather prediction even spills over into politics. The government of India briefly stopped issuing weather forecasts when people blamed the party in power for inaccurate predictions. Poor weather forecasts resulted in fewer votes!)

Atmospheric scientists are political and scientific realists. They know the public expects reasonable predictions, so they have trained us to understand that weather cannot be predicted with any great confidence for more than a few days into the future. Even when a weather prediction extends just twenty-four or forty-eight hours into the future, weather forecasters express their predictions in probabilistic fashion. For example, they might say that on Tuesday there is a 30 percent chance of rain, but on Wednesday the chance rises to 60 percent. The American public accepts weather predictions as uncertain and understands that the longer the time frame of the prediction, the less certain its success.

Mathematical models are also used to predict global environmental change, particularly the extent of atmospheric warming driven by the increasing levels of carbon dioxide (CO_2) from the burning of coal and oil. Carbon dioxide holds heat in the earth's atmosphere, causing it to act like a giant greenhouse, trapping the heat. Melting glacial ice, rising sea level, changing climate, and changing ocean circulation, all possible products of global warming, are studied and predicted using mathematical models. Distrust of and conflicting results from climate change models have led to the controversy surrounding global warming theories.

Models that predict global change are based on a great number of assumptions about how the earth works. To some degree, all the assumptions have weaknesses and unknown elements. Some assumptions are little more than educated guesses, such as, for example, the amount of CO_2 that will be absorbed by the ocean as atmospheric concentrations of this compound rise. Will cloud cover increase as sea temperatures rise? If an extensive cloud cover does form, how much of the sun's radiation will be reflected into the atmosphere, and how will the heating of the earth's surface be affected? How would increased cloud cover affect future global rainfall patterns?

Because of all the uncertainties, the use of mathematical models must be flexible. When the Environmental Protection Agency (EPA) first predicted, in the mid-1980s, the amount of sea level rise associated with global warming, it suggested as much as a 12-foot increase by the year 2100. By 1993, the worst-case, year 2100 scenario had been reduced to 6 feet, with a 2- to 3-foot rise deemed most likely. By 1995, the worst-case, year 2100 scenario had been reduced to 4 feet, with a 1.5 to 2 foot rise deemed most likely. The numbers changed as the basic assumptions changed to reflect changes in estimates of the future importance of CO_2-producing industries.

There is a big difference between climate change models and coastal engineering models. Weather and climate models solve the basic equations of motion, temperature, heat flux, condensation, and other real-world processes. They are based on accepted principles of physics. So many equations and concepts are involved, in hopes of minimizing error, that climate models can be run only on super computers.

GENESIS, on the other hand, is not based on physics. It is an empirical model, based on observations, most of which are made in wave tanks. Wave tanks are not oceans, however, and processes observed in wave tanks are poor imitations of ocean processes. Also unlike the climate models, GENESIS solves only a very few equations. Coastal engineers have reduced the surf zone to a simple system. These equations are so simple that the whole GENESIS program can be run at home on one's personal computer and is available on floppy disks for anyone who requests it from the Coastal Engineering Research Center.

Once all the equations and data are safely tucked into a humming computer, there is a tendency among both scientists and engineers to forget how weak the assumptions are and to look only at the numbers spewed by the machine. But when mathematical models used to predict beach changes are taken apart, assumption by assumption, one can see how very tenuous the results actually are.

Perhaps the success of the space program has led people to believe that we can solve any problem; no corner of nature need remain a mystery for long. But in looking back at the Corps' experience with models, we cannot find a single successful use of a mathematical model to predict the behavior of an engineered beach. At Folly Beach, South Carolina, the Corps based a two-million-yard reduction in replenishment sand volume on the GENESIS model. According to the model, the beach would not need nourishment for eight full years, but after only one year the Corps' district officials conceded that the predictions were inaccurate. For the Presque Isle, Pennsylvania, offshore breakwater project, the Coastal Engineering Research Center used mathematical models to show that sand would continue to flow along the beach behind the breakwaters once these structures were in place. It was, from a geologic standpoint, an impossible conclusion (see chapter 7). Sure enough, sand flow was halted and downdrift erosion began immediately upon construction of the breakwaters. At Oregon Inlet, North Carolina, a CERC mathematical model that predicted the success of artificially moving sand across the inlet (by dredging) at proposed jetties was criticized by the National Park Service's oversight panel of scientists, the "Inman Panel," as lacking basic important elements of nearshore sand movement (see chapter 9). Lack of confidence in the Corps' mathematical models is the primary reason the Inman Panel has objected to construction of the jetties.

Why Mathematical Models Cannot Predict the Behavior of Sand

Understanding the processes of the surf zone requires an understanding of the behavior of three very different media—air, water, and sediment—and their very complex interactions under constantly changing conditions. Mathematical models of beach behavior suffer because science and engineering are at a rudimentary stage of understanding surf zone processes and have no way to measure most of them. The models do not take into account the uncertainty of storms and the interaction of different processes going on at the same time. And they make the incorrect assumption that all beaches are the same.

Models versus the Real World

To get around the lack of understanding of the interaction of air, water, and sand, modern engineering models make unrealistic assumptions. Shoreline environments in the world of models are extremely simplified. In models, waves are typically neat and uniform, of equal height, and equally spaced (monochromatic waves) and usually come from the same direction. All sand movement in the nearshore zone is caused by waves and longshore currents. Shore-perpendicular bottom currents do not exist. The shoreface (the nearshore zone extending to a water depth of 30 feet) is a smooth feature with no offshore sandbars, covered by sand of uniform grain size. At the base of the shoreface is a "closure depth" beyond which very little sediment is transported. In most mathematical models, storms do not occur, but if they do, they occur at exactly the average frequency of storms in the past. In other words, there are no surprises. Storm waves are just as neat and evenly spaced as fair-weather waves, only they are higher. Beaches do not lose sand into the dunes by wind action or across the land by storm-wave overwash.

In the real world, sand is lost from the beaches through the complex interaction of wind, wave, overwash, and longshore and offshore currents. The state of the beach is important in determining the amount of sand that will be moved. The first storm of the winter along the mid-Atlantic Coast commonly causes far more shoreline retreat than subsequent storms. That is because the first storm removes the summer accumulation of sand washed ashore by the fair-weather waves. Waves, especially storm waves, are highly irregular, occurring at many wave lengths and heights, and may come from several directions at once. The surf zone, especially during storms, is in a "confused," highly complex, and dynamic state. Sand moves up, down, and across the shoreface through a combination of waves and many types of storm-driven bottom currents, some of which can carry large amounts of sand far beyond the assumed closure depth, well out onto the continental shelf. Waves and currents work together, with waves kicking up the sand and currents carrying it away. And in this fashion, even large particles can be carried by relatively weak currents. On some shorefaces, linear troughs on the sea floor, perpendicular to the shoreline, indicate the considerable or even overriding importance of sediment movement by offshore-moving currents. The shoreface is not smooth but is covered by sediments of various grain sizes. Often the shoreface shape is controlled by rock or mud outcroppings. The irregular shape and thickness of the shoreface sediment cover have a strong effect on wave patterns in the surf zone. A number of other factors may influence the transport of beach sand, including seasonal changes in the beach profile, the presence of erosion-inhibiting shell pavements, the presence or absence of offshore bars, and the wave-enhancing effect of offshore rock outcrops. Even the activities of burrowing organisms, expulsion of water by filter-feeding, bottom-dwelling animals, and formation of biological mats and slimes (e.g., algae) influence sediment transport.

The direction of wave approach is controlled by the shape of the sea floor (which can change a bit from year to year) and by the ever changing direction of storm waves. Currents are superimposed on the surf zone by various processes. One such process is the return of storm waters (the storm surge ebb) that have flooded adjacent land. A second is seaward-flowing bottom water that has been elevated in the surf zone by the sea level rise, forced by the winds that pushed water ashore. There is also surface water movement of rip tide currents and the actions of local winds and tides. As waves and currents erode and deposit beach sand, pavements of large shells that resist the currents may be formed by the winnowing away of the finer sand, causing a temporary decrease in the amount of sediment in motion. Under the right conditions of waves and currents, small landslides of beach sand may occur, carrying sand far out to sea. None of these processes are adequately considered in coastal engineering mathematical models.

For use in mathematical models, one cannot simply classify storms on the basis of the size of the waves, because each storm, like each beach, has a large and unique set of interacting forces. A storm of the same magnitude will cause quite different beach behavior on two different beaches; on the same beach, the same magnitude storm will result in greatly different beach responses in different seasons.

Weaknesses of Models

From a coastal geologic and oceanographic standpoint, bad assumptions and poor environmental measurements are going in and bad numbers are coming out of the coastal engineering mathematical models. Some of the specific and fatal weaknesses of mathematical models used by coastal engineers are listed below:

- **Isolation of natural processes.** Mathematical models used to describe beach behavior generally assume that the processes that move sand and shape the beach do so independently of other processes. The "principle of superposition," as it is called by engineers, allows individual processes affecting the dynamic beach to be isolated and evaluated separately. Although this may make sense from a mathematical standpoint, it does not apply to the natural beach system. Oceanic forces act in concert with one another and simply cannot be isolated realistically.

  A few simple principles about waves and sediment transport are generally accepted as understood: big waves move more sand; steeper waves are likely to move a higher proportion of sand in an offshore direction; and, up to a certain point, the greater the angle of breaking-wave approach to the shoreline, the more sand that will be moved laterally.

  To predict sediment movement, modelers commonly use some sort of greatest wave-height average, such as the highest tenth or highest third of the waves during a twenty-year period along a given shoreline reach. Anyone who has watched a storm-tossed surf zone with waves arriving simultaneously from several directions knows that something more than a simple average wave height is needed to describe how waves and sediments interact. A large body of oceanographic research has revealed that much sediment movement near the beach is not related to waves at all but, instead, must be described by combined waves and currents. Waves suspend sand, which is then carried by currents.

  How do modelers determine average wave characteristics? In the past, determination of average wave height has most commonly been made by "wave hindcasting." In hindcasting, wave height is estimated by ascertaining what sort of waves were most likely formed by the wind and weather conditions known to have occurred in the past and by assuming that the same sort of weather, hence the same heights of waves, will prevail in the future. Another method is to measure waves with a wave gauge somewhere offshore. Both approaches result in an estimate of what the waves are like in deep water. But shallow-water waves are what actually move sediment, and they obtain their character as they drag across the nearshore bottom on their way to the surf zone. The shape and nature of the bottom (rock outcrops, offshore bars, sediment grain size) determine what the breaking waves will be like, but these sea floor characteristics are poorly known, at best.

• **Representation of complex nature with artificial simplicity.** To compensate for the lack of data from the natural surf-zone environment, researchers observe the behavior of artificial beaches under controlled and isolated conditions in large wave tanks (LWTs). LWTs allow measurements to be taken of sand movement under particular wave conditions, but they lack currents of any kind. Nonetheless, the mathematical formulations gained by describing such sand movement become integral parts of mathematical models.

Although certain valid general principles of beach behavior have been verified in some of the Corps' early wave tank studies, it is doubtful whether such data have any application as currently used in mathematical models. No proof is ever presented that the waves, sediment, and fluid characteristics of a wave tank are representative of nature, yet the Corps refers to LWTs a few yards across and one or two yards deep as "prototype-scale." The real prototype, of course, is the beach!

There is no way that a wave tank can even begin to simulate the very large number of events occurring simultaneously in three dimensions (length, width, depth) over time in a real surf zone. LWTs are restricted in all dimensions. Unless all processes are simulated together, wave tanks will continue to be what they are today: great devices to impress politicians and elementary school students with crashing waves but little help in making real-life predictions.

• **Failure to consider inherent uncertainties of natural processes.** In technical parlance, mathematical models, to be useful, should be probabilistic and not deterministic, expressing results as a range of values rather than as a single value. The mathematical models used by the Corps are, without exception, deterministic. Model results should have "error bars" or some indication of the uncertainty of when the next "big one," that is, the next major storm, will occur.

On most beaches and in most engineering projects on beaches, storms are the cause of almost all important changes. Storms can remove huge chunks of replenished beaches overnight, cause beaches to disappear in front of seawalls, and cause new inlets to form. But we never know when the next storm will occur, how big it will be, or how long it will last.

Unfortunately for coastal inhabitants, storms are impossible to predict more than a few days in advance. Even when the timing of storms is accurately predicted, their magnitude is often miscalculated. The two greatest U.S. Atlantic coast northeasters of this century, the Ash Wednesday storm of 1962 and the Halloween storm of 1991, were not predicted by weather forecasters to be the huge storms that they were. To account for the possibility of a storm removing a large portion of a replenished beach in a single swoop (as has happened in recent years at both Ocean City, New Jersey, and Ocean City, Maryland), mathematically predicted beach behavior must allow for the uncertainties of storm frequency and magnitude.

The models produce only single-number estimates for such variables as the volume of sand required for a replenished beach, the rate of loss of a beach downdrift of a jetty, or the cost associated with replenished beach maintenance. For example, the cost of the northern New Jersey beach replenishment project, the Seabright project discussed in chapter 4, beginning in 1995, is predicted to be $3 billion for 33 miles over fifty years. It is also predicted that additional sand will have to be pumped up every six years to maintain the beach. At present, the Corps gives the U.S. Congress and local governments only such absolute estimates as these. Beach behavior predictions, however, should reflect the uncertainties associated with storm prediction. In the case of New Jersey, it could be said that there is a certain chance, expressed as a percentage, that the replenished beach in New Jersey will cost $3 billion over fifty years and a certain percentage chance that it will need new sand every six years. Or the uncertainties could be expressed as costs of $3 billion plus or minus some number of dollars and a nourishment interval of six years plus or minus some number of years.

In the early 1990s, two major replenishment projects in Ocean City, Maryland, were hit hard by major storms within two years. The Corps' Baltimore District declared the projects a success because the artificial beach protected beachfront buildings from direct wave attack. This was great news for a privileged few oceanfront property owners and city officials. But from another viewpoint, that of Congress and the American people, the projects were financial disasters. Within just three years, *one-third* of the amount of sand originally projected to be needed over *fifty years* was gone. Instantly, the long-term cost of maintaining a beach at Ocean City was increased dramatically. Had probabilistic rather than deterministic estimates been made, Congress and the public might have had more realistic expectations and budgeted accordingly. Or perhaps they would have decided the project was too expensive, risky, and uncertain to support at all.

- **Failure to consider chaos theory.** In the last couple of decades, chaos theory has revolutionized our understanding of the predictability of natural processes on the earth's surface. A natural system is said to be chaotic when very small perturbations have a strong impact on the eventual outcome. For some natural systems, like the weather, minor enhancements or very slight irregularities in one of the many factors controlling atmospheric conditions have been shown to have a huge eventual effect. Chaos is often described by the "butterfly effect," referring to the possibility that a butterfly flapping its wings in the Panamanian jungle could set off a chain of events leading to the turn of a hurricane into the Florida peninsula. The behavior of chaotic natural systems, like weather, can be usefully predicted only over the short term.

  Beach evolution is also a chaotic phenomenon. Very small changes in wave patterns, bottom sediment types, bottom currents, bottom shape, and a host of other factors may well cause very large changes in the ultimate shape of the beach and in the ultimate amounts of sediment transported or deposited during a storm. No coastal engineering mathematical model has recognized chaos, much less captured it.

- **Universal applicability (or the failure to recognize variety in nature).** Mathematical models of beach behavior are assumed applicable to any and all beaches on any and all shorelines. With adjustment, mainly for differences in grain sizes and wave climate, the same general models are applied to beaches on volcanic islands, carbonate banks, barrier islands, and cliffed coasts. But the list of variables that would affect beach behavior on these different types of coasts is so long that a separate, complex mathematical model would be needed for each beach.

A Close Look at One Model Concept: The Shoreface Profile of Equilibrium

A relatively simple mathematical relationship that well illustrates some of the problems inherent in mathematical models is the *shoreface profile of equilibrium*. The shoreface profile of equilibrium is the ideal shape of a nearshore zone or innermost continental shelf that forms in response to a particular set of wave, current, and sediment supply conditions. The concept of the shoreface profile of equilibrium provides the basis for virtually all coastal engineering models of beach sediment behavior. For example, designers of replenished beaches assume that the sand used to build an artificial beach will take on a new profile of equilibrium in a more seaward location. The predicted required volume of sand, therefore, is that volume needed to form the new, more seaward, profile.

The equilibrium profile concept states that the cross-sectional shoreface shape can be described by the equation:

$$h = Ay^n$$

where h is distance offshore, y is water depth, A is a constant related to grain size, and the exponent n is a curve-shaping parameter assumed to be 0.67. The model's failure is found within the constants n and A. The value for n is an average of a wide range of observed real-world values gleaned from representative profiles. Actual observed n values range from 0.03 to 1.1, making the mean value of n inaccurate for many profiles. The constant A is said to be related to the grain size of the sediment covering the shoreface, but by looking back to the original studies that were supposed to have confirmed this relationship, we find that the asserted relationship between beach profile and grain size does not exist (Figure 3–1).

The shoreface equilibrium profile equation assumes that the shoreface shape is controlled entirely by the grain size of the sediment covering a smoothly curved surface; therefore, every shoreface in the world covered by sand of a given grain size will have the same shape. Yet parameters as diverse as grain size, sediment supply, size of waves, size and frequency of storms, and location of outcropping rock and mud layers actually control the shoreface shape. No single parameter could possibly predict the shape of all the world's shorefaces.

The profile of equilibrium concept assumes that no beach sand will escape in a seaward direction beyond a *closure depth*, typically assumed (on the U.S. Atlantic and Gulf coasts) to be somewhere between 12 and 30 feet of water depth. The logic behind this is that all sediment movement on the shoreface is accomplished by the interaction of waves and sand on the sea floor. Sand will tend to move by diffusion from areas of high wave energy (the beach) to areas of low wave energy (the lower shoreface). The outer edge of this zone of sediment movement is called the closure depth. But this assumption ignores currents that move along the sea floor carrying large volumes of sediment at *all* depths. Oceanographers and geologists have shown that large amounts of sediment can be moved offshore by bottom currents during storms. Rob Thieler, a researcher at Duke University, has documented that at least 2 to 3 million

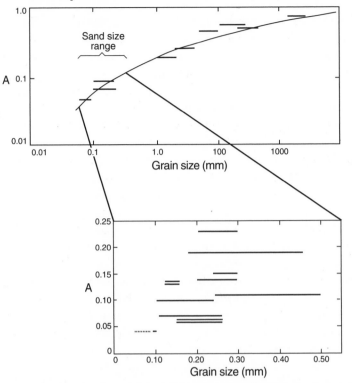

Figure 3–1. The upper graph shows the relationship between *A* (in the equation $h = Ay^n$) and grain size used by coastal engineers to determine the shape of the shoreface profile. Grain size in the upper plot ranges from mud to boulders. To make the lower graph, we went to the original data source (a University of Delaware master's thesis) and plotted all the data in the sand-size fractions using an arithmetic scale. We considered only the sand sizes because that is what is on most North American shorefaces. The lower graph shows that there is no relationship between A and grain size; however, coastal engineers assume that grain size determines the shape of shorefaces worldwide.

cubic yards of replenishment sand from Wrightsville Beach, North Carolina, has moved across the shoreface and now resides permanently on the continental shelf well beyond the closure depth of 28 feet assumed in the replenished beach design by the Corps' Wilmington District.

Miles Hayes, coastal geologist from the University of South Carolina, documented the transport of huge volumes of sediment across much of the continental shelf seaward of the Matagorda Peninsula in Texas during Hurricane Carla in 1961. Paul Gayes, of Coastal College in South

Carolina, discovered that the shoreface off Myrtle Beach, South Carolina, was covered with small seaward-extending gullies as a result of the return of the storm surge from Hurricane Hugo (1989). (As discussed in chapter 5, Gayes is finding similar gullies off Folly Beach, South Carolina.) The largest gullies, with reliefs of 3 or 4 feet, were found off street ends where particularly large volumes of storm-surge runoff returned to the sea. Don Wright, of the Virginia Institute of Marine Science, measured storm-driven currents of considerable strength with two current-measuring tripods on the shoreface off North Carolina's Outer Banks. After the 1991 Halloween storm, one of his record-keeping tripods was lost, and the other ended up in the surf zone. The surviving tripod's fragmentary record indicated the occurrence of strong seaward-directed currents capable of carrying large volumes of sand. The record on the rescued tripod also indicated that a lot of landward movement of sand occurred during the waning phases of the storm.

These examples, and other evidence, cast doubt on the validity of the shoreface profile of equilibrium concept for predicting real-world behavior of specific beaches, but it still is the most fundamental underlying assumption, the mainstay, of all coastal engineering models of beach behavior.

The Modelers: Who's Doing All This Stuff, Anyway?

Currently, the leading practitioners of mathematical prediction of beach behavior in the United States are Robert Dean and Nicholas Kraus. Dean, chairman of the Department of Ocean Engineering at the University of Florida at Gainesville and a member of the National Academy of Engineering, is considered by many to be the nation's leading coastal engineer. His approach to the problem of beach design is to use relatively simple mathematical models, typically referred to as analytical models. He developed the model basis for the relationship between beach length and replenished beach durability: the longer the beach, the longer the presumed life span of the beach. He has also led the way in applying the concept of the shoreface profile of equilibrium in a large variety of coastal engineering applications.

Nicholas Kraus, of Texas A&M University at Corpus Christi, uses more sophisticated and complex mathematical models known as numerical models. Working with others, he developed two of the most widely hailed numerical models used in coastal engineering: GENESIS and SBEACH. SBEACH is a model used to predict future storm erosion changes on both natural and engineered beaches. As we noted earlier, GENESIS is used to predict the behavior of beaches with groins, jetties, or other engineering structures. Ironically, SBEACH assumes that all sediment movement is on- and offshore, and GENESIS assumes all sediment movement is alongshore. In reality, offshore, onshore, and alongshore transport of sediment happens at the same time.

Kraus lived in Japan for twelve years and received his Ph.D. from the University of Tokyo. Before moving to Texas A&M, he spent most of his engineering career at the CERC, where he led the Corps' plunge into ever more sophisticated numerical models. He has published countless technical papers and documents devising and revising mathematical models to predict the behavior of sand. In our view, Dean and, especially, Kraus, in their efforts to predict beach behavior, are promoting the general application of concepts with severe limitations. They are, in essence, building widely used houses of cards.

A.W. Sam Smith is one coastal engineer who disagrees with Dean and Kraus. Smith is an Australian, born in New Zealand, who passed the New Zealand engineering exam with little formal education beyond high school. (As a result of his feat, the law was changed to make sure that those who passed the exam at least have a bachelor's degree in engineering.) Later, in a bow to professional trends, he went back to school, at age sixty, and earned a master's degree in civil engineering. For more than twenty years, he has practiced civil engineering on Australia's Gold Coast (the Australian equivalent of Miami Beach) and has acted as a long-term consultant to the local city council on problems of beach erosion and restoration. He takes great pride in pointing out that he lives 900 yards from the beach and visits it every day.

Smith believes in observing and imitating nature and is entirely skeptical of mathematical models. His rejection of models is not just a matter of casual opinion. He is what the Aussies call a field engineer, one who conducts all of his research and data collection on the beach, rather than in a laboratory or wave tank. He monitors the behavior of his beach and logs the data on a daily basis into what has become a vast Gold Coast data bank. His objections to the American approach are based on his simple observations: "On the real thing I seldom or never actually see, feel or sense any of the beach process assumptions so widely used by the U.S. mathematical modelers. . . . The more I learn, the more I realize how precious little we know."

In many reports to the Gold Coast city council, and in a sizzling editorial in the spring 1994 edition of the *Journal of Coastal Research* (an international scientific journal), Smith warns against the American system of models and wave tanks. One of his major criticisms is that very few American engineers question the models or bother to revisit their original assumptions to check their validity. His editorial points out: "Most of the literature continues to roll ahead on the back of pure theory. . . . Now something like 90 percent of the papers we peruse have as their only basis a mathematical model of some kind and, clearly to many, the model itself has become more important than the real thing." "Indeed," Smith continues:

> a sinister development that has accelerated over the last five years has been the model and its predictions syndrome. Some researcher assembles a mathematical model and then applies it to some data, usually only laboratory data. He then makes the data fit the model by calculating constants or factors until it balances. Then he turns around and runs the analysis in reverse using all the necessary fudge factors determined for the calibration in the first place and finds that he has ended up exactly where he started, all with the identical result. He then calls these results of simply reversing his calculations his complete model predictions and thus marvels at how good his model is. In fact he has only generated a closed loop and has got nowhere. As far as addressing reality is concerned, most of these classes of papers are quite useless; nobody else using different data can ever attain the same fudge [factors]. . . . The problem is that real-life data is being suppressed in favor of publishing papers based upon theory instead, but in the end none of the theory is worth anything unless it does match and predict real life. But without the real-life data being available—how do we know?

University of Arizona geologist Victor Baker agrees with Smith but views the problem from a different standpoint. Baker studies the geology of rivers. He argues that mathematical models of the behavior of earth-surface processes apply only to a very restricted set of conditions, defined by the various assumptions that underlie any model. Therefore, they should not be used to predict the behavior of rivers. Baker believes a thorough understanding of its past behavior would lead to more successful intuitive estimates of how a river, beach, or glacier will behave in the future. Common sense is a major component of Baker's approach.

In a 1994 technical paper Baker adapts an argument that a sequence of defensive reasonings used by proponents of models makes modelers immune to common sense. We have repeatedly observed the identical pattern of reasoning in reference to modeling of beaches. In the following paraphrase of Baker's description of this behavior, we have taken a lot of liberties with the original wording, including the substitution of a beach context for rivers.

1. When a coastal engineering model is criticized for its assumptions trivializing the complex and poorly understood processes on beaches, the engineer will assume the posture of a down-to-earth engineering practitioner. The engineer will note that we cannot wait until everything is known because we need results now, however crude, in order to make critical engineering decisions.

2. Next the coastal engineer may be asked: Why then, given the simplifications and distortions of reality implied in the model's basic assumptions, should he employ all the sophisticated mathematical machinery to get that crude result? Why not use some simple procedure instead? In response the engineer will change into a meticulous theoretician and extol the merits of mathematical rigor.

3. And when asked how one knows that the rigorous models really give information relevant to beach behavior during storms, the engineer transforms into a seasoned coastal engineer. He puts his critic to shame for not being aware of the empirically established, time-honored ability of these models to represent beach-storm response and of the good service they have rendered engineers in years past, etc. At this point the argument returns to item 1 above.

The coastal engineering profession is partly shielded from the criticism of geologists and geographers because of the differences between earth scientists and coastal engineers. Two different worlds are involved. The natural critic of the highly quantitative coastal engineering profession is a highly qualitative group that is very uneasy about the engineering models but cannot communicate their concerns in a mutually acceptable language.

Critical differences are also found between coastal engineers and other modelers, such as meteorologists. Meteorologists study the same atmospheric storms that are responsible for creating the waves and currents that cause most of the movement of beach sand. At professional meetings, atmospheric scientists seem to be obsessed with revisiting the past to check their predictions. Their profession is very much tuned to judging its own successes and failures in order to improve its performance. Coastal engineers, on the other hand, are tuned to the future. A vast American experience with sand movement around jetties and off replenished beaches remains unmonitored, undocumented, and unstudied.

Why do we continue to rely on models for predictions of beach behavior? It is partly out of an undying optimism and a strong belief in the models, as well as a strong belief that nature can be described by mathematics, ignorance about nature, and simply because modeling is the "state-of-the-art" thing to do.

The litany of ready responses to criticisms of coastal engineering models includes: "Do not throw the baby out with the bath;" and "Yes, there are some problems, but these models are the best we have until something better comes along." The Corps' usual response to criticism about the lack of error bars in their numbers is that Congress cannot deal with uncertainty in cost estimates. But politics should not drive science; neither science nor engineering should produce numbers that cannot be defended.

FOUR

Beach Replenishment

From the sunny beaches of California, east to the rocky shores of Maine and south to Florida, sand is being pumped and trucked onto beaches in hopes of maintaining broad expanses of sand to attract tourists and protect buildings from storm waves (Photo 4–1). Generally accepted as more aesthetically pleasing and less environmentally damaging than hard stabilization structures such as seawalls, beach replenishment—bringing new sand to a dwindling beach—has been growing in popularity since the early 1960s as "the solution" to beach erosion.

In many seaside resorts, tourism has been saved and even resurrected by such artificial beaches. Without beach replenishment most United States East Coast hot spots—Atlantic City, New Jersey; Coney Island, New York; Ocean City, Maryland; Virginia Beach, Virginia; and Jacksonville Beach and Miami Beach, Florida—would be beachless, concrete fortresses (Photos 4–2 and 4–3). Without beach replenishment to replace sand trapped by artificial harbors, breakwaters, and jetties, the Southern California coast would consist of a series of short stretches of wide beaches interspersed by long stretches of narrow to nonexistent beaches downdrift of coastal engineering structures.

Federal and Corps of Engineers involvement in beach replenishment got started in 1962, when the historic Ash Wednesday storm devastated beachfront property from northern Florida to southern Massachusetts. Because of the particularly severe damage along the New Jersey Shore, Congress authorized the Corps to begin a beach replenishment program, largely to restore beaches there.

The replenishment process basically takes sand from a "borrow" area, such as an offshore sand deposit, an inlet tidal delta, or an upland sand source, and places it on an eroded beach. The amount of sand is generally determined through the use of computer models, and the selected amount is put on the beach according to an engineering design. Sand is

Photo 4–1. Seashell collectors watch closely as a sand-water mixture is pumped onto Wrightsville Beach, North Carolina. Sand was obtained from a nearby inlet. (Photo courtesy of the Duke University Program for the Study of Developed Shorelines)

brought from borrow area to beach by pipeline, dredge, or dump truck, then smoothed into a beach profile by bulldozers.

To replenish or not to replenish is a critical decision in this time of rising sea levels and expected acceleration in that rise. It is a critical decision for the future of our beaches. Preservation of beaches for future generations is always an underlying rationale of beach replenishment projects, but, as stated in chapter 2, relocation of buildings may ultimately be the way to preserve beaches in developed areas.

As in all things, success is in the eye of the beholder. Thousands, sometimes millions, of dollars per mile are spent putting sand on beaches. Some view replenishment as throwing money—and sand—directly into the sea. Others believe replenishment is worth every penny because it restores, however temporarily, an eroded beach. Miami Beach, replenished in the early 1980s, received two awards that serve to illustrate. In 1985, the Corps' Jacksonville District received an award of merit for the Miami Beach replenishment project from the Florida Shore and Beach Preservation Association. In the same year, the Miami Beach project received the Golden Fleece award from U.S. Senator

Photo 4–2. Miami Beach, Florida, circa early 1970s. Along most of this shoreline no beach existed prior to beach replenishment in 1981, not because of natural shoreline erosion, but because of seawall placement beyond the high-tide line by oceanfront hotel owners. (Photo courtesy U.S Army Corps of Engineers)

Photo 4–3. Miami Beach, Florida, in 1981. This photo was taken immediately after the completion of the replenishment project. The beach at this point is wider than the natural beach was. The replenished beach has lasted for fourteen years, but in 1995 renourishment was being considered. (Photo courtesy U.S Army Corps of Engineers)

William Proxmire for distinction as a "ridiculous expenditure of taxpayer money."

The Corps' first task in a beach replenishment project is to establish the proposed project's environmental and economic feasibility. Highly optimistic estimates of long-term costs and durability of replenished beaches, however, have resulted in meaningless cost-benefit ratios. Although the Corps is charged with evaluating the relocation/retreat alternative, seemingly objective analyses of the relative cost of moving buildings back are skewed by overly optimistic replenishment cost estimates. Replenishment frequently leads to more development in greater density within shorefront communities that are then left with a future of further replenishment or more drastic stabilization measures.

The National Experience

Several years ago, with colleagues Tonya Clayton and Lynn Leonard in the Duke University Program for the Study of Developed Shorelines, we surveyed the national beach replenishment experience. As of 1988, approximately ninety East Coast barrier island beaches, thirty-five Gulf Coast beaches, and thirty West Coast beaches had been replenished. The total number of individual projects or pumpings is much larger because beaches require frequent nourishments (the term for replenishing a beach again and again) to keep them intact. For example, by 1995, Wrightsville Beach, North Carolina, had been nourished fifteen times since 1939, and nearby Carolina Beach, North Carolina, thirteen times starting in 1955. Ocean City, New Jersey, has been nourished at least forty times, with Virginia Beach, Virginia, coming in a close second, both starting in 1951.

Finding records of replenishment projects was an arduous task. Record keeping about replenished beaches is arcane, selective, and incomplete on the federal level and more so on the state level. Some replenishment projects carried out by individual beach towns without Corps or state involvement seem not to have been recorded at all.

As of 1987, at least 400 million cubic yards of sand had been emplaced on more than 400 miles of U.S. shoreline. The Atlantic barrier-island coast has the greatest length of replenished shoreline, more than 270 miles, followed by more than 100 miles along the Gulf of Mexico coast, and more than 30 miles on the Pacific Coast. No similar studies of beach replenishment experiences on the Great Lakes or in New England have been made to date. By 1995, the total national cost may have approached $4 to $5 billion, although the dollar amount is probably somewhat less for actual replenishment costs using new sand sources. The $4 to $5 billion figure includes beaches replenished with sand taken from normal maintenance dredging of navigation channels.

Funding for artificial beaches involves a combination of federal, state, and local moneys, the greatest part of which is usually federal. For the Corps to be involved, justification for replenishing a beach must fall into one of several authorization categories: (1) flood control (storm protection); (2) emergency repair; (3) navigation (pumping sand on a beach obtained from navigation channel maintenance); (4) beach erosion control; and (5) mitigation of damage caused by some other Corps project, most often jetties.

Listing replenishment operations according to the authorization category under which they are funded reveals some sleight of hand in the wrangle for funds. Each Corps district seeks money under the category most likely to be funded by Congress. The truth is often stretched to shoe-horn a beach project into a particular authorization category; for the same beach, the category may vary widely from nourishment to nourishment, even though nothing really changes on the ground. The intensity of this scramble for funding (and one of the difficulties involved in tracking down replenishment histories) is exemplified by the history of replenishment authorization categories from 1965 to 1987 in Wrightsville Beach, North Carolina (Table 4–1, Photos 4–4 and 4–5).

In its *Shore Protection Manual* the Corps reports that Wrightsville Beach received 4.6 million cubic yards of sand in two seperate pumping operations between 1965 and 1984. But we found that a total of 6.9 million cubic yards had been pumped onto this beach in at least six separate nourishments in this time frame. Thus the Corps omitted from its own records 2.3 million cubic yards, one-third of the total volume of the fill, pumped onto Wrightsville Beach. The reason: projects were done under

Table 4–1.

Authorization Categories for the Funding of Beach Replenishment Projects at Wrightsville Beach, North Carolina, 1965–87.

Number of Projects	Type of Authorization
3	Flood Control
3	Flood Control, Navigation, and Emergency
1	Emergency Repair
1	Mitigation

Photo 4–4. A replenished beach at Wrightsville Beach, North Carolina. A continuous vegetated dune at the back of the beach is sometimes referred to as the storm berm. (Photo courtesy of the Duke University Program for the Study of Developed Shorelines)

Photo 4–5. The replenished beach at Wrightsville Beach, North Carolina, experienced rapid erosion, resulting in a large erosion scarp (the cliff to the right). Small scarps often form on natural beaches after storms, but because of rapid erosion beach scarps are ubiquitous, and diagnostic, of a replenished beach. (Photo by William Cleary)

the navigation authorization category. In that category, the district receives little or no beach design money; sand is simply pumped onto the beach and spread around with bulldozers in a relatively low-cost operation when depositing of dredged material on the beach is determined to be the cheapest method of disposal. Although sand is emplaced as in a "real" replenishment, such as those done under the "storm protection" or "erosion control" funding categories, the Corps does not consider it replenishment.

To justify a large federal share in the cost of a 1981 nourishment on Wrightsville Beach (when the state was unwilling to pay its share), the district claimed that more than 90 percent of the sand loss had been caused by interference from the south by Masonboro Inlet's north jetty (constructed by the Corps); the city could thereby seek emergency funding under Section 111, which is reserved for damage mitigation. That conclusion was unlikely. The Masonboro Inlet jetties are at the downdrift end of the beach and therefore probably prolonged, rather than decreased, the replenished beach's durability. In fact, many beach replenishment projects include groins and jetties for the purpose of increasing beach durability. Even if the jetty had been responsible for the problem, there is no known way to quantify its share of the blame. Nevertheless, when the time came for the next nourishment, the Wilmington District once again concluded that the downdrift jetty was partly responsible. This time it was blamed for 67 percent of the erosion problem. In both of these cases Congress approved mitigation funding. The extra money was just enough to replace the state share with federal funds.

Regionally, various sand management philosophies seem to guide the individual Corps districts. The disposal of sand dredged during the maintenance of navigation channels and boat basins is handled in different ways on the Pacific Coast and the Atlantic and Gulf Coasts. Sand conservation drives Pacific Coast districts. In California, a state with few natural harbors, most boat basins, marinas, and harbors are either cut into the mainland, protected by engineering structures that project into the sea beyond the shoreline, or both. Sand obtained by construction and by harbor maintenance after construction is almost always put on nearby beaches. The sand could be dumped at sea at a lower cost, but the extra expenditure is justified because the harbors and their associated structures are responsible for the downdrift (usually to the south) erosion problem. Without this Corps transfer of sand, called sand bypassing, the beaches of Southern California would be practically nonexistent.

The Atlantic and Gulf coast Corps districts do not make bypassing sand an integral part of maintaining harbors and inlets. Sand from harbors and inlets is routinely disposed of at sea by hopper dredging. Hopper dredges fill their holds with sand and steam offshore for the continental shelf, where their load of beach sand is dumped well beyond the littoral system that would carry it back to the beach. From Florida's east coast inlets alone, more than 65 million cubic yards of dredged sand has been dumped offshore. This sand no longer participates in the dynamics of beaches, islands, and inlets; erosion rates inevitably increase. Florida has outlawed hopper dredging, but it is not clear that the state's edict will be followed by the Corps unless the state pays for the difference in costs between dumping the sand offshore and pumping the sand onto beaches.

Atlantic and Gulf coast districts cite the congressional decree that sand will be disposed of in the cheapest manner possible, arguing that pumping onto beaches will add to the cost of sand disposal. The tremendous costs to society of the erosion problem downcoast from inlets are ignored. While the California Corps wastes not a grain of sand, the Atlantic and Gulf Corps districts throw away huge volumes of beach sand, leading to serious coastal erosion.

The Local Story

In addition to regional and local differences in coastal management approaches, each replenished beach has a different story. Myriad factors, including politics, economics, and oceanographic processes, shape a community's beach replenishment history. Following is a series of "snapshots" from around the Atlantic and Gulf of Mexico coasts and in some foreign locales, illustrating the huge variability among community approaches to beach replenishment:

- South Seas Plantation, Florida, and Jupiter Island, Florida. These communities pay for their own artificially nourished beaches without federal, state, or local government funding, thus avoiding the public access requirement that comes with public funds.

- Palm Beach, Florida. Perhaps the nation's most exclusive barrier island, Palm Beach has almost no beach left since seawall construction led to its demise. Rather than replenish the beach, Palm Beach opted for an expensive concrete offshore breakwater, called a P.E.P. reef, that within a year of installation was causing serious erosion.

- Ocean City, New Jersey. This community may have had the greatest number of replenishments of any American beach, simply because the community owned its own dredge during the 1960s and 1970s. The hometown dredge ceased operations when the community could no longer get federal permits to dredge within the lagoon behind the island.

- Gold Coast, Australia. The beach replenishment here, where only local funding is available, is an example of the advantages of local control. Gold Coast engineers have, based on 20 years of intense study of beach sand pathways, an excellent understanding of local beach dynamics. The result is rapid response to repair erosion hot spots with detailed plans in place for major beach loss in typhoons. For example, the engineers know that, along their coast, most storm-related sand loss is naturally replaced in a year or two.

- Virginia Beach, Virginia. This community may be the American equivalent of the Australian Gold Coast in replenishment practices. For a number of years, Virginia Beach has replenished its beach using land sources, dump trucks, and its own money. As many as 100,000 dump truck loads per year have rumbled through the streets during the off season. Until recently the city managed its own beach without engineering and financial help from the Corps. The result has been a flexible replenishment program, able to respond to widely varying annual losses of beach sand. Corps replenishment projects tend to be much less flexible, but have the advantage of federal funding.

  In 1972, a joint ad hoc committee comprised of representatives from the city and the Corps studied the history of replenishment at Virginia Beach and determined that, at Virginia Beach, small annual nourishments were superior to large nourisnments spaced several years apart. Larger volumes of sand disappeared more rapidly. In 1995, without evidence that would contradict the 1972 report, the Corps, more attuned to big projects, has chosen to put large volumes of sand on the beach at three-year intervals. If the committe's conclusions were correct, this approach will require more sand and more money.

- Hunting Beach State Park, South Carolina, and Perdido Key, Alabama. These are among a few rare instances where beaches without buildings have been replenished. The replenishment sand from Hunting Beach, a state park, disappears quickly; the island has been replenished five times since 1968. The 4-million-cubic-yard project on Perdido Key, a national park, was deemed necessary because of long-term erosion caused by dredging the shipping channel into Pensacola, Florida.

- Atlantic Beach, North Carolina. Many beaches have benefited from dredging associated with Corps maintenance of navigation channels and harbors. Usually, these replenishment projects are done only after the Corps has determined that placement of dredged sand on the beach is the cheapest method of disposal, or if the state or local government pays the added expense of beach disposal. Atlantic Beach obtained four small, *free* beach replenishments because the Corps had run out of places to dump sand dredged from Morehead City Harbor.

- Corpus Christi, Texas. In Corpus Christi, a natural, fine-sand beach was replenished with coarse sand. Coarse sand produces steeper beaches; families with small children, the traditional users of the beach, were very unhappy with the resulting unsafe beach.

- Hilton Head, South Carolina. The major sources of sand for beach replenishment are lagoons, inlets and their associated tidal deltas, the continental shelf, and inland sand pits. The American practice is generally to take sand from wherever it can be obtained. On a number of barrier islands, including Hilton Head, replenishment sand has been obtained from the ebb or offshore tidal deltas a few hundred feet offshore. Although this is a ready and cheap source of large amounts of sand, it is too close to the beach. Mining tidal deltas will eventually reduce the island's natural beach-sand supply.

- Holland. The Dutch require that all sand for replenished beaches be obtained at least 12 miles offshore. This is to avoid interference with nearshore wave patterns and the sand supply of the beach. This would be a good idea for Americans, too, but current Marine Minerals Service (MMS) regulations require that any sand obtained from beyond 3 miles off an American shore be sold only to the highest bidder. No exceptions are made, even for public works such as replenished beaches. This has effectively halted any consideration of dredging in deeper water for replenished beaches.

- Fisher Island, Florida. Bright white oolitic sand from the Bahama Banks is being considered by a number of southeastern Florida communities and has already been used on the small beach fronting Fisher Island, the next island south of Miami Beach.

- New Zealand, Hawaii, Taiwan, and Japan. Sometimes communities go a long way for sand. Sand shipped from New Zealand was used on some Oahu, Hawaii, beaches. The Japanese have imported beach sand from Taiwan.

- Vero Beach, Florida. Vero Beach turned down a Corps replenishment project even though funding was assured. The reason: fear that the replenishment sand would move seaward (a very likely possibility) and cover offshore rocks and coral heads, very important ecologically and to local divers.

- Naples, Florida. In 1994 Naples abandoned $10 million in matching federal funds for a proposed $17.5 million nourishment. Michael Stephens, a consulting engineer working for the city, noted that the study and authorization time for the project would run somewhere between four and eight years, and said, "We can't afford to wait until the year 2000 and beyond before putting sand on the beach." So the city is funding its own beach.

- South Carolina. After Hurricane Hugo, the Corps and the state of South Carolina, in a massive, ill-directed sand-moving project, took sand from wide beaches on a number of islands and put it on narrower portions of the same islands. Most of this sand disappeared in a few months. In Maine, such a sand transfer near Wells Harbor was blocked by the court action of property owners adjacent to the widest beaches.

- Cape Hatteras, North Carolina, and Hunting Island, South Carolina. In another case of taking away island to make beach, the Corps dredged embayments in the islands to obtain replenishment sand. Ponds now occupy the sand removal sites.

- Miami Beach, Florida. Environmental impacts associated with beach replenishment abound but are most severe in southern Florida, where attached organisms on rock outcrops on the sea floor are common. Such fauna and flora cannot move, hence cannot escape encasement in mud and sand from replenishment projects. Coral heads off Miami Beach continue to be smothered on the continental shelf as the waves pound the artificial beach made up entirely of soft calcareous skeletal material, grinding it into mud and washing it over the corals.

How Long Will the Beach Last?

The durability of individual replenished beaches (the time span before the beach effectively loses its storm protection or recreation function) has been highly variable. Following the replenishment operation completed in 1981, Miami Beach remains more or less stable, requiring very little nourishment. It is the most durable replenished beach on the United States' Atlantic and Gulf of Mexico coasts. Miami Beach's durability is possibly attributable to the irregular grain shape of the coral fragment sand, which causes the beach to be tightly packed and hard to the touch; walking on Miami Beach is almost like walking on pavement. At the opposite extreme, a 1982, $5 million beach in Ocean City, New Jersey, disappeared in 2.5 months (Photo 4–6). California's beach replenishment experience has been quite varied; a number of beaches seem to have lasted twenty years or more (for example, in the Santa Monica area), while others have disappeared quickly. The difference is because many of California's beaches are pocket beaches tucked between protective rocky headlands.

Replenished beaches always erode unevenly along their lengths, a major reason there is disagreement on the success of beach replenishment. Tybee Island, a barrier island at the mouth of the Savannah River

Photo 4–6. A scene on the boardwalk at Ocean City, New Jersey, where in 1982 a $5 million replenished beach was lost in 2.5 months. (Photo courtesy of the Duke University Program for the Study of Developed Shorelines)

in Georgia, is an example. Before its 1976 replenishment, the Tybee beach was suffering serious erosion problems at both its north and its south ends. Although the shoreline of the central portion of the island was stable, the entire 3.5-mile island beachfront was replenished. The new beach disappeared almost entirely within a few months at the north and south ends of the island where the erosion problem existed, but remained along the island's center. Sixty percent of the beach was lost at the ends, 40 percent remained in the center. Thus, like the description of an elephant by blind men, the durability of a replenishment project can vary according to where one takes the measurement.

According to our definition of beach durability, 26 percent of replenished U.S. Atlantic Coast barrier island beaches (from the south shore of Long Island to Miami) were effectively gone in less than one year, while 62 percent lasted between two and five years, and 12 percent (all in southeast Florida) lasted more than five years (Figure 4–1). Replenished beach durabilities along the U.S. Gulf of Mexico coast and Pacific Coast are much the same, though some individual Pacific Coast replen-

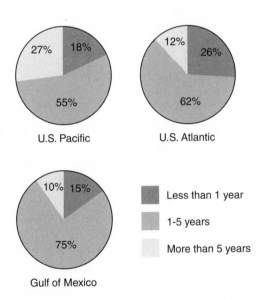

Figure 4–1. Pie diagram showing our view of the useful-beach durability of replenished beaches on three U.S. coasts. Beach durability is greatest on average along the Gulf of Mexico coast, but several individual replenished beaches on the Pacific Coast have lasted more than fifteen years. On the Atlantic Coast, virtually one-quarter of the replenished beaches have had a useful durability of less than one year (all beaches in that category are north of Florida).

ished beaches have persisted for over two decades. On the Atlantic Coast, there are strong regional differences in beach durability. South of Cape Canaveral, Florida, a beach typically lasts seven to nine years. Between Canaveral and the Georgia line, five-year durability is typical. For Georgia, North Carolina, and South Carolina, two to four years is typical, but for Delaware, Maryland, and New Jersey, only one- to three-year beach life spans can be expected.

Table 4–2 shows a comparison of some of the Corps' durability predictions for some planned beach replenishments with our predictions for the same beaches based on our knowledge of regional beach durability. The Corps' beach life span estimates are much longer, in some instances more than ten times greater, than ours. With two exceptions, we predict the beaches will be entirely gone before the time predicted as the nourishment interval. The beach "durability estimate" that we attribute to the Corps will not be found in the Corps' publications. We have calculated the estimates based on Corps data. The nourishment interval referred to in Table 4–2 is the expected time span between beach nourishments. It is a predetermined point at which about one-third to one-half of the replenished beach has eroded. If you know the interval, that is, if you know how frequently the Corps intends to add sand to the beach after the initial replenishment, and you know the volume of sand the Corps plans to use for each nourishment, you can calculate the rate of beach sand loss that the Corps has predicted. Knowing this predicted rate of loss, one can come up with a total predicted durability of the artificial sand body placed on the beach, assuming no further nourishment occurs. This is a rough but useful indication of the Corps' view of beach durability for a particular project.

Our replenished beach durability numbers are based on the Duke University Program for the Study of Developed Shorelines' survey of U.S. Atlantic Coast beaches, taking into account the strong regional differences in replenished beach durability. Thus, our numbers are based on the local experience and assume that the beaches in question will behave as neighboring replenished beaches already have. Estimates based on local experience, an admittedly rough assumption, are, we believe, generally more reliable than those based on mathematical models, for the reasons discussed in chapter 3.

Another view of beach success or failure is based on a comparison of estimated and actual costs or estimated versus actual sand requirements. Two of the most replenished beaches in the United States are Carolina Beach and Wrightsville Beach, North Carolina. From the standpoint of the two communities, these have been successful replenishments be-

Table 4–2.
Predicted Nourishment Intervals and a Comparison of Predicted Replenished-Beach Life Spans. In all cases, life spans are estimated assuming no additional nourishment will occur. Note that with two exceptions we estimate that the beaches will be completely gone before the nourishment interval (column 1) occurs. The nourishment interval is the point in time when the Corps assumes that 1/2 to 1/3 of the beach will be gone and it is time to bring in the dredges.

Beach	The Corps' Nourishment Interval (years)	The Corps' Beach Life Span estimate (years)	Our Beach Life Span estimate (years)
Seabright, NJ	6	30	1–4
Ocean City, NJ	3	11.5	1–3
Sandbridge, VA	one time	6–7	1–3
Topsail Beach, NC	2	12	2–5
N. Myrtle Bch, SC	8	36	3–5
Myrtle Beach, SC	8	36	2–4
Garden City, SC	8	12	2–4
Folly Beach, SC	8	24	1–3

cause, since 1965, beach sand has almost always been in place. But they are particularly glaring examples of cost overruns. Wrightsville Beach experienced a 650 percent cost overrun relative to the cost estimate given to Congress. Carolina Beach cost 1,300 percent (inflation corrected) over the cost estimate given to Congress. In a 1994 report (discussed in chapter 10), the Corps states that the Carolina Beach project was underestimated by only 100 percent.

In early design documents, the Corps' initial estimate of the total volume of sand required for fifty years' maintenance of the new Ocean City, Maryland, beach was 15 million cubic yards. This volume estimate provided the basis of the cost-benefit ratio. Within three years, the beach had gobbled up about one-third of the predicted fifty-year need.

Although the reasons cited by the Corps for the poor performance of replenished beaches vary, "unexpected" or "unusual" storms are the predominant excuse. Calling storms "unexpected" demonstrates a fundamental misreading of the natural system. It also demonstrates irresponsible engineering. The possibility of coastal storms of a broad range of strength and frequency needs to be considered in the design phase of projects, by projecting estimates as ranges rather than as absolutes, with plusses and minuses attached to all estimates of cost, sand volume, and beach durability (see chapter 3). The public's acceptance of the unusual storm excuse may be an important reason the Corps has failed to show any real effort to learn from past mistakes. It has been able to convey the impression that beach losses during storms are a natural disaster, a "tragic act of God," or a bit of bad luck. For example:

- "This beach [Miami Beach] should last indefinitely providing a major storm doesn't come by," Jacksonville District engineer as quoted in *Time* magazine.

- "We've had some unusual weather that probably accelerated the erosion slightly, but we're pleased with the way things are going right now," Savannah District engineer as quoted in the *Savannah (Georgia) Evening Press.*

- "One thing we had not counted upon was that a major storm would occur just as the project [Port Mansfield, Texas] was completed, so the experiment was not entirely successful," Galveston District Office.

The Corps seems to have succeeded in assuaging the anger and indignation that erupted when two projects back to back at Ocean City, Maryland (grand total cost between 1988 and 1994, including storm repair, $63.5 million) suffered significant losses within less than a year of emplacement. The Corps argued that both of the storms that caused the beach sand losses were unusually severe and that 96 percent of the sand was just offshore, "still in the system," protecting buildings and on its way back ashore.

Within the last ten years, the Corps has added this "it's just offshore" argument to performance evaluations of all its beach replenishment projects. Starting about 1985, the Corps began to report the percentage of replenishment sand offshore (underwater) in combination with the amount of fill remaining onshore to come up with the amount of sand remaining on the beach. By comparing differences in the offshore area of the beach, before and after replenishment, one can see, or one can at least believe one can see, how much sand lies in the underwater portion of a project after a storm.

Whether or not the offshore sand is actually from the replenished beach (in Ocean City, sand could have come from the continental shelf or from Delaware), the question remains whether the offshore sand makes any difference. Does underwater sand contribute to the storm buffering ability of a beach? A little bit. The real storm buffer of a replenished beach is the uppermost beach and the storm dune, or berm, as it is sometimes called. Offshore sand, even if it is in the surf zone, will be passed over by the storm floodwaters, or surges, that push the surf to the upper beach or further inland.

Does underwater sand make a better recreational beach? Not at all. To the beach goer looking for a place to set up a beach umbrella, offshore sand is of no use. Nor is it of any use to the business community that is hoping for a prosperous beach season.

Building a Beach: Replenished Beach Design

Beach replenishment entails more than simply dumping sand on a stretch of shoreline. Sophisticated computer models and other analytical techniques are used by coastal engineers to determine the volume of fill, the sand grain size, and how often fill will need to be added. But does this system of design work?

The one replenishment design principle that coastal scientists and engineers agree on is that the stormier the seas, the higher the loss rate of the artificial beach. The Bahama Banks, a prominent bathymetric feature located east of Florida, shelters south Florida's east coast. The banks are one reason east Florida storm waves are lower than those along New Jersey beaches, which do not have the same bathymetric protection and are more exposed to the full brunt of storms. But local factors can complicate that picture. For instance, no one can explain why the replenished beach at Jupiter Island has lost large amounts of sand in three years, while 80 miles to the south, Miami Beach has remained in place for over a decade (Figure 4–2).

Miami Beach

Figure 4–2. Line drawing to full scale showing the beach and shoreface off Miami Beach, Florida, to a depth of 30 feet. The small bump at the landward end of the profile is the replenished beach. This diagram gives an idea of how small replenished beaches are relative to the size of the shoreface and the zone of active sand movement.

Calculation of the required sand volume for a replenished beach is based on an assumption that the new beach will establish a shore-perpendicular profile of equilibrium extending down to closure depth, usually ranging from 15 to 30 feet of water depth, beyond which very little sand will be lost in a seaward direction. Beach design also assumes that there will be "profile adjustment," an initial high loss of sand immediately following beach emplacement. Some profile adjustments involve the loss of more than half the original beach width. After profile adjustment, the rate of loss, or erosion rate, of the beach is assumed to be the same as that of the pre-replenishment natural beach. The combination of erosion rate and presumed profile adjustment determines the "nourishment interval," the length of time in which about one-third to one-half of the visible replenished beach is expected to errode.

Other factors involved in beach design include grain size of the pumped-in sand, called the fill, as compared to the natural or "native" beach sand, and overall length of the replenished area. It is generally assumed that the coarser the sand, the lower the rate of sand loss from the beach, hence, the smaller the volume of sand required to achieve a stable offshore profile. Similarly, it is also generally assumed that the greater the length of a beach, the longer it will last.

On the basis of our studies of replenished beaches as well as our understanding of modern oceanographic principles, we have concluded that virtually all of the just described design principles that the Corps uses to predict beach durability are wrong. We have discussed these in more detail in chapter 3.

The concept of *closure depth* lacks validity because well-documented currents that move perpendicular to the beach are capable of carrying sand well beyond the defined closure depth.

Initial profile adjustment, or the initial high loss of sand as the profile comes to a new shape, has not been documented by observations of replenished beaches. At some locations, profile adjustment may occur, but, at others, particularly in south Florida, it is not apparent. The so-called profile adjustment may simply be the beach's response to the first storm that goes by.

Based on comparisons before and after replenishment, the *erosion rate* of replenished beaches appears to be almost always greater than the natural beach's erosion rate. The assumption that pre- and post-replenishment erosion rates are the same is an important reason predictions of beach replenishment durability are optimistic more often than not.

It would seem to be common sense that the finer the *grain size*, the more rapid the sand removal from a replenished beach, but this may not be the case. Geologist Paul Komar, in a study of Oregon beaches, showed that the coarser the sand on natural beaches, the steeper the slope of the beach, and the steeper the slope, the greater the erosion rate in storms.

The longer the replenished *beach length*, the longer its durability is a design tenet based on the assumption that replenished beaches erode from their ends only. Replenished beaches, however, tend to erode in a pattern similar to the natural beach. Sand may be lost from any portion of the beach, not just the ends. Simple graphs of beach length versus beach durability for Atlantic Coast replenished beaches indicate that beach length is not an important factor in durability on the Atlantic Coast.

Most replenished beaches probably disappear in steplike fashion. The size and frequency of the steps are controlled by the size and frequency of the storms that strike the beach. Not surprisingly, storm occurrence is thus *the* major factor determining durability of replenished beaches. But uncertainties about the frequency and magnitudes of storms are not considered by the Corps. No matter how solid the engineering, the uncertainty inherent in the coastal environment, particularly prediction of storm frequency and strength, must be reflected in planning and design documents as well as in congressional debate.

There is a more realistic approach to replenished beach design, and the Dutch and Australians are following it. Neither country depends on the tenuous and outdated assumptions or the complex mathematical models used by the Corps and the rest of the American coastal engineering community.

The Dutch take at least ten years' worth of profiles of an eroding shoreline to learn how much and in what fashion it is eroding. They then assume that the beach will continue to erode in the same fashion and calculate the volume of sand required to hold the beach in place for a designated number of years, adding 40 percent of this volume to allow for profile adjustment if it occurs.

The Dutch base their replenishment design on the behavior of the beach in question, not on a generalized mathematical model assumed to be applicable to every beach. In other words, they learn from nature and follow its dictates. The Corps rarely makes more than short-term and cursory observations of the behavior of a beach before replenishment. Because American coastal engineers assume the validity of a general coastal model, they see no real need to observe how individual beaches work.

Led by A.W. Sam Smith, the Australians use basically the same approach as the Dutch. Smith, whose views are discussed in chapter 3, and his colleague, Angus Jackson, observe the way the beaches react to storms, and they let that information determine their replenishment design and construction techniques. They have observed that after big typhoons, a large offshore bar forms along some Gold Coast beaches just beyond the surf zone. So, as the first step in replenishment, the Australians pump in a similar artificial storm bar. The offshore bar not only protects the new beach for a while, it also slowly moves, grain by grain, adding some of its sand via natural processes to the artificial beach. Like the Dutch, the Australians attempt to mimic the natural system as closely as possible.

Standing guard over current U.S. design principles is the Corps' Coastal Engineering Research Center. Most replenished beach designs by Corps districts are approved by CERC, which basically insists that the standard mathematical model approach be used. CERC accepts only those project designs that follow guidelines published in the Corps' *Shore Protection Manual,* modifiable only by more recent numerical models designed by CERC. More than any other single publication, the manual has held back progress by preventing any creative diversions from standard U.S. coastal engineering practice. Consulting engineering firms do not dare tread outside the manual's boundaries for fear of lawsuits if their design goes awry. At the time of this writing, a new *Shore Protection Manual* is underway, one that we fear will continue the emphasis on use of mathematical models rather than field experience.

Prevention of Storm Damage

Under federal regulations, storm protection makes a beach replenishment project eligible for federal assistance; recreational benefits do not. But in reality, virtually every community, as far as we know, wants a beach for recreation. As former congressman Mike Synar of Oklahoma astutely observed, it is the Chamber of Commerce folks that come to lobby for beaches in Congress, not the emergency preparedness officials.

There is no question that replenished beaches do reduce storm damage to buildings in beachfront communities. Once an artificial beach is in place, storm waves must chew their way through the replenished storm berm or dune before they can get to the buildings. Too often, however, claims of damage avoided become part of the funding clamor. The state of South Carolina, the city of Myrtle Beach, and director of the Coastal Engineering Research Center Jim Houston have all claimed that the replenished beach at Myrtle Beach saved many properties from Hurricane Hugo's wrath. A 35mm slide that seems to have been shown at recent public hearings by city officials in virtually every U.S. Atlantic and Gulf coast beachfront community contemplating replenishment reads: "The $4.5 million the city spent on the fill [replenished beach] has been saved tenfold or a hundredfold in property damage reduction. . . .—Myrtle Beach City Council member."

The beach in question was a very small one, put in place at city expense. The claims were apparently based on a consultant's report, following the hurricane, that compared property damage in communities to the south (Garden City) and the north (North Myrtle Beach) to that in Myrtle Beach proper. This comparison was decidedly misleading. The communities used for comparison are at lower elevations and have entirely different types of construction: beach cottages versus the more substantial concrete-and-steel high rises of Myrtle Beach. But what is particularly unsettling about these claims of damage mitigation is that, according to our own field observations, this very small replenished beach at Myrtle Beach was mostly gone before Hurricane Hugo struck (unless one counts underwater sand).

Not true!

After the winter storms of 1992, the city of Ocean City, Maryland, and the Corps claimed that more than $94 million in property damage was prevented by the replenished beach. But Hurricane Hugo, a much larger storm with a ten-foot storm surge, did only $10 million worth of damage in Myrtle Beach, a similar community, making the undocumented $94 million Ocean City estimate of damage questionable. The Ocean City estimate of damage prevented seems to have been pulled out of the air, but it has been widely quoted to justify the huge cost overrun of the city's new beach.

Future Projects: Have We Learned from Our Mistakes?

Inevitably, in public debate over a proposed replenishment project, an opponent points out the Corps' record of cost overruns and underestimated beach durability. The typical response is: "We at the Corps have made some mistakes in the past, but we've learned from them." Our analysis, however, finds that Corps predictions of the costs of building and maintaining a replenished beach are increasingly in error (for example, the huge cost and sand volume underestimates of Ocean City, Maryland, and Folly Beach, South Carolina).

The New Jersey coast beach replenishment project (called the Seabright project here and under construction at the time of writing) serves to illustrate. It is the largest single replenished beach ever to come off the Corps' drawing board, one that some in the Corps' New York District have said is comparable in magnitude to the Panama Canal. It affords a good indication of how the Corps will approach the shore in the future.

Seabright, New Jersey, is a small town on a long, low, narrow spit. Although it is the closest Jersey Shore community to New York City, it boasts only 1,600 year-round residents, most living in small, single-family houses. Seabright was once a summertime destination for New Yorkers; a train from the city delivered passengers directly to the beach. Today, hardly anyone comes to Seabright to swim. Seawalls built to protect the buildings eventually caused the loss of the beach.

The beach replenishment project involves the creation, by 1998, of a 140-foot-wide beach from Seabright to Asbury Park, a distance of 33 miles. The Seabright project design typifies the "moving target" about which Corps of Engineers' critics, such as the Inman Panel that reviewed the Oregon Inlet, North Carolina, jetty project, complain. The moving target is the constantly changing plan for a given project; you criticize one plan only to find another plan operational.

In March 1994 the status of the Seabright project a few weeks after U.S. Senator Frank Lautenberg turned over a ceremonial spadeful of sand and two months before pumping was due to begin was summarized in a startling article in the *New York Times* by Jon Nordheimer. "The cost of the entire 50 years of the 33 mile project had been presented to the public as just topping $1.1 billion," Nordheimer wrote, "but figures revealed this week by the Corps show that the cost will be $1.029 billion just to restore the first 12 miles. . . ." In one week, the reporter estimated, the fifty-year cost had tripled to $3 billion.

The next week district officials claimed to a reporter from the *Asbury Free Press* that the Corps had been using the higher cost estimates all along. By our reading of the earliest design documents on the Seabright project, however, the estimated fifty-year cost was $250 million.

A replenishment project cost-benefit analysis depends on estimates of how often and how much sand will be needed. The Corps calculated that the nourishment interval for the Seabright beach would be six years, and Gilbert Nersesian, district coastal engineer, was quoted in the *Times* article as sayings, "With calmer periods, repairs might be required only every 10 years or so." Based on the history of New Jersey beaches, we believe that the nourishment interval will more likely be one to three years. Norbert Psuty, coastal geographer from Rutgers University, predicts the new New Jersey beach should last for two years or so. If our experience-based estimate of beach life span is correct, and if the Corps is serious about keeping a beach on this New Jersey shoreline reach, they should be planning for fifty-year costs of approximately $6 to $12 billion (the total will vary with storms, of course).

Bruce Bergman, district director of planning, told the *Times*, "[Corps of Engineers] projections are that we will protect more capital than we spend on repairing beaches." Replenishment is not supposed to be a one-for-one, cost-for-value proposition. When beach replenishment costs approach property value, it is time to consider moving buildings, especially in this time of rising sea level and accelerating erosion rates. If our society were to predicate replenishment viability on whether putting in a new beach is cheaper than the value of the protected coastal property, the Corps would have a beach replenishment budget rivaling that of all other military activities.

According to the *Times* article, the New York District avoided the difficult questions related to public access along this heavily developed shoreline, the closest New Jersey shoreline in reach of the eight million overcrowded souls from New York City: "Two miles of new beaches in Seabright will have access paths spaced 2,500 feet apart with virtually no place to park, no public facilities and no lifeguards. Another half mile is occupied by private beach clubs that were given the right to keep nonmembers off the new sand. Only 12 public parking spaces exist along the two miles." Dery Bennett, executive director of the American Littoral Society, is quoted as saying, "Access at the Jersey Shore means parking, if there's no place to park you don't have access." Bergman stated: "Limited parking and concerns about local traffic bottlenecks would be overcome in part by a state plan to have shuttle buses between satellite parking at Sandy Hook [the national seashore to the north, where parking is already insufficient] and the new beaches." New Jersey state officials assert that no such plan exists.

Corps planner Bergman told the *Times* that replenishment will avoid "the untold environmental costs when the ocean breaches a barrier beach and flows directly into inland bays and rivers." A similar justification was used to boost the benefits in the cost-benefit ratio for the proposed Sandbridge, Virginia, replenishment project. The Corps' contention that replenished beaches can be justified because they will prevent environmental "disaster" in the form of new inlets is questionable for the following reasons: (1) such breaches are not natural disasters but natural changes to be expected on all barrier islands; (2) they are unlikely in northern New Jersey because most of the 33 miles of shore-line is mainland with no lagoon behind it; (3) replenished beaches do not prevent breaches from occurring, (although large seawalls might); and (4) if storm breaches were to occur in developed areas, the new inlets would be artificially filled. Such a breach did open on the barrier island north of Westhampton, New York, and the Corps plugged it. After Hurricane Hugo in 1989, a breach on southern Pawley's Island, South Carolina, was plugged within days. After Hurricane Hazel (1954) three inlets were immediately plugged. We know of no inlet, newly opened across a developed barrier island, that has been allowed to remain open. Corps planner Bergman's concern about the environmental damage from a newly opened inlet is unwarranted.

By December 1995 it was clear that the beach was disappearing much faster than predicted. The following quotes taken from a flurry of artricles, mostly in August issues of *The New York Times* and some local New Jersey newspapers, demonstrate that the Corps' defense of the diminishing beach played out in the usual fashion.

- "A big chunk of material is gone. It's probably more than we anticipated," James Mullins, resident construction manager.

- "Unsettled weather activity as sea caused the shoreline recession," but "We expect a good portion of the washed-away sand to return once conditions calm down," Gilbert Nersesian, New York District, Chief Coastal Engineer.

- "It did its job. The beach is supposed to be sacrificial," Peter Shugert, Corps spokesperson.

  Others viewed the rapidly disappearing beach differently:

- Norbert Psuty, Rutgers University coastal geographer ". . . doubted if the sand would return. I am sure most of it has been pulled into the offshore zone in such deep water it can't come back."

- "When they say it's going according to plan, I think they're just whistling past the graveyard," Dery Bennett, American Littoral Society.

- "We'll [the beach] be back to the rocks by Easter," Joseph DiCroce, local attorney.

Meanwhile, the Monmouth Beach borough council was taking steps to reduce beach use by the general public, illustrating the tenuous nature of the federal requirement for public access to replenished beaches. The council was acting in response to a petition that warned: "All kinds of people will be wandering around if we encourage them to stop and park."

Environmental Problems

The environmental effects of beach replenishment remain a relatively undocumented area of study. Several researchers are working to quantify these effects, but relatively little has been done compared to the immense effort put into the engineering aspects of beach replenishment. Replenishment is clearly not without environmental costs, however. Water turbidity, or cloudiness, caused by suspended sand and mud released during artificial beach construction can harm sea life. Corals have been not only smothered by settling mud but also destroyed by dredges and other beach-building machinery. Benthic (bottom-dwelling) organisms are displaced and lost when sand is taken out of the water and placed on the above-water beach, where, in turn, organisms that live in the beach sands are smothered. No one yet knows what the long-term, cumulative impacts of such displacements will be.

Intuitively, replenishment is the environmentally preferable alternative to seawalls and other hard structures that do nothing to preserve the beach and nearshore. The environmental benefits that have been proclaimed, however, particularly the restoration of sea turtle nesting habitat, have not yet had the experience necessary for objective evaluation.

Salmon and Turtles

In 1951, Pilkey, as a member of an explorer scout troop, visited a dam that was under construction on the Columbia River along the Oregon-Washington border. A ramrod-stiff U.S. Army Corps of Engineers colonel in a freshly starched uniform, almost covered with glittering brass battle ribbons and other awards from his recent service in World War II, gave a lecture to the troop. In a loud voice, brimming with confidence, the colonel explained how the dam was going to work. The part of the project he emphasized was the new type of fish ladder designed to keep the famous Columbia River salmon run prospering.

Alas, the superb presentation did not translate well into reality. Despite the colonel's confidence, the fish ladders were a massive failure, and, although they were not the only problem, today there is almost no salmon run in the Columbia, except for hatchery-released fish.

We fear that sea turtles may be headed for the same fate as the Pacific Northwest salmon. In the early 1980s, Pilkey heard another colonel, commander of the Corps' Jacksonville District, describe the Miami Beach replenishment project. This colonel was also tall, ramrod straight, and bemedaled, but by this time, thirty years after the lecture at the Columbia River dam, such things were less impressive. Miami Beach was the largest such project ever and was billed, perhaps correctly, as the wave of the future for the eroding shorelines of Florida. Because the fate of sea turtles is a critical environmental issue, the colonel emphasized that the creation of new nesting areas for the turtles was among the major benefits of the new beach and others to be built along the coast. Prior to replenishment, the surf zone was lapping against the seawalls of Miami Beach, leaving no space for turtle nest excavation.

Like that of the fish ladders along the Columbia River, the idea seemed to make perfect sense. Unfortunately for the sea turtles, as for the salmon, theory does not always translate into practice. The artificial beach composed of calcareous shell fragments at Miami Beach is far too hard for sea turtle nesting.

On other, less compacted, replenished beaches the fate of nesting

Photo 4–7. An erosion scarp on Folly Beach, South Carolina, shortly after the beach replenishment was completed in 1993. Erosion scarps present problems for nesting sea turtles, who cannot climb them to lay their eggs on the upper beach. (Photo by Michael Moeller)

turtles remains unclear. Scientists have found that the characteristics of beach sand determine the sex of hatchlings, and replenished sand often differs in some respects from natural beach sand (for example, replenishment material may have a higher mud content than its natural predecessor). Most important, perhaps, is the frequent formation of erosion scarps on replenished beaches (Figure 4–7). Such scarps or small cliffs block the turtles' path to the high, dry area of the beach. Is it possible that because of scarps, sediment types, and other still unknown factors in replenished beaches, the turtle population will be damaged or destroyed a few decades from now?

FIVE

Folly Beach: Reclaimed Heyday?

The red flare, clearly visible on a bright, sunny, May afternoon in 1992, followed a long, lazy arc from the police chief's flare gun, up and back down, dousing itself in the sea. The chief was bobbing in a skiff presumed to be 810 feet offshore from the Folly Beach Holiday Inn, where the most important dignitaries in all of Folly Beach and Charleston County, South Carolina, were assembled onshore. Lining the seawall with the local elite was an assemblage of legislators, bureaucrats, reporters, citizens, and curious surfers.

The promotion of the Folly Beach replenishment project was under way. In a grand effort to persuade everyone of Folly Beach's status as the victim of a Corps navigation project, the Charleston County Committee to Save Folly Beach, a group formed by the city's beach replenishment proponents and made up of every county and local dignitary possible, had invited county, state, and federal officials to an exhibition of the island's sorry situation. For Folly Beach had been wronged. According to the city's engineering consultants, Billy Edge, now of Texas A&M University, and Bob Dean of the University of Florida, erosion along Folly Beach was entirely attributable to the presence of the Charleston Harbor jetties, built by the Corps in the late 1890s, 8 miles to the north of Folly. But for the jetties, said Edge, the Folly Beach shoreline would be 810 feet seaward of its present position. That day, the assembled crowd could look to the right and to the left at nothing but long lines of rock and rubble revetments, seawalls, and groins as far as the eye could see. Some were large, some small, most were dilapidated, and all were ugly. The beach was largely gone except for narrow slivers of sand in a few places at low tide. There was only one solution, the committee said. To atone for its past sins, the Corps would have to replenish the beach on a massive scale.

The creativity of the Folly Beach dramatization was no surprise to those who knew the island's colorful history. But many of the assembled guests may have been unaware of some of the background leading up to the event. Given the long history of erosion on Folly Beach, discussed later in this chapter, the conclusion that the Charleston Harbor jetties had caused 810 feet of erosion, or even half that, was unlikely. Whatever its cause, Folly Beach had been living with its erosion problem for many years; when development began on Folly in the 1920s and 1930s, shoreline retreat was well underway and apparent to all concerned. The appropriately named Atlantic Avenue is now under water, and Arctic Avenue, once the second road from the beach and now the beachfront road, has lost three blocks. Houses were moved or abandoned as the shoreline retreated landward, until some property owners decided to fight the encroaching sea. Though the residents, not the Corps, attempted to stop the retreating shore by armoring it, the result was the same: the ugliness of a seawall-and-rock-littered beach.

Folly Island lies a few miles south of Charleston along the incomparably beautiful barrier island shoreline of South Carolina (Figure 5–1). Except for Myrtle Beach, which sits on the mainland astride an Ice Age barrier island left stranded by a higher sea level, the entire open-ocean shoreline of the state consists of barrier islands. Some of them, such as Capers Island near Cape Romaine, are very low in elevation and a few tens of yards wide, sparsely vegetated with flora capable of withstanding daily salt spray, and actively migrating back toward the mainland. Others, such as Hilton Head near the Georgia border, are more stable, have high dunes and dense mainland type forests, and are more than a mile wide.

Plundered for its beauty, no state's shoreline is more threatened by the American rush to the shore than South Carolina's. High-rise buildings line the shores of Myrtle Beach and Hilton Head Island, and smaller buildings jam the beaches on dozens of other island communities. Their retreat impeded by coastal engineering structures, South Carolina's beaches are shrinking. By 1988, fully 25 percent of the state's developed shoreline (and nearly 100 percent of Folly Beach) was lined with coastal armoring, mostly in the form of privately built rock revetments. The rate of shoreline armoring in South Carolina, all since World War II, is astounding. By comparison, New Jersey took 150 years to armor 50 percent of its developed shoreline.

Despite that, South Carolina has a coastal management program that has made some notable accomplishments. For one, through the Beachfront Management Act of 1988, seawalls and all other kinds of hard stabilization have been banned. Seawalls may be maintained but once de-

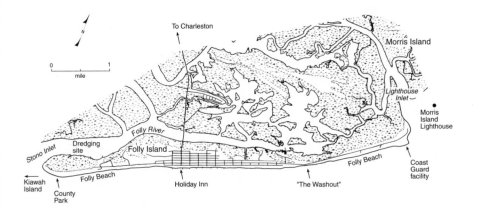

Figure 5–1. Index map showing location of Folly Beach, South Carolina. Folly Beach is a 6-mile island between Morris Island and Kiawah Island. The Charleston Harbor jetties, built at the turn of the century, have increased the rate of erosion at Folly Beach.

stroyed cannot be rebuilt. Folly Beach is the only community in South Carolina exempt from the retreat provisions of the state's coastal management laws. Destroyed seawalls may be rebuilt on Folly and were following Hurricane Hugo.

Under the leadership of the highly vocal city mayor, Bob Linville, a retired used car salesman, Folly Beach has become something of an outlaw city in terms of compliance with coastal management regulations. In addition to rebuilding seawalls, it has gained other exemptions. Although houses on pontoons are illegal in South Carolina, they can be found at Folly Beach. Although it is illegal to disturb wetland areas, marsh grass is mowed on areas of Folly.

The spectacle arranged by the Charleston County Committee to Save Folly Beach spurred action at the congressional level. Perhaps in a political move to protect the Charleston District or perhaps to assuage the local constituents, U.S. Senator Ernest F. Hollings of South Carolina managed to push the beach replenishment project through Congress two years ahead of schedule. The project was authorized and funded at the same time (a rare occurrence—authorization usually comes several years ahead of funding) as a "congressionally added project." Thus, the word to the Corps was, "Hurry up and get it done, now!"

After all the debate and showmanship, and nearly sixty years after the

Corps issued its 1935 report to Congress entitled "Beach Erosion at Folly Beach, S.C." (better known as the MacArthur Report), in 1993 Folly got its new beach. The $12.5 million replenishment placed 2.5 million cubic yards of sand along approximately 6 miles of sand-starved Folly Beach shoreline. The mathematical model GENESIS was applied to Folly Beach by the Corps' Coastal Engineering Research Center in Vicksburg, Mississippi, to predict required sand volumes and beach durability. Because of GENESIS, the Corps decided to add 2 million cubic yards less than it would have otherwise, which proved to be a major error. And while the mathematical model correctly predicted the location of one erosion hot spot, at Folly Beach's Holiday Inn, it failed to predict two others.

Sand pumping from the lagoon behind the south end of the island began in January and ended in April of 1993 (Photo 5–1). The new beach, designed to protect the community from the effects of a "five-year" storm had a storm dune (berm) width of 15 feet with an elevation of 9 feet and an overall "design" beach width of 135 feet with an elevation of 7 feet. Dredging and sand pumping were done by T.L. James and Company of Louisiana, old hands at beach replenishment. Nine dilapidated wood-and-rock groins were replaced with 250-foot, sheet-steel structures with concrete caps.

The federal government paid 85 percent of the project costs, while the county and state governments paid 15 percent. Folly Beach did not share in the initial expense, but it is responsible for a portion of nourishment expected to be needed every eight years (for which the city sets aside $100,000 each year). The approximate costs as of December 1993 broke down to: actual sand placement on the beach, planting of dune grasses, and groin construction and rehabilitation, $9.3 million; planning and design, $1.9 million; administrative costs, $700,000; monitoring, $280,000. An additional $250,000 was added to cover a settlement with the owner of the Atlantic House Restaurant. The Atlantic House, for many years a landmark at Folly Beach, was destroyed during Hurricane Hugo. Shoreline erosion had made it an over-water restaurant sitting on pilings, which allowed the waves to roll under the building. The owner wanted to rebuild the restaurant in its former position, but the town wisely ruled against construction in the surf zone. The court viewed the situation differently, however, and the city was directed to compensate the restaurant owner for an infringement of his property rights.

Although the replenished beach at Folly Beach (Photos 5–2 and 5–3)

Photo 5–1. The old and the new Folly Beach. In the distance a fleet of bull-dozers can be seen spreading the pumped sand onto the beach. In the fore-ground is one of the many old seawalls, with the high tide lapping up against it. (Photo by Michael Moeller)

was new at the time of writing, its story is an old and familiar one. Folly Beach is like hundreds of other replenishment projects on our coasts; only the names and the details are different. Yet if ever there was a community that might profitably have saved its beaches by moving buildings back from the shoreline instead of embarking on the long road to replenishment, it is Folly Beach. The retreat alternative to solving the erosion problem would have been relatively easy there; in 1991–92, most beachfront buildings were small and cost relatively little. But the few local voices that were raised in support of the retreat option could barely be heard over the roar of support for a federal- and state-funded replenished beach.

We toured Folly Beach with Gered Lennon, a 45-year-old geologist, Indiana native, University of South Carolina graduate, College of Charleston instructor, and long-term resident of Folly Beach. Gered is a former professional staff geologist of the South Carolina Coastal

Photo 5–2. A view of the replenished beach immediately after emplacement just north of the Holiday Inn. Notice the wide dry beach. (Photo by Michael Moeller)

Photo 5–3. A view from almost the same location as Photo 5–2 showing the replenished beach two years later. Note that the groins are exposed and the high-tide line is at the base of the vegetated storm berm. At this location, because walking on the vegetated storm berm is forbidden, there is no recreational beach at high tide. (Photo by Michael Moeller)

Council, the state agency charged with enforcing South Carolina's coastal management law. His 1982 Jeep Wagoneer station wagon (nicknamed "the Gold Buddha") has an old coastal car smell, the slight odor of exhaust fumes mixed with marsh mud. As we drove along the bumpy streets, Gered, a well-known figure on Folly and a recent candidate for city council, returned the waves of his neighbors. We had to listen carefully to make out his quiet articulation over the low background roar of his almost-working muffler as he gave us a lesson in island history, geology, and politics.

We started our tour at the county beach park at Folly Island's south end. Looking farther to the south across Stono Inlet we could see Kiawah Island, site of a private and exclusive planned community. Some say Kiawah Island was developed with the most environmental sensitivity of any beachfront community in the southern United States, though environmentally sensitive development of a barrier island is perhaps an oxymoron. Unfortunately, Kiawah's sound building covenants were abandoned when the island's ownership changed. The new owners, Landmark Developers of California, anticipating South Carolina's 1988 Beachfront Management Act's restrictions on new development, carved this beautiful island into literally hundreds of lots. As a result, the island was largely unaffected by the new law. Ownership has since changed again.

Before we got under way, we asked Gered to tell us about the person who named Folly Island with such foresight. With a polite laugh, Gered said that, although the name seems appropriate today, *folly* is an Old English word substituting for "volley" and actually meaning a tree-crested dune ridge. The tree-lined dunes of South Carolina's barrier islands were once reminiscent of a volley of ships or soldiers standing in the line-formation combat style of the day, he explained. Lookouts on approaching ships seeking the channel to Charleston Harbor were told to look for these island "follies." Folly may have been the first of many barrier islands along the southeastern United States seaboard to acquire the name. There it stuck.

The island was also briefly called Coffin Land. According to Gretchen Stringer-Robinson's history of Folly, *Time and Tide on Folly Beach, South Carolina*, a 1780 map shows Folly as Coffin Land. Stringer-Robinson writes, "It was customary in the 1800's for ships with plague or cholera victims to leave the ill travelers on barrier islands when approaching a large port. After conducting their business, the ships would then return and pick up the survivors, burying the dead on the island."

Today, Folly Island, about 6 miles long and a half mile across at its widest, presents rows of houses along its oceanfront rather than the tree lines of old. Most of the island is low lying, with an average 5-foot elevation increasing to little over 8 to 10 feet at the higher points. Almost the entire island can be described as highly hazardous, vulnerable to the brunt of storms. In some parts, however, the original high wooded dune ridges have been preserved, affording some elevation and protection to the houses nestled among them.

As we began our trek, Gered pointed out the signs of the Union occupation of Folly Island during the Civil War. More than eighteen thousand Union soldiers braved the mosquito- and malaria-ridden island as they prepared to assault Fort Wagner on Morris Island, Folly's neighbor to the north. The soldiers occupied their time by digging trenches, setting up batteries, and excavating still visible drainage ditches to reduce the mosquito population. Fort Wagner, a major obstacle in the way of anyone intending to assault Charleston from the sea, had been reconstructed just before the Union attack. The assault eventually made on the Morris Island fort (chronicled in the movie *Glory*) was preceded by the largest naval bombardment and the most successful amphibious assault ever made up to that time, and it served as a model for future engagements.

In 1896, the Corps completed construction of the Charleston jetties between Sullivan's Island and Morris Island to stabilize the entrance to Charleston Harbor. Before the jetties were in place, sand moved naturally from north to south and from island to island, across the tidal delta at the entrance to Charleston Harbor. After their construction, the jetties blocked the north-to-south sand movement. Beaches to the north, such as Isle of Palms, then grew and built seaward. To the south, however, the jetties caused the virtual removal of the original Morris Island immediately south of the inlet and its change to a landward-migrating strip of sand.

Although Folly Beach, the second island south of the jetties, enjoyed approximately thirty-five years of accretion following jetty construction, its shoreline returned to a pattern of erosion when the sand supply began running out. In the 1935 MacArthur Report, the Corps identified a long-term retreat rate of about 7 feet per year from records covering an eighty-four-year period. Even though Folly had a history of erosion predating the Charleston jetties, people built beachfront houses and a large resort there beginning around 1920. Development was somewhat limited until 1957 when a pipeline supplied fresh water directly to the island from the mainland.

In the 1950s, groins were built by the South Carolina Highway Department at 1,000-foot intervals. At that same time, a few seawalls began to sprout along the beach. In the 1960s, the Highway Department placed groins between the existing groins, so that groins jutted out to sea every 500 feet along the beach. Thirty years later, and before beach replenishment, the Folly shoreline had been reduced to a sequence of construction debris and rubble revetments, old seawalls, and dilapidated groins. The seawalls, each designed and paid for by individual homeowners, had grown in hodgepodge fashion in the time-honored process of Newjerseyization. Rocks lost from the engineering structures began to clutter the ever shrinking beach, endangering the dwindling population of swimmers. "Special devices" sold by modern snake oil salesmen touting bright new ideas for trapping sand carpeted sections of the beach; these inevitably failed and added to the clutter, disarray, and general ugliness. Soon, along most of the ocean shoreline, the beach was completely submerged at high tide during normal tidal cycles. Folly Beach soon became the most armored beach in the southeastern United States, rivaled only by some Jersey Shore communities in degree of ugliness.

At the same time that Folly residents were trying to fight back the sea, Folly Beach became *the* place to be during the 1940s and 1950s. Thousands of revelers came to dance first to the music of Benny Goodman and later of Fats Domino at the grand entertainment pavilion and pier that stood at the present-day site of the Holiday Inn. But beach loss continued as sand was washed from in front of the seawalls. As the beach went, so did the crowds. The town's character slowly changed from a mainstream resort to a fringe haven. In the 1960s, it became the "hippie beach." At other times, it was the "biker beach." In 1975, Folly Beach became an incorporated city, though in a strange bureaucratic twist, the state highway department continues to be responsible for road maintenance. Into the early 1990s, the tiny community of fewer than two thousand permanent residents (although thirty thousand people may crowd the island on a summer weekend) radiates an independent and warm spirit.

In the 1970s and 1980s, Folly Beach politicians, led by Mayor Richard Beck and then by Mayor Linville, began the drumbeat of victimization, identifying the Corps-built Charleston jetties as the cause of shoreline erosion and the loss of the community's beach. To prove their point, Mayor Beck and the city hired Eric Olsen, a coastal engineer, who made the "scientific" link between the jetties and erosion at Folly Beach.

Coastal engineer Billy Edge picked up Olsen's work and made an elaborate anti-Corps case for the city. The fact that the erosion problem was evident when people first began building houses in harm's way was ignored. So was the fact that for decades people successfully coexisted with a retreating shoreline. The resulting assertion, that the Corps owed the city a beach, was like blaming the railroad for running over someone sleeping on the tracks.

Some erosion could indeed be blamed on the Charleston Harbor jetties, but the question was: How much? Unfortunately, it is impossible to accurately separate jetty-induced erosion from natural erosion. The Corps initially denied that the jetties were responsible for any of the erosion on Folly Beach. By the mid 1980s, however, the Corps reported that the jetties were responsible, after all, for just over 50 percent of the erosion problem, and, therefore, the United States owed Folly Beach a new beach under the damage mitigation authorization category.

Then, in September 1989, came Hurricane Hugo, changing the life of our guide Gered, his family and neighbors, and the very makeup of the town. The southern third of the 26-mile-wide eye of the storm passed directly over Folly. Storm surge pushed an estimated 10 to 12 feet of water over the island. All houses near the beach were substantially damaged, including Gered's rented beachfront abode. Some houses disappeared, apparently having been washed to sea as the waters poured back over the island when the winds reversed. Only those houses built within the protective dunes in the interior of the island survived relatively unscathed. Five years later, Gered and some city officials consider Hugo to have served as an urban renewal program. By the time of Hurricane Hugo in 1989, the front row of houses, mostly post–World War II, were little more than small cottages and shacks. Property values soared almost immediately after the storm; damaged and destroyed $40,000 cottages were replaced with $250,000 edifices. Property took another jump in value after the replenishment. People, mostly retirees "from up north" were moving to Folly Beach, attracted by the replenished beach and real estate prices that were still very low compared to nearby exclusive Kiawah Island. Each new costly house, each jump in property prices, strengthens the case for continuing replenishment even if the cost were to become three to five times greater than the Corps' original estimates.

As we bumped along Arctic Avenue, Gered showed us a number of examples of the island's changing post-replenishment waterfront, including apparitions locally known as pocket beaches. Before the replenishment, five oceanfront lots were vacant and without seawalls. So the shoreline had receded well back into those lots in the classic "end-around" effect, in which erosion occurs on adjacent property around the ends of a seawall. Then the beach was replenished up to the seawall line, leaving giant depressions between the replenished berm and the road that contained pools of stagnant water. With the development boom, however, these pocket beaches are considered desirable real estate.

On our tour, we saw that the northern third of the island is so narrow that in places the beachfront road marks the lagoon-side boundary of the island. We stopped at the "washout" at the island's narrowest point to clamber up the substantial seawall—rebuilt, post-Hugo, with state funds to protect the road leading to a few dozen houses at the island's north end. From that vantage point, we could see dozens of surfers taking advantage of a good wave day. Because of the relatively steep nearshore zone, Folly Beach has good surfing waves and is the most popular surfing spot south of Cape Hatteras, North Carolina.

A long, narrow strip of stubs of American beach grass, panic grass, and sea oats had recently been planted atop the storm berm at the back of the beach. As we stood watching the surfers at the washout, Gered warned us that, because of a Folly Beach law forbidding disturbance of "dunes," we would be fined $200 if caught walking across the new grass. At that very moment, a member of the city's seemingly over-staffed police force informed Gered that his parked car was pointed in the wrong direction. Then the young officer moved on to ticket several others.

The stubby strip of grasses, known as the dune, was part of the original replenishment plan but was not planted until six months after the sand pumping had been completed. The dune grasses were added to trap windborne replenishment sand so as to build up beach elevation. Unfortunately, by the time they were planted, the beach was already narrow. And that made sand accumulation unlikely. In some places, the erosion of the nourishment sand had undermined this dubious project within a year of its completion. At the washout, for example, there wasn't even a berm left to plant grass on—it had washed away by the time the grass contractor got on the beach, according to City Administrator Vicki Zick. In other areas, the berm was already too narrow to plant. In still other areas, the beach profile was so unrecognizable that the contractor just stuck plants into the beach as best he could, she said.

In an effort to protect the new dune, the city informed oceanfront residents that they would have to construct dune overwalks to reach the beach in front of their house, alleging that it was a state requirement (which state officials flatly deny). Only a few people spent the $3,000 for private overwalks, but the general effect of the requirement was an immediate reduction in both public and private access to the beach. Of the public access points, about half were effectively closed to all but those willing to risk the penalty for being caught, surfboard or beach umbrella in hand, on the "dune." According to Zick, "No one really knew where the sand dune started or stopped."

Our final stop on the Gered Lennon guided tour was an abandoned Coast Guard station at the north end of the island being slowly reclaimed by trees, bushes, and blowing sand. We walked by a pile of cow bones eroding from the inlet shoreline, the remains of an old Union garbage dump from Civil War times. Gered surmised that the cows, though consumed by Yankees, were probably of Confederate origin. Looking farther north toward Morris Island and the Charleston jetties, we glimpsed the amazing sight of the Morris Island lighthouse standing far from the land. Morris Island literally migrated out from under its lighthouse, which today provides spectacular evidence of jetty-induced erosion in its location—400 yards out to sea. What better evidence could there be for the dynamic and flexible nature of barrier islands and the foolhardiness of building on them?

After our tour, with a long list of questions in hand, we went to Charleston to speak with Corps representatives. When we arrived for our meeting with Frances Limbaker, the Charleston District's Folly Beach project manager, we suspected that, given the reputation that Pilkey enjoys at Folly Beach (the City Council passed a resolution condemning his statements about their beach), the Corps representative might suddenly be "unable" to meet with us. Instead, he had invited five people to join in; thus, the meeting included Limbaker; his boss Don Herndon; project engineers Millard Dowd and Amy Denn; David Rich, the district's chief public relations officer; and Vicki Zick, Folly Beach city administrator. True to our experience with other Corps districts, the Charleston District Corps personnel were obliging and gracious, giving us several hours of their time, answering our questions, and sending us away with armloads of documents. We were told about the good relationship between the Corps and the city of Folly Beach and how well the project was doing. We also left with the feeling that we had not heard the whole story.

At Folly Beach, talking with the local residents and city officials, we heard what the Corps was not telling us. Locals told of a fast-disappearing beach, of the lack of cooperation by the Corps, and of a trail of misunderstandings and broken promises. According to Vicki Zick, the general feeling is that what Folly Beach thought they were getting is not what they got.

Throughout our meeting with the Corps' Charleston District officials, Zick, a dynamic, outspoken individual known for her tenacity in finding answers for tough questions, was very quiet. Perhaps she was remembering the "partnering session" she had participated in during the early stages of planning for the replenishment project. Then, under a federal directive to the Corps, all of the parties officially involved in the project got together for a day at the Folly Beach Holiday Inn. Under the leadership of a specialist from Washington, DC, representatives from the Corps, the city of Folly Beach, the U.S. Fish and Wildlife Service, and the South Carolina Wildlife and Marine Resources Department—more than fifty people in all—spent a day taking personality tests and participating in work sessions intended to help make their cooperative venture more effective.

Frances Limbaker, perhaps also remembering the partnering session, repeatedly described the Charleston District as the "design agent" for the city of Folly Beach. After the meeting, Zick characterized the Corps' role in the Folly Beach replenishment project as something far less cooperative. She described the relationship as one of being forced to play by rules written by the Corps, "the only game in town."

As an example, Zick told us that the city had specifically requested special attention for the Holiday Inn, an imposing structure visible for miles and perched at the seaward end of the highway leading into town. The nine-story building was constructed with a fast-tracked variance from the town's 35-foot maximum building height regulation, and out on the beach behind a seawall that towered 18 feet above the beach (Photo 5–4). From its opening day, the hotel, a physical and financial atrocity with which the city was stuck, had been skating on the edge of bankruptcy. Folly Beach had to do its best to coexist; for the largest building in town to be an abandoned hotel was unthinkable. A high priority for the city was to keep a healthy beach in front of the hotel (Photo 5–5). According to Zick, "In the true spirit of 'partnering' we implored the Corps to add sand in this area, since it was in the center of town, a magnet area for beach tourists, and vital to the economic survival of the Holiday Inn. . . . We never knew until the midnight hour that sand pumped in front of the Holiday Inn was being [emplaced] solely to allow the dredge contractor a support berm for his pipeline" (Photo 5–6). A request by Folly Beach to spend its own money for a new groin to hold this segment of replenished beach in place was denied because

Photo 5–4. A 1995 low-tide view of the Holiday Inn and its seawall. There is no beach here at high tide. The view is from the south end of the seawall, showing the so-called downdrift offset of the beach where the downdrift beach has been starved of sand by the seawall, causing rapid retreat. (Photo by Michael Moeller)

Photo 5–5. A close view of the Holiday Inn beach in 1995 at low tide. No dry beach exists. Prior to replenishment, Charleston District officials had assured the Folly Beach mayor that he could invite his constituents to join him for a beer on dry beach 150 feet seaward of the Holiday Inn. (Photo by Michael Moeller)

Photo 5–6. A 1993 photo in front of the Holiday Inn seawall of the dredge pipe, broken when more than 100 feet of beach disappeared in a single storm that struck during replenishment. In the background are two of the newly completed groins. (Photo by Michael Moeller)

construction of a new groin was considered potentially environmentally harmful. This, after the Corps had endorsed and completed the reconstruction of nine adjacent groins.

The 1992 project design maps for the Folly Beach replenishment project, shown to us by project engineer Millard Dowd, clearly indicate that the district never planned to maintain a beach in front of the Holiday Inn, only to put enough sand in front of the hotel to temporarily lay the pipes that carried replenishment sand from the borrow site to the beach. The city's understanding was different. City Administrator Zick told us that the Corps assured Mayor Bob Linville that, once the project was complete, he could invite people to walk 150 feet seaward from the Holiday Inn and join him for a beer. Zick said, "We listened. We listened carefully."

After the meeting we also learned the rest of the story concerning beach performance. Don Herndon of the Corps had told us that the new sand (emplaced between January and April 1993) had shown its durability by surviving two storms, including the March 1993 "storm of the century." He did not tell us that those storms occurred while the dredge was still there. The contractor had to backtrack twice, each time after a storm had washed away a large part of the new beach. After building a 150-foot-wide beach twice (the dredge pipes broke apart on the rocks and wall in front of the Holiday Inn after the first storm took away the beach), the contractor put out a 200-foot-wide beach to add a margin of safety and get the pipes safely past the Holiday Inn. One year after project completion, the Holiday Inn had no beach at high tide. At the time of this writing, what was left of the new beach had gone through two winters, but they were winters without important storms. Even under relatively calm conditions, the new beach is steadily and rapidly retreating at a rate far exceeding design predictions.

The haste imposed on the Corps by U.S. Senator Hollings is evident in several aspects of the project. Part of the project plan was the rehabilitation of existing groins along the middle stretch of the Folly shore to help contain replenishment sand. Not surprisingly, groins do a much better job of trapping sand if they are finished before sand is pumped onto the beach. At Folly, however, the project was so rushed that sand was being pumped as the groins were being built. They were officially completed one month after sand pumping was completed.

The rehabilitated groins are much larger versions of what once were low-lying piles of stone that allowed a lot of sand to pass through and over them. The new groins are relatively impermeable and will ultimately increase erosion rates at the south end of Folly Beach. Miles

Hayes, a University of South Carolina geologist, argued years ago that Kiawah Island was attached to the sand supply of Folly Beach. At this point, it is impossible to say whether Kiawah will experience a net addition in its sand supply because of Folly's lost replenishment sand. Millard Dowd told us that Kiawah Island will neither benefit nor suffer from the Folly Beach replenishment project "within our lifetime." Time will tell.

Very fine sand was used to replenish Folly's beach. At the behest of the South Carolina Wildlife and Marine Resources Department, the new beach was plowed to a depth of three feet to make it softer for turtle egg laying. For months afterward beach strollers sank ankle to calf deep in beach sand that would surely have caused a turtle to disappear beneath its surface had one attempted to come ashore. The softened sand certainly increased the initial rate of beach erosion but probably had no effect, negative or positive, on turtles. Immediately upon completion of the replenishment operation, a large vertical erosion escarpment appeared that would have stopped cold in its tracks any turtle that tried to come ashore. Absence of storms and strong along-shore drift over the first winter after the project allowed the scarp to dissipate, but a stormy season will soon form a distinct erosion scarp or expose the seawalls once again.

The fine sand size is related to its source, the project borrow area. The Corps selected as its borrow area a navigation channel behind the southern end of Folly. Although in the early days of replenishment, lagoonal areas behind islands were commonly used as borrow areas, a surfeit of fine-grained sediments, including large amounts of mud, and the high potential for serious damage to important fisheries, led the Corps to find other sources. Dredging and removing sediment is a very disruptive activity in the relatively quiescent estuarine environment. Today, the preferred borrow areas are inlets or offshore sand deposits.

When the Corps sought the necessary interagency agreement for the use of the old navigation channel, it did not prepare an environmental impact statement for the borrow site. Even though the cross-sectional area to be dredged was thirty-two times larger than the old channel, the Charleston District explained the lack of an environmental impact statement by saying that no one requested one during the public comment period. In our view, here as elsewhere, the Corps chose minimum compliance with environmental regulations, waiting to be told, rather than taking an environmentally sound managerial initiative.

One way in which the Corps avoided an environmental impact statement was by sidestepping the federal authorization requirement. By selecting a borrow area within a navigation channel maintained by the Corps for shrimp boat traffic, authorization was already in place for a channel 9 feet deep and 50 feet wide. From that point, only state permission was necessary. In the state-granted dredging permit for the area, the approved borrow area was 32 feet deep and 600 feet wide. The Corps' interpretation of the permit was somewhat more liberal; the borrow area was dredged to a width of 1,200 feet.

Perhaps one reason that the Corps enlarged the borrow area was related to problems they encountered in finding suitable sediment. The borrow area was initially approved on the basis of nine core samples. Those were just enough to show that, although suitable "beach-quality" sand was present, a lot of mud was, too. When one area was determined, in mid-project, to be completely unsuitable, dredging was moved to another site. The Corps actually knew very little about the sediment within the borrow area, and, in effect, prospected for sand during replenishment.

Much to the city's dismay, the Corps may need to find another borrow site for renourishment operations. After the beach had been replenished, the Corps received a letter from the U.S. Fish and Wildlife Service telling them to stop violating the 1991 Coastal Barrier Improvement Act by dredging within their environmentally sensitive jurisdiction.

During our meeting at the office of the Corps Charleston District, Vicki Zick listened, stunned, as Don Herndon told us that if the Corps had to find a new borrow site for the next nourishment because of the Coastal Barrier Resource System rules, the project's cost-benefit analysis would have to be redone. Zick knew immediately that sand could only be more costly for future nourishments. Continental shelf sand requires larger, more costly dredges, able to withstand the wave energy of the open ocean. Herndon's implication was that if this economic review were to find that an increased cost of obtaining sand outweighed the benefits of the replenished beach, the Corps would abandon the project. Folly Beach residents were counting on an agreement good for fifty years.

The Corps had promised Folly Beach a new beach that would last for fifty years (with some additions of sand every eight years or so). The overall erosion rate of the replenished beach assumed by the Corps in its engineering design was such that the last grain of visible sand would disappear twenty-four years after project completion if no renourishment occurred. In fact, Folly Beach will be lucky to keep any usable beach above the high-tide line for five years. Certainly the entire beach will be gone long before the eight years predicted as the nourishment interval (discussed in chapter 4).

The distinction between nourishment interval and total beach durability is a critical one. David Rich, the Corps' Charleston District spokesperson, implied to us (and in numerous statements to the public) that the eight-year nourishment interval was actually the predicted lifespan of the entire beach.

During our meeting at the Corps' Charleston office, Don Herndon explained that the nourishment interval is used simply as a predictive estimate, primarily for accounting purposes. And he acknowledged that sand might need to be added to the beach more or less often than eight years. Zick was aware that the city now faced the prospect of raising much more money much more quickly than planned for coming nourishments. Even if future renourishment expenses were not increased by having to go to the continental shelf for sand, the beach will cost far more than predicted simply because it is disappearing so much faster than predicted. Neither in planning sessions nor through other communications with city officials had Charleston District officials previously expressed any uncertainty about the eight-year nourishment interval, defining it as the time when the beach would need small additions of sand.

Within the first year of the project, Folly Beach residents reported that, outside of the erosion hot spots where the entire beach was gone, they watched their beach go from a dry-beach width (above the high-tide line) of 200 feet to one of 75 feet. Gered Lennon reports, based on surveys by the College of Charleston's Department of Geology, that by April 1994, about half of the fill had moved out of the beach system. The Corps assured everyone that the sand was still all there, just offshore, still providing storm protection for the city (Figure 5–2). In our meeting, project engineer Dowd said that 93 percent of the beach was in place, counting the sand underwater, in the summer of 1994. By the summer of 1995, the Charleston District was claiming that 89 percent of the beach remained.

Dowd's 93 percent of the amount of sand remaining within the beach system is inconsistent with the monitoring that geologist Paul Gayes is doing at Folly on the Corps' behalf; Gayes is finding that sand is going offshore through gullies and other sea-floor pathways, where it is unrecoverable by the waves that would carry it back to shore.

Not surprisingly, perhaps, neither Gered nor the other residents of Folly Beach have drawn much comfort from the Corps' assurances of

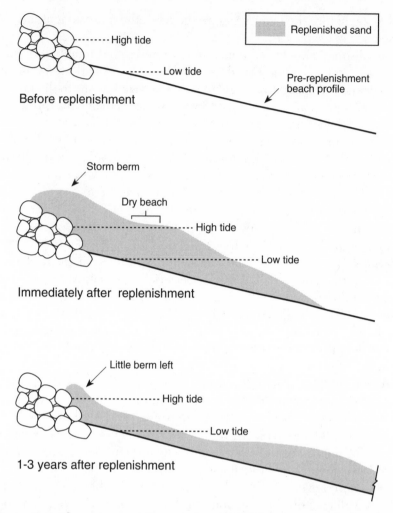

Figure 5–2. The uppermost diagram shows Folly Beach as it was before the replenishment project. As can be seen by the position of the high- and low-tide lines, Folly Beach had no exposed sandy beach at high tide and only a narrow beach at low tide. As a part of the replenishment, shown in the middle diagram, a storm berm was constructed as well as a dry beach above the normal high-tide line. The lowermost diagram shows the situation as it existed along the central portion of the project about one year after completion of the replenishment project. Claims by the Corps that most of the sand remained, as in the lower diagram, ignore the fact that the two main purposes of the new beach—storm protection and recreation—have not been achieved.

offshore sand. Administrator Zick found the Corps' post-project decla-
ration of a protective underwater beach inconsistent with "the way they
sold this project" to Folly residents. According to Zick:

> We fully expected the beach at elevation 7 feet to stay intact
> [during the eight year "nourishment interval"] and were re-
> peatedly told by the Corps that whenever the berm was threat-
> ened, the next renourishment would be triggered. This all
> played into our expectations about building sand dunes, cre-
> ating vegetation walkovers, etc. It also set the pace for making
> contributions to a . . . fund for the second renourishment pro-
> ject eight years down the road. Now bear in mind, none of us
> had any expertise or preconceived notions about beach re-
> nourishment in general, but learned all that we knew from
> conversations with the Corps. Then, when—less than a year
> later—much of the dry beach was already underwater, we got
> pretty nervous. The Corps instructed us not to panic. It
> pointed out that certain areas of the beach were "hot spots,"
> and that all the sand was accounted for in the near offshore or
> in the Folly River. Never mind that this is not where we, locally,
> wanted the sand to be. But we quietly wondered why the
> Corps seemed to be talking differently one year after the pro-
> ject was completed than it did in the year prior to start of con-
> struction. Had we known what the Corps said they knew from
> the start—that the dry beach was going to erode this rapidly—
> we would not have been so excited about sand dunes, vegeta-
> tion, and walkovers.

When city officials asked, the Corps initially replied that sand would
be added when the dry-beach width was less than 50 feet. When erosion
continued to narrow the visible beach, city officials recall, the Corps said
that a dry-beach width of less than 35 feet would trigger renourishment.
From what the Corps had told the city to expect from the project initially, the city was ready for renourishment within six months after project completion. In 1995, however, with little dry beach remaining and
the storm berm largely gone, the district once again told Zick that the
beach was working just as planned.

Lack of communication extended to finances as well. Zick's request
for a financial role or even just an accounting of expenditures to date was
not honored. During the course of the project, the Corps made with-
drawals on the city's escrow account established for that purpose but did

not let the city know how the money was being spent. The city simply received copies of one-sentence letters written to the bank, such as:

> I, _____, District Engineer, Charleston District, U.S. Army Corps of Engineers, do hereby make demand for $700,000 under NationsBank, Charleston, South Carolina Escrow Account (Folly Beach Shore Protection Project Construction Fund) issued on behalf of the City of Folly Beach, South Carolina.

Zick's reaction: "Given that the Corps had access to $2.3 million of our money, I guess I expected a little more accounting information than was provided. So much for being partners in this project!"

At the time of writing, two years post-replenishment, the Folly beach steadily disappears. Looking to the north and south from the eighth floor of the Holiday Inn, the view is much as it was pre-replenishment. Waves splash against the Holiday Inn seawall. Zick and her colleagues sit in their offices, two blocks from the sea, and wonder what they are going to do without a beach. Without the beach, the $250,000 houses, built on a promise of a fifty-year protective beach, stand exposed to the onslaught of winter wind and wave. Without the beach, future summer tourist seasons will be slim indeed. Without the tourist season, raising the funds necessary for renourishment will be even more difficult.

What we view as a spectacularly unsuccessful beach is said by the Corps to be working as expected. In a forthcoming technical paper, researchers with the Coastal Engineering Research Center state, "After one year the shore protection project is performing as designed. . . . About 95 percent of the beach fill volume . . . can be accounted for . . . landward of the 3.8 meter contour [at about a 12.5-foot water depth]. . . . Beach widths at the end of the 1993–1994 winter season were 40 meters [about 130 feet]." This is very close to the predicted 144-foot (44-meter) beach width. We are puzzled by the reported average 130-foot beach width, given our own observations and the accounts of local residents and scientists.

To Congress, when seeking approval of the project, the Corps indicated that the city of Folly Beach would be protected by a dry beach with a berm of a size capable of withstanding a certain strength of storm. To city officials, whose primary interest is a beach for recreation, the Corps spoke of a wide swimming beach that would not need much new sand for eight years. When it became clear that the dry swimming beach and the storm berm would soon be gone, far ahead of schedule, the

Corps reported that the city was still protected from storms because almost all of the sand (95 percent, according to CERC) was still in the system, held in the underwater portion of the beach. The Corps does not really know where the sand has gone, and, in this case, their claims contradict preliminary monitoring results. Even if the replenishment sand were to reside on the lower beach, it would provide neither the level of storm protection promised to Congress nor the community's recreational beach.

The Corps has been able to claim success to Congress and in technical papers only because reports are made without consultation with local city managers and local citizens.

SIX

Sargent Beach, Texas

If there is ever a contest to determine which American beach community looks the ugliest, Sargent Beach, Texas, will certainly be a top contender (Photo 6–1). Sargent Beach can be found along the Gulf of Mexico shoreline at the end of winding Texas State Road 447, about 170 crow-flown miles northeast of Corpus Christi and 20 miles southwest of Freeport. The town is little more than a few dozen fishing shacks and cottages perched atop dredge-spoil mounds that line both sides of the Gulf Intracoastal Waterway (GIWW), part of the National Intracoastal Waterway (ICWW) system.

Several miles of well-compacted mud ledges, originally formed in the marsh behind a former shoreline, outcrop on the beach and shoreface (Photos 6–2 and 6–3). The mud is picked up by waves breaking on the beach, giving the waves a distinct brownish hue. There are brown caps rather than the usual white caps of open-ocean beaches.

Along some stretches, the only sand is a 2- to 3-foot-high ridge lining the uppermost beach above high tide. Where the sand beach is sufficiently broad, tracks of 4 x 4 vehicles abound, the result of an old Texas beach-use tradition.

Along with an abundance of shells, the beach is strewn with a wide variety of flotsam and jetsam including hard hats, plastic milk cartons, and children's toys. Most of the shells contained within the mud and sand on the beach are of lagoonal rather than continental shelf species. Oyster shells are the most common, because oysters flourish along the margins of salt marsh. When an oyster dies, its shell becomes incorporated into the marsh sediment and is eventually washed out of the mud by the rapidly retreating Gulf shoreline. The unusually high oyster shell content of the beach sand is one sign that this is one of America's more quickly eroding beaches.

Photo 6–1. A typical view of Sargent Beach. The buildings on the left are perched on dredge-spoil piles along the Gulf Intracoastal Waterway. The Gulf of Mexico is 200 yards to the right. (Photo courtesy of the Duke University Program for the Study of Developed Shorelines)

Photo 6–2. A view of the rapidly eroding shoreline at Sargent Beach. Salt marsh mud layers accumulated in quiet inland waters are now at the sea's edge. In this photo virtually no sandy beach exists. (Photo courtesy of the Duke University Program for the Study of Developed Shorelines)

Photo 6–3. Another view of a 40-foot-per-year retreating shoreline. Here a small amount of sand is present on the beach. Vegetation that once existed well behind the beach has been killed by the salt spray as the shoreline moves steadily inland. (Photo courtesy of the Duke University Program for the Study of Developed Shorelines)

Since most of Sargent Beach's fishing shacks and cottages are built on the spoil mounds, ownership, in a practical sense, is indeterminate. The U.S. Army Corps of Engineers still claims the right to use the mounds as dump sites for dredge spoil.

In the late 1960s, a development of fifty or so moderately priced summer houses was started on the low-elevation strip of land between the intracoastal waterway and the Gulf shoreline. Finger canals provided each house with waterfront and ready access to the Gulf. The community was a spectacular failure. About forty of the original fifty houses have been destroyed by storms or erosion (Photo 6–4). Their legacy is a beach littered with pipes, septic tanks, and assorted posts, pilings, and other house fragments. Five rows of beach houses are nothing but memories and debris.

Nevertheless, a new feature will soon be present at Sargent Beach: an eight-mile seawall along the Gulf shore. Construction began in 1995 on what will be one of the world's longest seawalls, second in the United States only to the massive Galveston wall. It will be the longest wall ever built at one time in the United States.

Why build a seawall for a virtual anti-resort? The reason is not the

Photo 6–4. A lonely remnant of a community of beach cottages at Sargent Beach. This cottage perched at the edge of the rapidly eroding shoreline is awaiting its inevitable fate. (Photo courtesy of the Duke University Program for the Study of Developed Shorelines)

threatened houses or the rapidly retreating shoreline. A retreating shoreline on such a remote area of coast is not of any particular concern to our society. And the preservation of the remaining private houses would not justify such a large expenditure of tax money. The crisis at Sargent Beach is a shoreline that is about to catch up with the intracoastal waterway, a shipping lane for a number of south Texas industries, particularly petrochemical industries (Figure 6–1).

The waterway takes an eastward bend, closely paralleling the Gulf of Mexico shoreline, for about seven miles between Cedar Lakes to the northeast and the head of east Matagorda Bay to the southwest. In 1989, the waterway was separated from the Gulf by a strip of land 600 to 900 feet wide. The Corps estimates that, without intervention, the remaining land will be eroded, making this section of the waterway open ocean in approximately fifteen years.

Why not simply relocate the waterway landward by giving it a new course? To the west, inland of the waterway, lies the 24,500-acre San Bernard National Wildlife Refuge. Relocating the waterway there would mean the destruction of over 100 acres of salt marsh and the alteration of wetland drainage patterns over many more acres.

The erosion at Sargent Beach poses a real dilemma. Unlike other areas—Oregon Inlet, North Carolina, or Presque Isle, Pennsylvania, for example—there is no happy solution for Sargent Beach or the adjacent wildlife refuge. Furthermore, Sargent Beach is only the first of a number of stretches of the Atlantic and Gulf intracoastal waterway in immediate

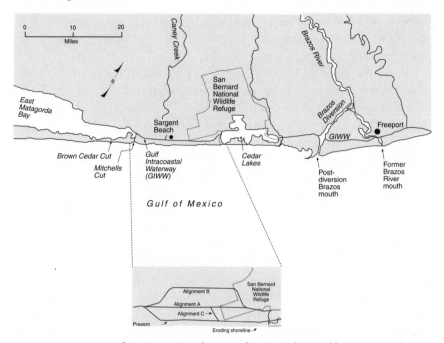

Figure 6–1. Map of Sargent Beach area showing the Gulf Intracoastal Waterway, Matagorda Bay, the boundaries of the San Bernard Wildlife Refuge, and the diversion of the Brazos River near Freeport. The inset shows the alternative to seawall construction that involved relocation of the GIWW as shown in this figure. The corner of the refuge that would be affected by the relocation is an area used for hunting.

danger of destruction by shoreline erosion. On the U.S. Atlantic Coast, the northern two miles of Assateague Island, Maryland, could migrate into the waterway within two decades. Jetties at Ocean City Inlet, to the north of Assateague Island, have starved the island of sand and caused its rapid landward migration. As sea level rises, likely at increased rates with global warming, other parts of the waterway and their seaward shores will be faced with similar problems. Before long, preservation of the waterway may require national attention, raising some important questions about whether the effort is worth the cost.

The Gulf Intracoastal Waterway

The idea for inland waterways in the United States is as old as the nation itself. The nation's leaders wanted protected navigable courses so military and merchant ships could avoid going offshore during wartime. In war or peacetime, merchants saw the value of inland transport for safer, quicker passage of goods.

Along the Gulf of Mexico, merchants clamored for a cross-Florida channel to avoid the long passage around the Keys. In 1888, the Caloosahatchee channel connected Lake Okeechobee with the Gulf, but by 1936 the prospect of a channel across the entire state was abandoned. The idea was revived in 1964, only to be abandoned once again, this time for environmental reasons. Numerous short channels were also constructed in Louisiana and Texas. In 1902, the Galveston and Brazos Navigation Company sold its privately constructed 11-mile channel near Galveston to the U.S. government. By that time, the Corps of Engineers was busy surveying other parts of the Gulf Coast for waterways. A description of the survey in the Corps' *History of the Gulf Intracoastal Waterway* depicts conditions as quite gruesome: "The Engineer employees encountered swampy terrain inhabited by wild turkeys, bears, panthers, alligators, and poisonous reptiles and infested with mosquitoes and deer flies. To conduct the distasteful task of exploring this unpleasant region, each surveyor counted among his essential accouterments rubber boots, snake bite kits, and side arms."

In 1905, the Interstate Inland Waterway League was formed by business interests with the goal of building a continuous waterway system to link 18,000 miles of navigable waters from the Great Lakes, through the Mississippi Valley, and along the Louisiana and Texas coasts. The league exists today as the Gulf Intracoastal Canal Association. Its work led to the 1925 congressional authorization of construction of a "Louisiana and Texas Intracoastal Waterway." That authorization embodied a new philosophy toward inland waterway systems. Until 1923, they were designed to connect open bays; from 1923 on, the focus shifted to building continuous landlocked inland channels.

By 1949, the waterway had been completed. The Corps of Engineers, which managed the waterway, and the Gulf Intracoastal Waterway Association could boast a navigable inland passage from Apalachee Bay, Florida, to the Mexican border.

Why All the Erosion?

Sargent Beach is on the western flank of the Brazos River delta. Unlike most of the Texas shoreline, this is a mainland coast, not a barrier island. On the adjacent continental shelf, geologists have detected a series of now submerged shorelines slightly older than the present one, indicating that Sargent Beach has been eroding for many years, perhaps two thousand.

The first accurate shoreline map of Sargent Beach was made in 1850. Since then, according to Bob Morton, a coastal geologist for the state of Texas, the overall annual erosion rate has been about 15 feet per year. According to Morton's research, that rate has climbed more recently to 40 feet per year, with a maximum of 60 feet per year. The present-day shoreline at the mouth of Caney Creek is 2,300 feet landward of the 1850 shoreline.

Overall, the year-by-year erosion rate of Sargent Beach's Gulf shoreline is quite regular, with a slight increase from northeast to southwest. The erosion rates on many barrier island shorelines are storm dependent. But, the long-term average rates of erosion here are steady regardless of whether a major storm occurs. In 1980, Morton has noted, Hurricane Allen caused a major loss of beach sand and formed mud scarps on the beach, but it fomented only a minor and temporary increase in the shoreline retreat rate.

One reason for the rapid rate of shoreline erosion is a general paucity of sand. The exposed marsh mud along Sargent Beach erodes quickly. The mud ledges do not disperse wave energy like a sloping sandy beach does, and that, in combination with mud's highly erodable nature, makes the ledges less resistant to wave attack. The fine mud grains are suspended by waves and easily carried out onto the continental shelf, out of the beach system. Sand, by contrast, tends to stay within the beach system except when caught in stronger storm flows.

Sargent Beach's rapid erosion is partly natural. But most of it, especially the recent increase in erosion rates, can be attributed to human activities. First, the inlet leading to Freeport, to the northeast, was dredged and jettied in the late 1800s. Eventually, sand trapping by the Freeport jetties must have reduced the sand supply to Sargent Beach and increased the erosion rate. In more recent decades, numerous dams built along the length of the Brazos River have trapped sand, reducing the sand load that reached the coast and, once again, increasing erosion at Sargent Beach. While less sediment flowed down the Brazos, there was continued siltation in Freeport Harbor. In 1929 the river was diverted away from the harbor. Although the old jettied river mouth at Freeport was kept open as the harbor entrance, the diverted river flowed into the Gulf through a new mouth six miles to the south.

The Brazos's new artificial channel deepened and meandered, bringing large volumes of sediment to the mouth of the river. Within a few years, a sizable delta protruded into the Gulf. Wave refraction, caused by the delta's seaward bulge, then reversed the direction of surf-zone currents, trapping shoreline sediment in the delta and starving Sargent Beach. The once continuous stream of sand flowing from the river to Sargent Beach was halted.

An estimated 500,000 cubic yards per year of sediment is now lost to erosion along the 10- to 12-mile stretch of shoreline near Sargent Beach. If the Brazos River sand were still coming south, the shoreline retreat rate would probably be closer to 4 or 5 feet per year, rather than the current 40 feet. Closer to Sargent Beach, privately cut inlets linking the Gulf to the intracoastal waterway have created passages for small recreational fishing boats, adding to the shoreline erosion. The first of these was Charpiot's Cut, dredged in the mid to late 1960s. It immediately caused local erosion as beach sand flowed from the shoreline into the inlet. Eventually, this sand choked Charpiot's Cut itself.

In the late 1980s, using an abandoned meander of Caney Creek, a new inlet called McCabe's Cut was cut between the waterway and the Gulf. Like Charpiot's Cut before it, McCabe's Cut was opened by local interests without an assessment of the potential environmental impact. The excavation increased the local shoreline erosion rate as tidal flow and wave action carried beach sand through the inlet and into the waterway. The Corps had to dredge almost continuously to keep the waterway open. The artificial inlet rapidly grew in depth and cross-sectional area and began to affect waterway traffic directly. In one case, a tug was sucked seaward through the inlet but went aground before being carried into the Gulf. The Corps insisted that local people close the inlet because of all the problems it was creating. After closure of McCabe's Cut and Charpiot's Cut, erosion rates of Sargent Beach immediately decreased.

In 1990, local interests opened Mitchell's Cut, a new inlet southwest of Sargent Beach, to replace McCabe's Cut. Mitchell's Cut occupies the site of an old inlet filled in long ago by natural processes. Because the reopened inlet is located well away from any buildings or structures, the erosion it has caused is not of local concern.

How to Save the Waterway?

The Galveston District of the Corps, charged with maintaining the waterway, considered four alternatives:

1. Let the erosion continue unabated and eventually sacrifice the seven-mile stretch of waterway.

2. Realign or straighten the waterway by dredging a new section to the west of its present course.

3. Replenish the beach along the entire affected length of shoreline.

4. Build a seawall on the beach along the seven miles of threatened waterway.

As we will discuss, public debate was essentially limited to two alternatives: realign the waterway or build a seawall.

Let Nature Take Its Course

The "do nothing," or "no action," approach may not be as drastic as it seems. Letting erosion continue would be the least expensive and the only truly permanent solution. The threatened stretch of the waterway would be lost, but is that so bad? Inland passage is not available along nearly the entire west coast of Florida. Eastbound vessels must leave the waterway at Carrabelle, Florida, and steam into the open Gulf. Sargent Beach, like the west coast of Florida, has a relatively low wave-energy environment, where, except during storms, waters are generally calm. Thus, we doubt that loss of the waterway along Sargent Beach would hamper shipping to a significant degree.

Another consequence of doing nothing would be the exposure of a portion of the San Bernard National Wildlife Refuge to the open Gulf, leading to the eventual loss of many acres of wetlands. Although wetlands preservation deserves high priority, should it be at the cost of other ecosystems, including, in the case of the seawall alternative, other wetland areas? How far should we go to protect specific wetlands?

A possibility not considered by the Corps would be to turn the "do nothing" approach into a "work with nature" approach by releasing sand trapped at the Brazos River delta. The rapid erosion at Sargent Beach is directly attributable to sand trapping at the artificially diverted mouth of the Brazos. If engineering efforts were successful in releasing sand from the delta, erosion would eventually slow at Sargent Beach. With an increased sand supply, Sargent Beach would continue to erode in its historically slow and fairly regular pattern. Although erosion-rate slowing might not happen in time to save the current waterway, this approach could be combined with the waterway alignment option to protect the wetlands of the wildlife refuge.

Realign the Waterway

Realignment of the threatened section of the waterway would entail straightening the approximately seven-mile jog and dredging a new section through the 2,400-acre Smith Marsh Unit of the San Bernard National Wildlife Refuge wetlands. The U.S. Fish and Wildlife Service, charged with refuge stewardship, has objected to realignment because it would mean the direct loss and potential degradation of many acres of wetlands. And these are not just any wetlands. In a reply to the Corps' request for comments on the proposed realignment, Michael Spear, service regional director, indicated that the Smith Marsh Unit "contains some of the highest value marsh for waterfowl on the refuge." What Spear does not mention is that this is also one of the refuge's three designated public hunting areas, where the service builds freshwater impoundments to attract waterfowl and then opens the area to guns.

In addition to interfering with waterfowl and their hunters, the new channel created by realigning the waterway through the Smith Marsh would interfere with the flow of fresh water over and through the wetland. Among a variety of consequences would be increased salinity to the seaward side of the new canal. To maintain the hydrology and salinity of surrounding wetlands, the Corps proposed an extensive siphon system to pump water from one side of the canal to the other. The service's costly demand that the nature of the marsh should not be changed and that any potential change must be alleviated by an engineering solution is ironic. As is the case in many wildlife refuges, the service has already extensively altered the nature of the San Bernard Refuge to help hunters and select wildlife species.

To offset the direct loss of a wetland, the National Environmental Protection Act (NEPA) requires that a new wetland of equivalent area and type be established. In this case, the Corps proposed construction of a marsh in nearby Matagorda Bay. To make a new marsh, mud and sand would be pumped into Matagorda Bay, harming the bay's bottom environment. Which is the more important ecosystem: bay bottom or salt marsh? A number of scientists also question the effectiveness of creating artificial wetlands to replace natural wetland systems. Combining the U.S. Fish and Wildlife Service's inflexible, no-wetland-change requirement with the NEPA requirement that dredge spoil be pumped 5 or 6 miles to Matagorda Bay to form new marsh makes the realignment alternative more costly than the seawall alternative. According to the Corps' calculations, the cost-benefit ratio was 1.8 for realignment and 2.0 for the seawall.

Beach Replenishment

The Corps deemed replenishment at Sargent Beach too costly. This is only reasonable given the shoreline's current average erosion rate of 40 feet per year. Furthermore, experience along the U.S. Atlantic Coast shows that replenished beaches tend to erode more rapidly than their natural predecessors. If this generalization applies to Sargent Beach, the replenished beach's erosion rate would exceed 40 feet annually, making the cost of repeated sand pumping virtually out of the question.

Again, however, there is an alternative for Sargent Beach akin to beach replenishment. Taking sand from the Brazos delta, where it is trapped by wave refraction around the newly formed delta, and putting it into the longshore transport system of the local beaches would increase the sand supply to Sargent Beach.

The Seawall!

Despite Corps efforts to amend the realignment plan to avoid wetland areas that the Service identified as particularly important, the Service became a seawall advocate. Constructing a seawall, it argued, not only would avoid the need to damage wetlands for a new waterway, it would also halt present-day shoreline retreat and marsh loss. The Service even went so far as to request that the seawall be extended east, seaward of the Cedar Lakes area, where it would protect another one of the three public hunting areas on the refuge.

The seawall design calls for an eight-mile low revetment about 300 feet seaward of and parallel to the waterway. The wall will be a low, sloping structure built primarily of concrete block, with several sections of concrete sheet pile where the substrate will not support the concrete block. Each concrete block will weigh approximately six tons and measure 3 feet x 5.25 feet x 5.25 feet. These blocks will be laid over a 2-foot-thick bed of finer rock. The base of the wall will be buried to a depth of 10 feet below the mean low-tide line. The top of the wall will extend 7 feet above the mean low-tide line, but, because ground elevation is about 5 feet, only about 2 feet of the wall will be above ground. The plan is to allow storm overwash but prohibit shoreline retreat. At each end of the seawall, landward-extending "wings" built at an angle to the wall to anchor the structure and prevent waves from washing around and eroding sediment from behind the wall, a phenomenon known as end-around erosion.

The Service's promotion of the seawall alternative led it to make highly questionable scientific arguments about the coastal ecosystem. In 1989, David Hankla, field supervisor of the Service's Houston office, wrote to the Galveston District: "A concrete steel or rock shoreline stabilization structure will provide a positive environmental benefit" by serving as a point of attachment for sedentary organisms, that, in turn, would provide a food source for mobile organisms. "This," he said, "would significantly compensate for the lack of benthic production on the beach and nearshore bottoms." It is the old notion that if we try, we can improve on nature.

The Corps' Galveston District, following the lead of the Service's biological expertise, noted the seawall's benefit to the ecosystem. In other shoreline-armoring projects, such as the proposed jetties at Oregon Inlet, North Carolina, the Corps has also proclaimed that an artificial rock structure on a sand beach would encourage the arrival of new species and enhance species diversification. Such logic assumes that increased diversity per se is an improvement on the natural system, ignoring the potential loss of native species and their habitat.

The Service was in the difficult position of having no happy or easy choices. Nonetheless, had it undertaken a rigorous analysis of all four erosion-control alternatives considered by the Corps, its arguments might have reflected a better overall management perspective. Such an analysis might have revealed that the potential damage to the ecosystem through seawall construction would be at least as serious as direct loss of wetlands. Instead, the Service narrowly focused on saving a piece of *its* wetland as it exists today, with little if any consideration for surrounding natural areas or the potential long-term consequences.

The seawall is impressive in design but will hardly be the panacea the Corps and the Service would have the public believe. It carries, in fact, potentially huge economic, societal, and environmental costs. Nonetheless, in the end, the seawall was the chosen alternative.

The Costs

- *Economic:* The cost of construction is estimated to be $81 million (1992 dollars). Even before construction began, the Corps spent approximately $16 million in planning, designing, and surveying activities. Over a fifty-year period, the so-called economic design life of the project, including interest, the average cost of the project will be $8.5 million a year. The cumulative total over the fifty-year period is, therefore, $425 million.

  Weighing benefits versus costs, the Corps came up with a positive ratio of 2; that is, for every dollar spent, there will be a return of $2 in benefits. A number of assumptions are built into this estimate, including a certainty that the predicted average annual costs are accurate. We believe that the cost estimates of the Sargent Beach seawall, as with other Corps shoreline projects, will prove to be low. There are two primary reasons: maintenance and repair costs will likely be greater than anticipated, and no consideration has been given to the inevitable need for seawall lengthening in a few decades.

Maintenance costs for any shoreline engineering project are difficult to predict. The Corps' estimates are usually low because the Corps consistently assumes maintenance under ideal conditions, without acknowledging that the storm-cushioning beach will be steepened and gone within a decade or two or three. The predicted average annual maintenance costs of around $800,000 per year are based on the assumption that about 20 percent of the concrete blocks would have to be replaced every ten years. But the Corps has little basis on which to predict how this particular type of wall will fare in the long term or when battered by severe storms. This wall, like every seawall, will unquestionably be damaged by a storm, though no one can say when that will happen. Many major storms could strike the Texas coast within the fifty-year design life of the wall. Even without damaging storms, when the fronting beach disappears, additional stone will probably need to be placed at the base of the wall as erosion undermines its foundation.

Among the other uncertainties characteristic of every Corps project are the vagaries of the federal funding process. Future expenditures for maintenance and repair are only forecasts until Congress approves them during its biennial appropriations process. Competition for limited funds among Corps districts is intense, and the Sargent Beach seawall is likely to slip into obscurity as a national priority when it goes into cost overruns and more stretches of the intracoastal waterway need similar attention.

- *Social:* If the social costs of the Sargent Beach seawall are similar to seawalls on other American beaches—and we know of no reason to think otherwise—we anticipate the following scenario of false hopes.

Once, and perhaps even before, the seawall is in place, an illusion of safety will be created. The value of the property behind the seawall will shoot up, and the house building will begin. Public access to the beach, already made somewhat inaccessible by the seawall, will be increasingly restricted. The popular Texan pastime of driving on the beach will no longer be possible at Sargent Beach. Forty miles of beach between Freeport and Sargent Beach will be cut off to vehicle access unless a new coastal road is constructed.

Water quality will also decline as surrounding waters are contaminated by run-off from paved roads and driveways, septic systems, and other sources. As more people build houses in Sargent Beach, more lives and property will be at risk when storms and high water besiege the town. As a result, more emergency personnel will have to endanger themselves to rescue the foolhardy. And more disaster assistance funds will be spent in obviously hazardous areas to help people rebuild and start the whole cycle again.

• *Environmental:* Seawalls are the most damaging form of shoreline stabilization, illegal in several states and strongly discouraged in most others. They exact a high toll on coastal and nearshore physical and biological environments. Scientists and engineers agree that, sooner or later, the beach in front of the seawall will disappear. Presumably, the shoreface, the underwater part of the beach, will steepen as well. Waves will then strike the seawall at full force, without a gently sloping shoreface and beach to dampen their energy.

Contrary to claims that the seawall will increase biodiversity along the Sargent Beach shore, a measure of biodiversity will actually be lost. The loss of the beach means the loss of the intertidal environment with all its faunal and floral uniqueness. According to a 1992 national study done for the World Resources Institute, a surprising number of rare, threatened, and endangered coastal species are restricted in their habitats to within 10 feet of the water line. These species, and many others, are being squeezed between rising seas and coastal development. A seawall gives them nowhere to go and nowhere to live. The study also identified commercially important fish and shellfish species that depend on coastal nearshore environments. Alteration of this habitat could thus have detrimental effects on commercial fisheries. At the very least, the biological implications of the seawall should have been thoroughly evaluated.

Another consequence of the seawall will be accelerated land loss downdrift, in this case to the southwest. In its environmental impact statement, the Corps' Galveston District fails to address the question, a startling omission, given that the downdrift impacts of seawalls are well documented. Bob Morton pointed out the exclusion in the Texas Bureau of Economic Geology's criticism of the Corps' environmental impact statement. The Galveston District's response: "There is little guidance on how to accurately assess downdrift effects from barrier structures since each case has its own set of complex parameters." In other words, the district decided that because it could not quantify downdrift effects, it would ignore them. This is a somewhat surprising response; typically, as discussed in chapter 3, the Corps predicts shoreline behavior under all kinds of circumstances using sophisticated mathematical models.

For the Corps to ignore downdrift land loss may be startling, but for the Service to do so is appalling. Over the long term (measurable in decades), the area that would be affected to the southwest of Sargent Beach is largely wetlands in Matagorda Bay, which is part of the National Wildlife Refuge system. Yet in its examination of the Corps' proposed alternatives, the Service appears to have failed to consider the potential loss of wetlands to seawall-induced erosion.

Part of the reason for the Service's failure to adequately investigate the potential downdrift effects of the seawall may lie in the misconception that the longshore current will simply continue to carry sand past the structure. Unfortunately, while this might happen briefly, no more sand will move to the southwest once the beach and shoreface fronting the seawall have disappeared and steepened. Thus, the service's plan to save wetlands in one location is likely to result in accelerated wetland loss elsewhere.

The Politics

The proposed seawall for Sargent Beach may be among the longest ever built in the United States, but the project, at least during its planning phases, was also among the least known to the public. Other major shoreline stabilization debates have been reported in the national media. For example, both Oregon Inlet, North Carolina, and Presque Isle, Pennsylvania, have been the subjects of articles in the *New York Times* and the *Washington Post* and have received international television coverage. The debate over Sargent Beach has remained unseen and unheard outside of Texas and has seldom made even in-state headlines.

One individual who tried, in his quiet way, to sound the warnings about an environmentally unsound project was 52-year-old Bob Morton of the Bureau of Economic Geology in Austin, which watches over the shoreline scientific interests of the state of Texas. Morton, a Tennessee native with a Ph.D. from West Virginia University (who nonetheless sports a Texas accent), is unofficially the state's official coastal geologist. For years, he has been involved as an expert witness for Texas in all sorts of shoreline cases, and he has helped the state force the relocation of buildings on Galveston Island that had been stranded on the beach by shoreline retreat.

Morton has been responsible for critiquing the various Sargent Beach design documents and environmental impact statements put out by both the Corps and the Service. In carrying out this task, he became highly skeptical of the process that led to the choice of the seawall over the waterway realignment alternative. Not one to take a highly visible public role, he quietly did his duty on behalf of the state and then watched with dismay as the shoreline environment was forgotten.

Among the few public comments on the seawall were those by the Sierra Club, which opposed the construction. Its participation, however, did not go beyond several letters of objection.

The lack of publicity and public debate may be a reflection of the dilemma surrounding the project. Given that the debate focused on two alternatives, either build the seawall or realign the waterway, opponents to the wall were forced into advocating the destruction of hundreds of acres of wetlands. We suspect that, had the long-term effects of the seawall been more thoroughly assessed, the tenor of the debate would have been different. Left out of the discussion were factors such as the potential for downdrift wetland loss, the blocking of vehicle access to 40 miles of shoreline, and the potential increased density of development along a dangerous, exposed shoreline.

One group of citizens made certain that the seawall was presented favorably. The Coalition to Save the Gulf Intracoastal Waterway is composed primarily of Sargent Beach property owners. Their spokesperson, William Templeton, enlisted the support of a number of corporations, including DuPont, Central Power and Light, Union Carbide, Hocht Celanese, Champlin, Koch Refining, and Valero Refining, among others, that ship petrochemical products via the waterway. The group mounted a highly successful campaign to make Sargent Beach a congressional issue. In an unusual partnership, Republican Senator Phil Gramm and Democratic then-Senator Lloyd Bentsen, both of Texas, cosponsored legislation to fund construction of the seawall. Bentsen once went so far as to arrive on the scene by helicopter and declare, before a cluster of news cameras, his support for the wall.

After winning congressional approval, the well-versed and well-funded coalition pushed to hasten the seawall's construction. Rather than assuming shoreline retreat to be a realistic 40 feet per year, the coalition consistently cited 75 feet per year until that unrealistic number became the accepted rate. The coalition further succeeded in lobbying for an additional $1 million in preliminary funding for the Corps from Congress.

In the end, the coalition expended a lot of effort, and no doubt a lot of money, to push a project that the Corps was obligated to do anyway under its mandate to maintain the intracoastal waterway. The coalition's apparent motive was to get a seawall in place as soon as possible. From the Sargent Beach property owners' perspective, the seawall will halt the rapid erosion that threatens their houses and will increase property values. Proclaiming the goal of saving a national waterway, however, is far more palatable to the public than increasing private property value at citizens' expense. A handful of individuals (in this case, property owners between the waterway and the Gulf) will be the primary beneficiaries of the Corps project.

The two agencies responsible for reviewing alternatives and recommending a course of action were left without a happy alternative. Both— particularly, in our view, the Service—failed to adequately assess the need to protect the immediate and surrounding coastal and estuarine ecosystems. The Corps has a long tradition of approaching environmental problems through structural engineering. The U.S. Fish and Wildlife Service focused on the maintenance of the present state of its own particular wetlands jurisdiction immediately behind an eroding shoreline, at the expense of the beach environment and another area of wetlands.

The Sargent Beach seawall represents another link in a long chain of projects that have led to ever increasing inflexibility and set more engineering along this stretch of the Texas coast. Engineering created the crisis at Sargent Beach through updrift jetty construction and river mouth diversion projects that severely restricted the availability of sediment to Sargent Beach. Now another engineering experiment will be imposed on this shoreline system.

The Future

Within two to three decades, the scene at Sargent Beach will have altered drastically. The visible "beach" will be nothing more than the concrete blocks of the seawall. Southwest toward the Matagorda Peninsula beyond the end of the wall, shoreline erosion rates will have accelerated and wetlands loss will be huge. A lot of money will have been made by

Sargent Beach property owners, their virtually worthless, erosion-prone, shoreline tracts having become valuable almost overnight as a result of seawall construction. Large, expensive buildings next to and behind the wall will stand vulnerable to the onslaught of the next severe storm, some perhaps rebuilt since the last storm. The cost of seawall maintenance will have greatly exceeded the original estimates because of "unexpected and unusual" storms. The shoreface in front of the seawall will be steepened. As a result, higher waves will strike the shore with greater force, and more overwash will penetrate the community. Taxpayers nationwide will know about Sargent Beach through federal disaster assistance, federal flood insurance payments, and seawall repair expenditures.

Three to five decades from the time of construction, the seawall will have been enlarged considerably. More rock will be placed in front of the deteriorating and undermined structure and more will be used to make the wall higher to protect buildings behind the wall. The additional protection will be needed because overwash will be occurring with increasing frequency. The seawall will also have been greatly increased in length, as the rate and extent of downdrift erosion will have become intolerable. Sargent Beach will be a beach community with no beach in sight for many miles.

SEVEN

Presque Isle:
The End of a Beach

In the chill of a November day in 1992, we walked across the big interior dunes of Presque Isle, Pennsylvania, with our guide, Paul Knuth, a fifty-year-old, soft-spoken coastal environmental scientist at nearby Edinboro University, the only other people we saw braving the cold were a few fishermen and joggers enjoying Presque Isle State Park.

Geologically and culturally, Presque Isle, near Erie, Pennsylvania, is a fascinating place. Technically known as a compound recurved sand spit, Presque Isle (French for "almost an island") sits atop and owes its location to a submerged glacial moraine, a deposit of sand and gravel left behind by a melting glacier about a thousand years ago. Jutting into Lake Erie, the Presque Isle moraine is basically a pile of sediment pushed into a long ridge by the same glaciers that scooped out the basin now occupied by the lake. After the glaciers receded, water filled the Lake Erie basin and waves began eating away the shoreline. The beach sand this erosion furnished was transported from west to east, moving out along the moraine. Over the past few thousand years, this sediment transport system has widened Presque Isle lakeward and lengthened it to the east, forming the peninsula's fingerlike eastern end, known as Gull Point. As wind and storm waves blew sand into the spit's interior, Presque Isle gained elevation. Erie Harbor, one of the best (and few) natural harbors on the Great Lakes formed in the lee of the spit.

Today, Presque Isle is a peninsula of more than two thousand acres of unconsolidated sand that protrudes into Lake Erie from an otherwise straight shoreline (Figure 7–1). The spit has seven miles of open-lake shoreline; its width ranges from a few tens of yards at the narrow neck that connects it to the mainland to as much as a mile in its midsection.

From the air, this "flying spit," as it is sometimes called, seems to float freely out into the lake.

Away from the roads and picnic areas, Presque Isle seems pristine. To Paul, it is a very special place. He spent a lot of his childhood here swimming, fishing, and exploring, often under the watchful eye of his grandfather, who was a member of the park maintenance crew on the Isle. On this day it seemed that he knew every tree, fallen log, dune, and animal burrow as he guided us off and on the hiking trails amid the blazing fall colors of black gum and cottonwood leaves.

As we stood atop a dune, Paul reminded us of the beach's vital role in the spit's evolution. He pointed out that every grain of sand on the spit (except those brought in by dump trucks) was carried across the beach by either storm overwash or wind. Presque Isle's original sand source from the eroding lakeshore bluffs to the west has been compromised, he noted, by erosion-control structures built to protect the expensive houses that line the bluff tops. Reducing bluff erosion in an attempt to save buildings has ultimately starved Presque Isle of much of its sand supply, thereby increasing erosion rates.

People have affected the park in other ways, too. The roads, picnic areas, parking lots, jogging and hiking trails, boating, wind surfing, fishing, designated swimming areas, and millions of visitors inevitably have brought associated environmental problems. Important on Paul's list of problems is polluted swimming water. The pollution's sources are unclear and have long been a matter of debate, but urban run-off to the west of the peninsula is a major suspect. Every major storm overflows urban sewer systems, releasing effluents into the lake to be trapped in beach sands. In the summer of 1992, beaches were closed ten times due to a high coliform bacteria count in the water. In 1993, the beaches were again closed numerous times. Behind the peninsula, within Presque Isle Bay (also known as Erie Harbor), four miles of park beach have been closed to swimming since 1940. Meanwhile, the lake fishery, for which Lake Erie was once renowned, largely disappeared after the principal fish species suffered a combination of overfishing, pollution, and lamprey eel predation.

As we continued our walk, oblivious in his enthusiasm to the bushes that grabbed at our clothing, he talked without pause. Now his subject was the critical role of vegetation in holding sand in place once it arrives on the land. As he walked and talked, Paul was clearly agitated by the constant apparently inescapable and low roar of machinery.

We finally broke into the open through a screen of cottonwood trees

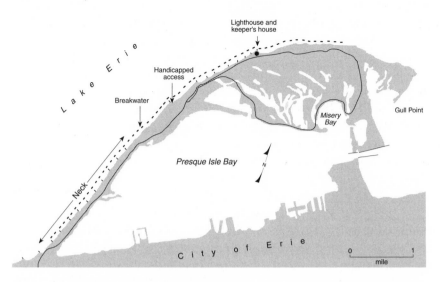

Figure 7–1. Map showing the location of the Presque Isle State Park and the positions of the offshore breakwaters.

to discover the source of the noise and a disheartening sight. The seemingly infinite panorama of Lake Erie was broken by the outline of swinging cranes plucking rocks from barges and carefully placing them on the offshore breakwaters. The roaring noise that had been pestering us came from sand-pushing bulldozers and graders. That was accompanied by the duller chugging sound from a tug just off the beach that was busy moving the stone-laden barges. It was a scene at odds with the beautiful dunes and woodland we had just crossed. The U.S. Army Corps of Engineers was putting in the last of fifty-five offshore breakwaters.

The Corps' noisy engineering project belies Presque Isle's ecological significance and rich cultural history. Presque Isle State Park was founded in 1921 and became the sixty-fourth congressionally designated National Natural Landmark in 1967. Joseph Miller, associate regional director of management and operations for the National Park Service, cited Presque Isle in congressional testimony as "one of the few areas in the world where ecologists may study the succession of plant life from a sand and water environment to a climax forest within a span of less than one mile." Its National Natural Landmark designation, one step short of being a national park, recognizes the area as "an example of scenic grandeur and of our natural heritage." Although the National Park Service (NPS) is charged with stewardship of the landmarks, it has no direct management authority over them other than to urge the protection and maintenance of their environmental integrity and to remove the landmark designation if conditions warrant. To carry out its stewardship responsibility, NPS assigns to each landmark a patron, a qualified individual who serves as the Park Service's eyes and ears.

Presque Isle's landmark status also recognizes it as "a habitat supporting . . . vanishing, rare, or restricted species." According to congressional testimony by Jean Stull, director of the Presque Isle Audubon Society, the peninsula supports over thirty bird "species of concern." Gull Point, at Presque Isle's eastern tip, may be one of the few significant fueling and resting spots between the Great Lakes and the Atlantic Ocean for a number of species of migrating shorebirds, including various plovers, sandpipers, whimbrels, and sanderlings. Presque Isle also supports many of Pennsylvania's rarest plant species and one of its rarest turtles. James Bissell, curator of botany for the Cleveland Museum of Natural History, found fifty-five "plants of special concern in Pennsylvania" on Presque Isle, "more rare plants than known from any other area in Pennsylvania."

The cultural history of Presque Isle is as rich as its natural beauty. The first recorded inhabitants were the Eriez Indians. These peaceful people were virtually exterminated in the eighteenth century by the more aggressive Iroquois tribe, who had fled westward to avoid extermination at the hands of advancing white settlers.

The French, who arrived in 1753, built Fort Presque Isle on the mainland overlooking the lake within the present-day site of Erie. Fort Presque Isle was not intended to be a settlement. It was built as part of a chain of fortifications stretching from just outside Pittsburgh to Lake Erie to deny British access to the Great Lakes, the water route to the rich Northwest. French control ended when the British captured Fort Niagara, first in the chain, in 1759. With their grand plan of blockade no longer viable, the French burned and abandoned Fort Presque Isle. The British rebuilt the fort in 1760 only to have it captured and burned to the ground by Indians during Pontiac's war three years later.

For most of the rest of the eighteenth century, except for construction of a mainland trading post, events passed Erie by. General "Mad" Anthony Wayne reoccupied the shore of Lake Erie in 1795 after his forces defeated the Indians at the Battle of Fallen Timbers near Fort Defiance, Ohio. In the same year, settlers established a mainland outpost that included a blockhouse and was called Presque Isle, eventually to be renamed Erie. Wayne died in Erie in 1796 after a long and very distinguished career in the service of the fledgling United States.

Presque Isle was an active site once again during the War of 1812. Between December 1812 and July 1813 timbers cut from the white pine stand along the shoreline in the lee of Presque Isle were used to construct Commodore Oliver Perry's main warships, the *Niagara* and the *Lawrence,* in Erie Harbor. While the ships were being built, Perry's soldiers dubbed their harsh Presque Isle winter encampment Misery Bay, as it is yet called today.

Once constructed, the two 260-ton fighting vessels with their 9-foot drafts were able to cross the 6-foot sandbar at the harbor entrance, each supported by two high-floating scows. Once in the lake, the *Niagara* and the *Lawrence* were joined by seven other smaller vessels to face the six-vessel British fleet commanded by Captain Robert Barclay, a one-armed veteran of Trafalgar. In the battle that took place off the Ohio coast, the Americans prevailed, though the *Lawrence* was destroyed. For the first time, the British suffered the indignity of capture of an entire fleet.

Having defeated the British, Commodore Perry moored his ships just offshore of Presque Isle and penned on the back of an envelope to his commanding officer his now famous quote: "We have met the enemy and he is ours."

In 1813 a large blockhouse was built at the tip of the peninsula to guard the Erie Harbor entrance. Six years later, a lighthouse built near the harbor entrance provided the first navigation aid. The present Presque Isle lighthouse, still in operation, was built in 1873.

Local residents of the day used the beaches of Lake Erie as highways. Specially designed wagon wheels allowed smooth and easy rolling for long-distance travel along the soft sand beaches. Storms and changing lake levels moved the shoreline around but no one was troubled by retreating beaches. Because houses were built away from the water's edge, eroding shorelines were not a threat. At this same time, the world's largest freshwater fishing fleet was established in Erie Harbor.

Another page was added to Presque Isle's notable history when it became the site of the U.S. Army Corps of Engineers' *first* beach erosion study in 1819. In 1829, the Corps dug a channel through the same sandbar at Erie Harbor's eastern entrance over which Commodore Perry's ships had been carried by scows, deepening the water from 6 to 9 feet to allow deeper-draft ships access. Knowing that sand would simply flow into and fill the newly deepened channel, the Corps also built a wooden bulkhead, a shore-parallel retaining wall, along Presque Isle's landward-facing shoreline.

Structural approaches and the hands-on method of shoreline management had thus taken hold. In its beach erosion study, the Corps noted that numerous breaches had opened temporary inlets at the neck, or mainland end, of Presque Isle. Breaches, like inlets along barrier islands, are formed when water is pushed into an area by a storm. Once the storm has passed, the water "seeks its level" by the least resistant path, be that by a waterway or through a narrow point of land, such as the mainland neck of Presque Isle. None of the Presque Isle breaches had ever threatened the spit's integrity; most were ephemeral and closed naturally as sand moving along shore filled the gap (Figure 7–2). Nonetheless, in the 1830s, the Corps built wooden seawalls along the open-lake shore of the neck to prevent breaching. The seawalls had little benefit, and in 1833 a breach sizable enough for small-boat navigation formed and remained open until 1852, when it is believed to have closed by natural processes. Another breach formed in 1917 and remained open until 1923.

In 1890, a long stone-and-sheet-steel pile groin was built at the Presque Isle lighthouse to prevent that structure from falling in. The groin succeeded in its purpose: to trap sand in front of the lighthouse. But it also caused rapid shoreline erosion to the east on nearby downdrift beaches. As storms ate away at the groin, it became short and low enough for some eastward sand flow to resume. The groin was removed completely in 1992 during offshore breakwater construction.

With the twentieth century, people came to the shores of Lake Erie with a new attitude toward coastal living. Rather than building at a distance from the shore as their forebears had done, they built right next to the lake for its expansive view, cooling summer breezes, and adjacent beach for strolling and swimming. The new residents soon found that a price for the lake view was exacted when the harsh north winds of winter whipped around their exposed houses. High lake levels, especially in combination with winter storms, brought the real threat of shoreline erosion.

The level of Lake Erie is controlled by the rainfall in the lake's drainage basin: high rainfall, high lake levels; low rainfall, low lake levels. The maximum recorded vertical difference between low water and high water is 4.7 feet. High lake levels inundate beaches, erode bluffs, and overtop seawalls and bulkheads. Low levels leave bluffs and beaches exposed, and worried waterfront property owners relax. Too often, quite unwisely, people build even closer to the lake during low water levels, putting themselves at risk of flooding during the next cycle of high lake levels. High lake levels can exacerbate the action of storms on the shoreline, causing more extensive, albeit usually temporary, shoreline changes.

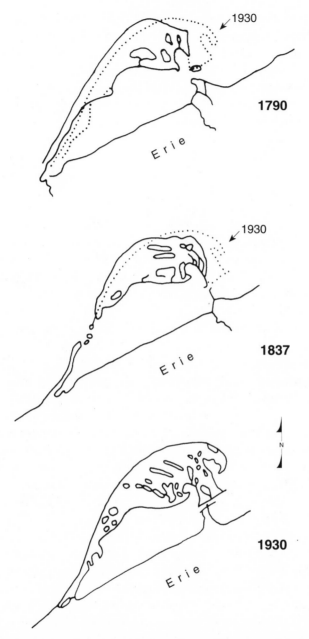

Figure 7–2. Evolution of Presque Isle from the earliest maps of this shoreline to the 1980s. The change in shape of the peninsula is an indication of the dynamic nature of this landform. During several periods of time the peninsula was breached, as shown in the 1837 diagram. The breaches were usually repaired naturally within a few years.

Many shorefront property owners, some in ignorance and some in arrogance, have dumped wagon or truck loads of rock in front of their houses or at the bases of bluffs in response to eroding shores. Today, mile after mile of Lake Erie shoreline is "protected" by rock, concrete, steel, and wooden structures. Much of the Lake Erie shoreline looks like a graveyard of broken seawalls. The long, wide, sandy strip has been replaced by much shorter and narrower stretches of sand between long reaches of rocky shoreline. These days nobody thinks of using the beaches of Lake Erie as walkways let alone as highways, even with four-wheel-drive vehicles. The beach, one of the main reasons for the twentieth-century rush to the shoreline, has largely ceased to exist except for a few rural reaches or state parks.

After surrounding beaches were replaced by seawalls and other structures, Presque Isle was left as one of the few, and arguably the most beautiful, remaining accessible relatively pristine stretches of Lake Erie shoreline. In 1993 alone approximately two million people picnicked, swam, and hiked along the beaches and trails of the small but beautiful Presque Isle State Park.

Nevertheless, the seawalls and other structures that destroyed Lake Erie's mainland beaches harmed Presque Isle as well. The shoreline stabilizers created barriers that blocked the flow of sediment along shore and between bluff and beach. Bluffs, like dunes, serve as a sediment source for the beach. When sand could no longer wash out of the bluffs to the beach, the sand supply for downdrift areas, including Presque Isle, was cut off. Hence, as Paul pointed out to us during our tour, shoreline erosion has increased along the length of Presque Isle.

From 1900 to the present, the state and the Corps have carried out a total of twenty-eight projects, large and small, to construct or maintain erosion-control efforts on Presque Isle, mostly with federal dollars. During the 1950s, the entire neck was lined with a large stone revetment. To protect the revetment a vertical sheet-steel pile seawall was later emplaced along its face. Along the front of the seawall were eleven large groins. These groins remain today but are usually covered and hidden from view by replenishment sand.

Large-scale beach replenishment has been under way on Presque Isle since the mid-1950s. It was the only method of shoreline stabilization used in the 1970s and 1980s. Over a period of thirty-eight years a total of 8 million cubic yards of sand has been dredged or quarried and trucked to the beaches of Presque Isle. Although the first project eroded rapidly, perhaps due to poor choice of sand, beach replenishment has been successful in keeping a recreational beach in place.

Each big winter storm occurring during high water levels has resulted in panicked letters to state and congressional representatives and doomsday editorials in the local Erie newspaper. Yet the storm "damage" has usually consisted of overwashing waves at the neck, a common phenomenon recognized by the Corps in the 1820s. When the storm recedes, real damage on the undeveloped spit is usually minute. Likewise, the urgency with which the local community has viewed erosion problems along the Lake Erie shore and, particularly, Presque Isle has come and gone with storms and lake levels. Erosion, frequent flooding, and storm overwash characterize the spit during high lake levels. In the mid-1960s, when lake level was quite low, erosion and flooding were negligible. In contrast, all hell seemed to have broken loose during the high lake levels of the early 1970s and mid-1980s.

In 1991 and 1992, offshore breakwaters were built at the end of each of the groins. As a result, the neck of Presque Isle is now protected by a rock revetment protected by a sheet-steel seawall protected by groins protected by beach replenishment protected by offshore breakwaters! The array of walls and groins on the neck of Presque Isle blocks the natural eastward flow of sand in the surf zone along the shore, making continual beach replenishment a necessity. No better illustration exists on an American shore of how shoreline engineering begets shoreline engineering.

A "Permanent Solution"

Erosion along the length of Presque Isle led to general fear that the spit would one day disappear unless something were done to stop it. People were understandably loath to lose their much loved and highly valued Presque Isle. Public officials repeatedly turned to their coastal experts— the local Buffalo District office of the Corps of Engineers, which, over the years, responded with a new structure or beach replenishment. Politicians called for a "permanent solution." In 1968, the Corps came up with thirty-three "concepts" for "a solution to the erosion problem at Presque Isle." These were boiled down to several categories:

- Do nothing and let nature take its course.

- Construct more groins and bulkheads to extend the groin field along the entire shoreline.

- Construct a continuous offshore breakwater.

- Continue beach replenishment.

- Construct segmented offshore breakwaters.

Several options were rejected almost as soon as they were considered. Letting nature take its course was dismissed on the premise that the natural flow of sand to the spit had been so significantly reduced that at least some annual artificial replenishment would be necessary. The Corps dismissed the "do nothing" alternative with statements such as: "If we do nothing, the erosion continues, trees fall into the water, and the beaches are lost." We consider this attitude irresponsible. Yes, erosion would continue, and trees would fall in, but the beach would not be "lost." As discussed in chapter 2, even on rapidly retreating shorelines, a beach is present unless it runs into a seawall or similar structure. Doing almost nothing might actually be a good choice in this state park, where a recreational beach is a high priority. Although some shoreline retreat and occasional breaches would continue, a beach would always be present.

The addition of more groins and bulkheads and the construction of a continuous offshore breakwater were also dismissed as too costly and environmentally damaging. Knowing the clearly detrimental aspects of both of these alternatives, we believe that they were probably offered as "strawmen." Groins and bulkheads would stop erosion in one area but exacerbate it along the shoreline. Groins already had a bad reputation on Presque Isle. The continuous breakwater would decrease water circulation along the beach (raising water-quality questions) and prevent natural sand replenishment of the beaches from offshore, leading to more erosion. Both alternatives would be aesthetically offensive.

The two other options that received serious consideration and debate were continued beach replenishment and segmented offshore breakwaters. The Corps had already selected the segmented breakwater alternative in 1973 but was directed, for financial reasons primarily, to reconsider the plan in 1983. Following a review, the Corps again opted for breakwaters over continued replenishment. After that, few changes were allowed in the design, no uncertainties of any kind were discussed, only positive aspects of the breakwater were mentioned publicly, and alternative approaches were downplayed.

The Breakwaters

Offshore breakwaters are walls built offshore parallel to the shoreline and designed to block or trip incoming waves. The resulting wave shadow on the shoreline causes the longshore current to slow and drop some of its sand load, thus building out the beach behind the breakwater. Breakwaters also trip big storm waves before they reach the beach.

Breakwaters can have profound potential long-term effects on beaches, as discussed in chapter 2. In California, the large Santa Barbara and Santa Monica breakwaters were constructed to form harbors rather than to retain beaches. These breakwaters, as have others in California, initially caused dramatic erosion on the downdrift shore. The damage was mitigated with costly sand-bypassing operations, that is, pumping sand from areas of accumulation to areas of erosion. A similar situation could arise on Presque Isle, where the supposed sand accumulation around breakwaters would have to be redistributed to an eroding Gull Point. One of the tenets of the Corps' breakwater design was that sand would travel past the breakwaters in sufficient volume to nourish Gull Point.

Segmented breakwater structures somewhat similar to the Presque Isle breakwaters have been constructed at Winthrop Beach, Massachusetts (five segments); Lorain, Ohio (three segments); Ashtabula, Ohio (three segments); East Harbor State Park, Ohio (four segments); and Colonial Beach along the Chesapeake Bay of Virginia (two sites with three and four segments, respectively). Holly Beach, Louisiana, provides an example of an open-ocean segmented breakwater. None of these even approaches the magnitude of the fifty-five-segment breakwater chain of Presque Isle. Clearly, the Presque Isle system of breakwaters is a new approach and is highly experimental in nature.

Denton Clark, chief of the coastal engineering section of the Corps' Buffalo District, brought the concept of offshore breakwaters to Presque Isle. Clark had visited Japan and was impressed with the Japanese success halting shoreline erosion with segmented detached breakwaters. But the Japanese installed the structures mainly on rocky shorelines, not on unconsolidated sandy shorelines such as Presque Isle. Furthermore, the Japanese objective is not comparable to the Presque Isle objective of saving the beach.

In Japan, more than two thousand segmented offshore breakwaters have been constructed for halting erosion and for forming safe anchorage for boats. For this small, wealthy, highly populated island nation, the belief is widespread that saving land area is more important than beach preservation. In an American state park and National Natural Landmark, like Presque Isle, the recreational beach is *the* priority. Therefore, it is crucial to assess what effect construction of a "permanent" structure will have on the recreational beach.

Two state agencies have the expertise and jurisdiction needed to make that assessment, the Pennsylvania Bureau of State Parks, responsible for managing Presque Isle as a state park, and the Pennsylvania

Geological Survey, the state's corps of geologists. The state parks bureau became a breakwater advocate. The state Geological Survey, for whatever reason, chose to remain silent and uninvolved. Some suspect that the political pressure for a "permanent" solution left no place for real discussion of alternatives.

Another influential staunch breakwater proponent continues to be the local newspaper publisher, the Erie Times Publishing Company. With articles and editorials carrying headlines such as "Army Corps Certain Breakwall Idea Sound," the paper strongly backed the breakwaters. A February 1989 editorial entitled "Breakwalls Protect Beaches" concluded that the breakwater project represented "real hope for preserving Erie's greatest resource. We think Gorecki's [the Corps' Presque Isle project engineer's] statements have considerable impact." In this case, the pro-development newspaper may unwittingly have dealt a strong blow to future development and the quality of life of its community.

Public opposition was at first quiet. In its 1986 "Addendum: Shoreline Erosion Control Project at Presque Isle Peninsula," the Corps reported, "There is no known public opposition to the construction of 58 [later reduced to 55] offshore breakwater segments at Presque Isle." Only environmentalists, a few local academics like Paul Knuth, and the occasional local citizen with a good intuition about the shoreline spoke out. But local opposition began to grow, largely as a result of efforts by Knuth and the Presque Isle Audubon Society to publicize weaknesses in the Corps' design plans. Major national news coverage was spurred by articles in the *New York Times* and a WNET television special.

In fairness, neither the *Erie Times* nor its readers have much experience with the societal debate about shoreline erosion. Pennsylvania's open-water shoreline is limited to 50 miles along Lake Erie. Citizens of states such as the Carolinas and Florida, with much lengthier coasts, are accustomed to questions of coastal management that involve large projects.

To provide a forum for public debate and source of coastal expertise other than the Corps, the Pennsylvania state parks bureau convened the Presque Isle Advisory Committee, of which Paul Knuth was a member. The committee quickly became a powerful player in the breakwater controversy. In its review of the Corps' erosion-control proposals, it raised a number of questions. For one, it was troubled that the Corps' plan was outdated and little modified since 1973, despite changes in the shoreline and nearshore environments of Presque Isle and the failure of prototype breakwaters (discussed below).

The Corps' segmented offshore breakwater proposal involved constructing fifty-five rock breakwaters, with gaps between them, along much of the spit's length. The Corps sold the segmented breakwater idea as a passive, permeable, nonintrusive, and permanent solution that would slow, *but not stop*, the natural longshore-current sand-moving system.

The Corps' design, finished in 1980, aligned the segmented breakwaters parallel to the shoreline about 250 to 350 feet offshore in a trough between the first and second along-shore sandbars (Photo 7–1). Prior to placement of the large boulders, a bedding layer of coarse stone (2 to 10 inches) was laid on the lake floor. All told, more than 600,000 tons of rock was used. Each structure was 150 feet long, 9 to 11 feet wide at the top, and 8 feet high above low lake-water level. They were placed 350 feet apart.

Allowing natural sand transport to continue was an important aspect of the breakwater design. If sand flow did not continue, continual replenishment would be required for downdrift beaches (Photo 7–2) and, ultimately, for the ecologically sensitive Gull Point. In its plan for

Photo 7–1. Aerial view of Presque Isle taken immediately after construction of offshore breakwaters in 1992. The breakwaters are responsible for the irregular shape of the beach, as sand piles up due to the lack of transportation. In 1995, a number of these sand accumulations extend out to the breakwaters, preventing sand transport altogether. (Photo by Jean Stull)

Photo 7–2. Trees are falling in and an erosion scarp has formed on the dune in one of the zones of erosion between the breakwaters. (Photo by Jean Stull)

the Presque Isle breakwaters, the Corps assumed that sand, although in reduced volume, would continue to be transported behind the break-waters in an east-west direction. That's because the design, the Corps reasoned, would prevent the formation of tombolos, above-water sand-bars extending from the shoreline to a breakwater. Tombolos would completely cut off longshore transport of sand (and make it easier for kids to get out to the breakwaters and clamber over the rocks). Yet because the breakwaters were placed in relatively shallow water close to shore, the prevention of tombolo formation could not be assumed. Only if the breakwaters were far from shore in deep water, such as those at Santa Monica, California, would tombolo prevention be likely.

The Corps allowed that some minor sand replenishment would still be required from time to time—but far less, it reasoned, than if the breakwaters were not present. The planned beach in the Corps' design had a minimum width of 75 feet with an elevation of 10 feet above low lake level. The Corps predicted that about 38,000 cubic yards of annual sand nourishment would be required to maintain a reasonable beach.

The committee, further concerned with the risks to adjacent beaches and Presque Isle's unique environment, revisited the beach replenish-ment alternative. The Corps' replenishment proposal involved bringing sand from the accreting eastern tip of the spit, the area known as Gull

Point, to replenish the beaches at the neck. This had been rejected by the Corps based on claims that the pumping and trucking operation would be costly, would have to be done repeatedly, and would intrusively violate the park's sanctuary. The Corps' rejection of this borrow site was appropriate; the disturbance within the unique natural area of Gull Point was deemed unacceptable to biologists and environmentalists. But, the committee noted, the Corps had another option—an offshore borrow site.

This large sand deposit provided Presque Isle an ideal resource for long-term beach replenishment. The large sand reservoir, with excellent beach and dune replenishment characteristics, exists offshore at a depth of 40 feet on the Presque Isle moraine. Unusual for the floor of Lake Erie, which is generally covered with a thick layer of muddy sediment completely unsuitable for beach replenishment, this sand deposit is known to contain at least 4.5 million cubic yards of the right grain size to furnish beach sand for decades to come. Locals have known of this deposit for a very long time; its sand has been dredged commercially for at least seventy-five years. Private contractors savvy about the various characteristics of the deposit can locate the particular type of sand needed for a particular type of project.

Replenished sand at Presque Isle travels along the shore, much of it staying within the beach system. Typically, enough sand is emplaced to create a slug of sand that moves along the shore causing noticeable and somewhat dramatic local changes. In contrast, on many ocean beaches, replenishment sand is rapidly lost in an offshore direction. Prior to breakwater construction, sand emplaced at the neck of Presque Isle, where most of the nourishment operations have taken place, was carried eastward by the longshore currents toward Gull Point, replenishing other beaches along the way.

Thus, replenishment worked well as erosion control at Presque Isle. However, the Corps' use of coarse, dirty gravel from upland deposits— unattractive to both beach goers and nesting shorebirds—made replenishment unpopular. Many public objections could have been overcome by using the higher-quality sand from offshore, as requested by the Presque Isle Advisory Committee and others, rather than the gravely material from upland sand deposits. Either way, there was no evidence that replenishment was losing the battle against erosion or that the strategy was excessively expensive.

Nonetheless, breakwater proponents repeatedly decried replenishment as inadequate, saying that breakwaters were needed to "save" the spit. One local newspaper carried dismissive statements by the Corps such as, "We've tried beach nourishment long enough," that ruled out the replenishment alternative. The Corps objected to the offshore sand site based on the added cost and difficulty of obtaining and transporting material.

The Corps' coastal research arm, the Coastal Engineering Research Center, had done numerous studies related to Presque Isle. One critical investigation, by Jeff Williams of CERC in 1982, verified the size of the large sand deposit offshore of Presque Isle. This investigation was done at the behest, not of the Corps' Buffalo District, but of the Ohio Geological Survey.

The Corps further argued before the advisory committee that it was not feasible from an engineering standpoint to move small amounts of sand from an offshore source to the beaches by hopper dredging. Once the breakwater construction project was under way and the funding assured, however, the Corps began replenishment in back of the breakwaters using the very method previously deemed unfeasible; it took sand from the offshore deposit previously declared too costly.

The Outside Consultant's Report

At the Presque Isle Advisory Committee's urging, the state hired Moffatt and Nichol Engineers, a private consulting firm from Raleigh, North Carolina, to conduct an independent analysis of the Corps' design. The Moffatt and Nichol engineers, James Walker and John Lesnik (a coastal engineer formerly with the Corps), were highly critical, concluding that there "has been insufficient evidence presented that the proposed structures will perform adequately." In almost every aspect of the project, the pair found the Corps' design lacking in up-to-date information. For instance, among its criticisms the Moffatt and Nichol report noted that the Corps had not updated its lake-level data after 1974; as a result, the lake-level information used to design the breakwaters did not "reflect over a decade of unprecedented high lake levels." Based on the type and amount of information provided by the Corps, Moffatt and Nichol could not determine whether breakwaters at Presque Isle were a good idea or not. Theirs was very like the experience of the Inman Panel in their evaluation of the Corps' proposed jetty construction at Oregon Inlet, North Carolina (chapter 9).

Because of the small size and wide, nearshore placement of the breakwaters, the consulting engineers warned that the breakwaters would not trap sufficient sand during high lake levels, thus requiring the added and unanticipated expense of extra beach replenishment. During low lake levels, "or if a considerable sand accumulation occurred behind the structures, park visitors (particularly children) may have easy access to the structures. . . . Swimming between them and even beyond them may be the only way to gain access to the water under those conditions. This would be an obvious hazard to the public, both from people falling on the structures and from being thrown against them by waves."

The state's response? The State Department of Environmental Resources accepted the Moffatt and Nichol report and then apparently ignored it. The state did not even ask the Buffalo District or the Corps' Coastal Engineering Research Center to respond officially to the report's damning allegations.

Cost-Benefit Assertions

The 1988 Moffatt and Nichol report also criticized the Corps for basing its economic justification on the assumption that the breakwaters would be exactly 75 percent effective at trapping sand. What if, Moffatt and Nichol argued, the breakwaters were only 50 percent effective in trapping sand? Would the project still be economically justified at a range of other percentages of effectiveness? As an illustration, Moffatt and Nichol referred to an earlier stabilization idea tested by the Corps at Presque Isle. In that test, conducted in 1985, the Corps covered a portion of the beach with gravel covered by a layer of sand, assuming that it would reduce the rate of longshore transport of sand by 65 percent. Instead of reducing sand movement, 60 percent of the gravel and 90 percent of its sand cover were lost *in the first year*. "Therefore," concluded the consultant's engineers, "the basic assumption upon which the economic justification rested proved to be unfounded."

The Corps' first cost-benefit ratio determination for the breakwaters was a barely favorable number (greater than one). The district was directed by federal budget officers to recalculate the ratio because it had included recreational benefits that were not allowable. Undaunted, the district recalculated without the substantial recreational benefits and, once again, came up with a barely favorable ratio. It assumed that the breakwaters would cost and function just as designed, and that sand would continue to flow from east to west behind the breakwaters—that downdrift erosion would not be a problem.

The Corps estimated the overall cost of the replenishment alternative by averaging the annual cost of all the replenishments carried out on

Presque Isle since the 1950s. That seems a logical thing to do, except for the inclusion of the huge 1955 project that used 4.5 million cubic yards of sand. The 1955 replenishment was at least ten times larger than any other Presque Isle project but lasted only a year or two, probably because the fill was composed largely of fine sand from dunes excavated for a marina on the bay side of the spit; the fine-grained sand disappeared almost immediately. Because the project was atypical of all other replenishment experience, it skewed the average to a higher cost estimate for replenishing the beaches of Presque Isle since 1955.

We believe the results would have been more accurate if the unsuccessful 1955 project had been excluded. Under this more realistic estimate, only about 150,000 cubic yards per year would be required to hold the entire 7-mile peninsula in place. This is a startlingly low amount of sand for a 7-mile reach of beach. By comparison, the rates of sand loss on ocean beaches at Carolina Beach and Wrightsville Beach, North Carolina, are such that 1.2 million cubic yards of sand would be needed each year to maintain a 6-mile stretch of beach. And perhaps three to five times more sand than that would be needed to sustain most New Jersey ocean beaches.

We question the Corps' assertions that long-term replenishment would have been too costly. And we challenge another Corps prejudice. Corps engineers Denton Clark and Richard Gorecki of the Buffalo District informed James Walker and John Lesnik of Moffatt and Nichol that obtaining sand from the offshore borrow site would at least double the cost of replenishment. Had the Corps not been unrealistically negative about this method, state and local officials, and the citizens of Erie, might have determined that the cost of using the offshore borrow site was much more reasonable.

Long-term cost comparisons among alternatives are difficult because they vary according to intangibles such as lake level, storm frequency, and the degree to which the Buffalo District's breakwater design expectations are realistic. A probable and realistic fifty-year cost for replenishment of Presque Isle is around $1 million per year, compared to around $3 million per year over fifty years for the breakwaters (in 1990 dollars).

The Prototype Breakwaters

The Corps also drew criticism from several observers, including Moffatt and Nichol, for inadequate testing of the proposed plan. To test the breakwater design, the Buffalo District constructed three prototype breakwaters in 1978 near the east end of Presque Isle. Within the first year, the breakwaters began to deteriorate when a large storm moved some of the stones. Other stones began to crack. A sand tombolo formed, despite a design intended to prevent tombolo formation. Within a few years after construction, all three breakwaters were completely buried by a slug of replenishment sand from a beach replenishment project east in the longshore sand transport system. Beyond the breakwaters, the downdrift section of the beach and dunes up to Gull Point experienced severe erosion directly attributable to sand trapping by the breakwaters.

Clearly, the prototype breakwaters' fate did not bode well for the long-term success of the project, yet those breakwaters were to be the downdrift anchor point for the additional breakwaters. The Moffatt and Nichol report questioned the Buffalo District's description of the prototype breakwaters as "complete successes." On the contrary, it determined that there was "insufficient evidence to conclude that the existing structures [had] accumulated sand and stabilized the beach." Instead, the consulting engineers found that the "downdrift beach [had] eroded, lake levels [had] risen, and sand [had] been repeatedly added to the system on several occasions." No design modification of consequence resulted from the failure of the prototype breakwaters.

In the face of the prototype breakwaters' obvious failure, the Corps, from the level of district colonel on down, repeatedly and blatantly asserted in public that the rapidly eroding shoreline east of the experimental breakwaters (downdrift) was not really accelerated erosion. Its denials came despite obvious signs of erosion, including the collapse of numerous older trees and the loss to Lake Erie of one of the largest dune systems along the open shoreline. In 1991, Richard Gorecki, the Buffalo District project engineer, told local newspapers that shoreline scouring east of the prototype breakwaters was filling in and would continue to fill in. Clearly, this was not the case. Within another year the erosion notch grew by a factor of four.

In another pre-project test included at the request of the Buffalo District, the Corps' Coastal Engineering Research Center conducted a modeling study of the Presque Isle system to predict the performance and effects of the breakwaters. In defending its breakwater plan, the district pointed to the work done by CERC as proof that sophisticated researchers agreed with the plan. The model, however, had actually produced inconclusive results. Undeterred, the Buffalo District called the results positive and repeatedly pointed to the model in meetings. Simply having a model was apparently enough. Rather than contradict the district, the CERC went along without a murmur, and individual engineers from its Vicksburg headquarters agreed with the impossible: that sand would flow behind the breakwaters.

Environmental Questions

Environmental concerns about the Corps' plans were wide ranging and included every aspect of Presque Isle's already stressed ecosystems. James Bissell of the Cleveland Museum of Natural History cited the importance to dune building of longshore transport along the lakeshore of the peninsula in a 1989 letter to Arthur Davis, secretary for the Pennsylvania Department of Environmental Resources. Bissell wrote that he feared "that the proposed off-shore breakwaters [would] severely curtail or eliminate the dynamics required for survival of the unique beach ecosystems." He further warned Davis, "In my opinion the Corps of Engineers has no basis for saying that the proposed breakwaters at Presque Isle will not have disastrous impacts on the rare ecosystems at Presque Isle because the Corps has no information about these systems." Bissell was also quoted in an April 30, 1989 *Pittsburgh Press* article as saying that the "existence of some of [nearly sixty plant species classified as endangered, threatened, or rare in Pennsylvania] was not known until . . . after Congress approved the breakwaters. . . ."

An environmental lightning rod was Presque Isle's National Natural Landmark status. Presque Isle's Landmark patron is Dr. Ed Masteller, a retired Pennsylvania State University biologist. In 1986 and again in 1988, Masteller notified the National Park Service that proposed breakwater construction and beach replenishment could have significant impact on the entire Presque Isle ecosystem. The Park Service did not follow through on Masteller's alerts, nor did its officials comment on the Corps' environmental impact statement for the proposed breakwaters. Had the Park Service weighed in, it surely would have urged the Pennsylvania Department of Environmental Resources not to allow construction of the breakwaters. Such inattention is surprising because the Park Service was the first government agency at any level to institute a policy (in 1972) prohibiting the use of hard erosion-control structures, such as seawalls and breakwaters, on shorelines under its management. National Park Service policy, therefore, should not permit construction of the offshore breakwater proposed for Presque Isle at a national seashore. The agency had long recognized the economic futility and environmentally damaging consequences of shoreline armoring.

At a June 1990 congressional field hearing on Presque Isle's National Natural Landmark status held in Erie, U.S. Congressman Peter H. Kostmayer of Pennsylvania, then chair of the U.S. House of Representatives Committee on Interior and Insular Affairs' Subcommittee on Oversight and Investigations, opened the hearing with this question: "Will management strategies stabilize the beach area at Presque Isle and enhance the recreational and intrinsic value of the peninsula, or will the projected [breakwater] system destroy the unique geological and ecological features of the peninsula that made it a National Natural Landmark to begin with?"

Local and regional environmentalists and biologists replied that the Corps had not adequately evaluated the breakwater construction's potential consequences to the peninsula's ecosystems. Bruce Kershner, of Great Lakes United a regional conservation organization, expressed a common concern when he argued that the breakwaters would be the final blow for an already stressed environment. Jean Stull of the Presque Isle Audubon Society summarized local environmentalists' frustrations: "Our questions over the years concerning this plan have gone unanswered. . . . Our recommendations for continued beach nourishment . . . with clean lake sand [from the offshore borrow site] . . . have not been seriously considered."

Politicians were divided, and the level of their division became clear during the June hearing. Pennsylvania State Senator Anthony "Buzz" Andrezeski spoke out against the breakwater alternative, while U.S. Representative Thomas Ridge, a Republican from Erie (who was anticipating a run for governor), spoke as a major proponent. Representative Ridge was responsible for obtaining federal funding for the project. Although he was told about them a number of times, he paid little or no attention to problems with the project.

In contrast, Senator Andrezeski asked, "What good will the breakwalls be if they are protecting beaches that people can't use?" The senator based his concerns on the fact that the breakwaters' construction plan was changed at a bureaucratic level from a twelve-year phased construction to an all-at-once two-year schedule, ostensibly because of finances. The twelve-year schedule had originally been proposed by the Buffalo District because, as Andrezeski stated, it would be "the least disruptive to the Park from an environmental standpoint and would have allowed close, careful monitoring of any hydrologic effects caused by" construction. Andrezeski's reaction to the schedule change: "In light of recent concerns about increased beach contamination, increased beach closings, and the threat of any invasion of zebra mussels, it is frustrating for us to be told that the only good reason for proceeding 'full speed ahead' . . . comes down to one thing—money!"

In the end, Kostmayer expressed great dissatisfaction with the Park Service's lack of vigilance and delivered a virtual tongue-lashing to Park Service representatives, ordering immediate submission of a report detailing the reasons for their lack of concern for Presque Isle. Before the report was submitted, however, Kostmayer lost his reelection bid to the U.S. Congress, and the matter was dropped.

Engineers for the Public Good?

Was the Corps a good advisor to the people of Erie? Did the Corps provide a "permanent" solution? No. All in all, the Corps failed to provide sufficient information for a comprehensive public debate on the merits of breakwaters. It claimed an understanding of breakwaters that does not exist. A recent Corps publication on offshore breakwaters (written by William Daly and Joan Pope of the Coastal Engineering Research Center) admitted as much, explaining that accurate prediction of eventual shoreline configuration is beyond the present state of knowledge. Corps personnel consistently professed certainty and optimism when they were not justified, and they made dismissive statements in press reports and other public forums about the beach replenishment or "letting nature take its course" alternatives. Most alarming perhaps, the Corps' publicly funded research was all directed toward proving the viability of the breakwater alternative. Even when the performance of the prototype breakwaters showed that design assumptions were incorrect, that indisputable evidence was alternately ignored and denied. As a result, the Buffalo District promised a permanent solution to the Presque Isle erosion problem but produced instead a beach-damaging, experimental project that may well cost much more than the replenishment alternative.

One of the arguments that won people over to the segmented breakwaters was the promise of a permanent, economically sound, environmentally benign solution for Presque Isle. But Paul Knuth and others experienced with the ways of beaches and shorelines knew that replenishment is the superior alternative in all respects: economic, environmental, and erosion control. The replenishment solution would also have left open the possibility of building breakwaters at a later time if replenishment failed.

Compared to breakwaters and other hard structures, replenishment is a less environmentally damaging, more flexible, and proven alternative. It avoids problems with aesthetics, safety, and water pollution, and it preserves the beach. It can be applied at different spots and at different rates, depending on the location and severity of erosion problems. Replenishment is a modern solution that has proven its merit on Presque Isle and other locations on U.S. coasts. The breakwater solution is a hard-stabilization approach that is now illegal in four ocean states and on all National Park Service seashores.

The Corps, of course, does not deserve all the blame for armoring the Presque Isle shoreline. The Buffalo District brought the Trojan horse, which was gratefully ushered in by local and state politicians anxious to be perceived as part of the Presque Isle "solution." Newspaper files bulge with photos of politicians wearing a concerned expression, standing on a storm-washed Presque Isle, declaring their desire to "save the peninsula." The fact that the peninsula did not need salvation did not seem to register.

Political courage is necessary for politicians who argue against structural erosion control. Because it is usually looked to when buildings are falling in and disaster is imminent, only a knowledgeable politician with foresight can be expected to endorse protecting beaches for future generations through less visible solutions. The desired effect of structures— immediate stabilization—is obvious. Because the severe problems associated with armoring shorelines with seawalls, breakwaters, and the like are often a decade or more in the making, they will probably arise on some other politician's watch. For an opportunistic politician, the Presque Isle breakwaters offered the chance to be today's hero without having to worry about being tomorrow's villain. Politicians in office today may have moved on in their political careers, or be out of politics altogether, before the complete magnitude of the disaster at Presque Isle is apparent.

However, it is the responsibility of the politician as policy maker to heed learned advice. And it is the responsibility of the Corps of Engineers to provide expertise in an unbiased manner. Based on the debate that surrounded the Presque Isle breakwaters, from the perspective of a coastal scientist, both the Corps and some politicians abused their trust to lead a thorough dialogue that considered the unique aspects of the geologic and ecological setting and balanced public interests with good science.

Good science and information about experience with similar structures along other shorelines thus found little place in the Presque Isle debate. The unique ecosystem of Presque Isle was largely ignored, and the public interest was not well served, if only because people were not given objective analyses on which to make informed decisions. Only political interests won at Presque Isle.

Irreconcilable Differences

A testimony to the often radically different philosophies held by the scientific and engineering communities, the Presque Isle breakwaters have received resounding praise from professional engineers. The Michigan Society of Professional Engineers awarded the Corps its 1993 Outstanding Engineering Achievement Award for the breakwater project. The National Society of Professional Engineers recognized the breakwaters as one of the "ten top U.S. engineering achievements of 1993" for the project's "overall contribution to the engineering profession and society." The Buffalo District has proudly entered the breakwaters into a competition of engineering projects by the Corps of Engineers throughout the world.

The National Society of Professional Engineers announced its award in a January 12, 1994, news release that gives insight into the engineering mentality:

> One of the largest projects of its kind, the segmented breakwater design is the result of over 22 years of planning and engineering studies. The system functions by reducing the incident wave energy that reaches the shoreline, thereby reducing sand losses and erosion. The project also allows for the natural movement of littoral sediments to continue to occur behind the breakwaters and for continued growth of the environmentally sensitive Gull Point area of the Peninsula. *The resulting shoreline is appealing and blends with the natural environment.* (emphasis added)

The level of misunderstanding within this professional engineers' society is profound. It accepted the Corps' impossible assertion that the breakwaters will allow beach sand transport to continue as before. It appeared to be completely unaware of the failure of the prototype breakwaters and of the private professional engineering firm's condemning report. And it mistakenly categorizes a coastal engineering project as successful after only a year in place when at least a decade is needed to render such judgment. Finally, there seems to be no appreciation of rare beauty, the incalculable value of a natural beach with an uninterrupted view of lake and horizon.

The Future

In 1993, Presque Isle Park's first complete season with its breakwaters, a number of tombolos formed and severe spot erosion occurred on some downdrift beaches. Corps backpedaling began almost as soon as the breakwaters were all in place. At the Coastal Zone '93 conference, a biennial meeting of coastal scientists, engineers, managers, and policy makers, held that year in New Orleans, a Corps engineer from the Buffalo District stated that the agency's breakwater design would be different if it had it to do again. In 1994, Corps publicist John Derbyshire noted that some changes might have to be made but said more time was needed to see how the shoreline finally adjusts. Derbyshire also explained away tombolo formation—a geologic process that the breakwaters were designed to prevent—by describing those breakwaters that formed tombolos as "too successful."

Knowledgeable observers have told us that within the first year some breakwaters were already showing the first signs of subsiding into the lake floor. Some rocks were cracking (the rocks on the experimental prototype breakwater were severely cracked after a few years). Swimming areas became much more restricted because of the breakwater hazard. To keep people away from the rock structures, the state instituted a three-wheeler patrol and put up numerous KEEP OFF BREAKWATER signs. Also, because the beach steepened in the vicinity of the breakwaters, available swimming areas had shrunk.

The true scope of the armoring disaster of Presque Isle will only become clear after two or three decades. By that time, some of the breakwaters are likely to be irregularly shaped piles of rock, broken and dismantled by storms and ice.

The unique ecological succession of a growing, evolving, changing spit, the basis of the peninsula's designation as a National Natural Landmark, will be no more. The level of pollution and the number of beach closings will increase as nearshore circulation decreases behind the breakwaters. Swimming will be restricted to relatively few locations where special efforts have been made to clear rock from the lake floor, and those areas will be roped off to hold back overly adventurous swimmers. A number of boaters and wind surfers will have come to grief on the rocks. A large number of injuries, and a few deaths on the rock piles, will have resulted in lawsuits against the state, which will succeed because the state can be shown to have repeatedly ignored warnings about the dangers before construction ever began.

Severe erosion will worsen at a number of hot spots, and the Presque Isle road will continue to be flooded by storms. The state will have spent a very large amount of money replenishing the beaches behind the breakwaters, clearing rocks from beaches, and removing tombolos as they quickly and inevitably form. The once beautiful beach will often have the appearance of a construction project. Gull Point will probably have largely disappeared (unless the breakwater chain is extended around the point); most certainly, the point will have undergone significant, potentially severe, ecological degradation. The portion of the tourist industry that depends on quality beaches will be significantly reduced, as it has been on heavily armored New Jersey beaches such as Seabright, Monmouth Beach, Long Branch, and Asbury Park.

Our society, with its short memory, is quick to forgive. Indeed, it seems to protect bureaucracies that fumble in their mission. The long struggle to get the breakwaters, the opposition's claims of incompetence, the Buffalo District's and the CERC's vain counter-assertions of certainty in their design assumptions will fade into history. If history repeats itself, the Corps district and local politicians will smooth over the fiasco by claiming that unusually large storms were the culprits. They will argue that things would have been even worse without the breakwaters. Already, this theme is being heard as in the Corps' publicist's statement that tombolo formation qualified some breakwaters as "too successful." Presque Isle State Park superintendent Harry Leslie has been quoted extensively in the local newspapers as viewing the breakwaters as "a positive addition to the park." Leslie praised the improved recreational beach (an improvement attributable to the use of high-quality sand from the offshore deposit), ignoring the degradation of the peninsula's natural significance—the reason the park was initially established.

The tragedy of the armoring of Presque Isle is the lack of vision on behalf of future generations. The public, and the Corps, needs a huge leap of understanding to fully comprehend former Governor of Florida Bob Graham's statement that "this generation does not have the right to destroy the next generation's beaches." Graham was referring to the seawalls and other hard stabilization structures that were invading and destroying Florida's beaches. Undoubtedly, at Presque Isle, the inexperienced present generation thought it was doing the right thing for future generations; the motivation to "save" Presque Isle in the face of seemingly critical erosion was a noble one. Public officials and the Corps are to blame for failing to include objective scientific and engineering expertise in the debate. That is an ignoble failure of public trust. The small battles lost by Paul Knuth and others are a major defeat for the citizens and future generations of Pennsylvania.

The Solution?

The state of Pennsylvania may one day have to think the unthinkable: take out the breakwaters. There will be a lot of cracked and displaced rocks, well-formed tombolos, eroded beaches, injured swimmers, and lawsuits before that will happen, but drastic means will be needed to rescue Presque Isle from a big engineering experiment and return it to a natural flying spit with a beautiful recreational beach.

EIGHT

Camp Ellis, Maine

Maine's long history of involvement with the sea persists in its industry,
countryside, and political battles. Seafood, including the famous Maine
lobster, has long been a major product of the state. Coastal pine trees,
some as tall as 150 feet, were once harvested for masts for English navy
vessels, and some road intersections still have strange, broadly curving
approaches designed long ago to accommodate wagons with 150-foot
loads.

Still visible in some coastal marshes are the remnants of hayricks used
to dry salt marsh "hay" before feeding it to livestock. The earliest industries of Maine used the region's small estuaries and rivers extensively as
sites for mills and as ports for shipping goods to all parts of the world. As
ships increased in size, small rivers that once provided access through
the marshes were abandoned in favor of larger, more permanent ports at
river mouths. One of those ports is at the mouth of the Saco River, a location known today as Camp Ellis.

Saco Bay is an arc-shaped, open-ocean shoreline reach, the western
side of which is formed by a seven-mile-long, unnamed barrier island
(Figure 8–1). A sandy beach, a rare commodity in a state known for its
"rockbound coast," extends along the entire seaside length of the island,
which is backed by salt marsh. Saco Bay is bounded at its south end by
the mouth of the Saco River and, to the immediate north of the river, by
the small community of Camp Ellis. The north end of Saco Bay is anchored by Pine Point just south of the mouth of the Scarborough River.

Old Orchard Beach, one of Maine's oldest resort areas, lies along Saco
Bay about halfway between the two river mouths. Beach goers from
more populous areas of Maine once traveled to Old Orchard Beach by a
train called the "Dummy." The Dummy had no roundhouse, so was
forced to make its return trip going backwards. The train's demise came
with the arrival of the horseless carriage. Old Orchard Beach's sandy

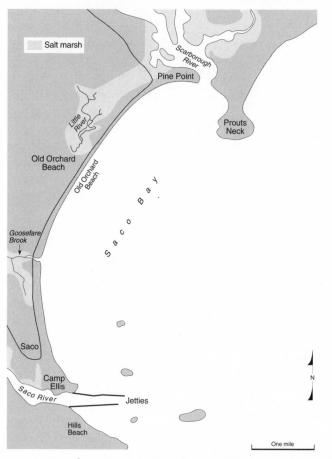

Figure 8–1. Map depicting Saco Bay, showing Hills Beach, Camp Ellis, Old Orchard Beach, and Pine Point. The jetties were first built at the entrance of the Saco River in 1867, then enlarged in subsequent years.

shore remains a summer resort area, but a little bit of the town's soul disappeared with the Dummy.

Industry was once an important presence in Saco Bay. Around the time of the Civil War, the owners of textile mills and other industries lining the Saco River demanded improved access to the estuary for commercial sailing vessels. In particular, industry required improved navigability through the inlet at the mouth of the Saco River to allow passage into the Biddeford-Saco Harbor. A huge sandy tidal delta in the river mouth made passage for large ships difficult and dangerous. Ships bringing coal and other raw materials in and carrying finished products out were delayed and even wrecked on the shifting shoals adjacent to what is now Camp Ellis.

Photo 8–1. Aerial view of Camp Ellis (top of photo) and the landward portions of the jetties. Sand is transported from south to north here as indicated by the pile-up of sand south of the jetties, to the benefit of the community of Hills Beach to the south (bottom of photo). (Photo by Joe Kelley)

In 1867, in response to the outcry by industries along the Saco River, the U.S. Army Corps of Engineers New England Division began construction of a large stone jetty on the north side of the river mouth. The purpose of the jetty was to maintain a navigation channel and reduce the cost of channel maintenance. Before the stone jetty was built, there were reportedly small wooden jetties in place.

When sand continued to accumulate in the navigation channel at the end of the new jetty, the Corps assumed that it came either from Old Orchard Beach to the north or from a deposit of sand just offshore on the inner continental shelf. To prevent channel clogging, the Corps reinforced and lengthened the jetty, eventually anchoring the structure to bedrock more than 4,000 feet offshore. Still sand accumulated in the channel at the end of the jetty. So, in 1891, the Corps began construction of a jetty on the south side of the channel to prevent sand from flowing in from Hills Beach.

By the end of World War II, Biddeford-Saco Harbor was of greatly reduced commercial importance. Industry was leaving the area, much of it going to the South. Over subsequent decades, as in so many other locations along the U.S. coast, commercial use of the harbor was replaced by recreational use. The harbor at Camp Ellis is now visited primarily by small recreational boats and a few commercial fishing boats (Photo 8–1).

The saga of the Saco River jetties and the Camp Ellis shoreline logged in the studies (Table 8–1) and jetty alterations (Table 8–2) over the last 120 years is a record of one of the oldest jetty pairs in North America. It also includes the general truths of shoreline stabilization outlined in chapter 2. And it is a history of the clash of engineering and scientific approaches to beach management, which at Camp Ellis led to a conflict between Corps and state policy.

Among other stabilization "truths," the Saco River–Camp Ellis jetties demonstrate that the negative impacts of shoreline structures may become evident only after a long period of time. In the case of these jetties, severe shoreline retreat ensued thirty-five years after the first jetty was originally built.

The jetty system has actually been a 120-year experiment founded on limited knowledge of the shoreline processes on a very complex rocky coast. Each of the Saco River–Camp Ellis jetty modifications has failed; shoreline erosion at Camp Ellis continues unabated, and the navigation channel continues to shoal.

The state of Maine, in an attempt to break the armoring cycle and based on its policy of beach preservation, attempted to implement a retreat from erosion at Camp Ellis rather than implement a stabilization solution. As we will discuss, although the state invited the Corps to join in this plan, the Corps refused.

The Studies

We can identify at least twenty-five studies conducted over a period of 100 years at the Saco River mouth and Camp Ellis shoreline (Table 8–1). These have resulted in at least seventeen major modifications and additions to the Saco River jetties. Most of the studies documented the process of channel clogging or adjacent shoreline erosion. Alternative solutions, including doing nothing, were considered, and benefits and costs were weighed, culminating in a "final solution" recommended to Congress. The early Saco River studies focused solely on the navigational hazards posed by the shoaling channel and anchorages. In more recent years, the reports have concentrated on the cause and the solution of the erosion on adjacent beaches.

The Corps has held two critically important assumptions as it studied and designed various jetty alterations and erosion abatement plans. The first is that beach sand is moving from north to south along the Saco Bay shoreline. If the Corps is correct, it would be unlikely that the shoreline retreat at Camp Ellis is caused by the jetties. Instead, the Camp Ellis beach should be widening as south-flowing sand is stopped by the rock walls. The Corps' second overriding assumption is that sand clogging the navigation channel does not come from the Saco River. Rather a glacial deposit on the continental shelf is seen as the major source. That sand, the Corps has postulated, moves in from offshore and is then moved from north to south along Saco Bay beach, eventually to clog the channel. The sand gets into the channel by moving through the jetty, over the jetty, or out along the length of the jetty and into the entrance.

The most detailed Camp Ellis study was released in 1955 and has served as a basis for all later studies. In that report's appendix is the observation that between 1859 and 1955 around six million cubic yards of sand disappeared from the beach and shoreface off Camp Ellis. During the same time period a similar amount of sand slowly accumulated seven miles to the north, off Pine Point (Photo 8–2). Had this critical piece of information been pursued, it should have tipped off the Corps that longshore drift is to the north instead of the south, as long assumed.

The Jetty Alterations

In recent decades, previous jetty alterations necessitated more alterations and engineering structures on adjacent beaches. Table 8–2 is a list of Corps construction projects at Camp Ellis; records do not exist of most beach replenishment operations. The Corps has carried out frequent small beach replenishments using dredged material from the channel. Meanwhile, dump truck replenishment has been funded by state or by local citizens. The channel between the jetties has been dredged numerous times, but little or no record has been kept of how much was removed or where the dredged material was deposited.

The Adjacent Beaches

What happened to the shoreline during all this engineering activity? Initially, the beach accreted to the north at Camp Ellis because the jetties forced the tidal delta at the mouth of the Saco River to break up and

Table 8-1

A Partial List of Corps Studies at Camp Ellis.

1882—Recommended repair and extension of the Saco River jetty; published as a
U.S. Senate document. U.S. Army Corps of Engineers. SD 44, 48th Congress.

1883—Survey to dredge the river and extend the jetty; unpublished. U.S. Army
Corps of Engineers.

1884—Preliminary examination to dredge a 6-foot Saco River channel; published
as a U.S. House document. U.S. Army Corps of Engineers. HD 37, 49th
Congress.

1909—Preliminary examination to deepen Saco River channel to 7 feet; published
as a U.S. House document. U.S. Army Corps of Engineers. HD 752, 61st
Congress.

1910—Summarized expenditures and progress to date, concluding that the economic benefits of maintaining the entrance at the mouth of the river
($350,000 at that point) did not justify the cost. Noted "a constant movement
of sand from north to south along the ocean beach . . . which has deposited
material in front of the original entrance channel." Published as a U.S. House
document. U.S. Army Corps of Engineers. HD 752, 61st Congress.

1920—Study at Saco River mouth, concluded jetties are not responsible for the
erosion on Hills Beach; unpublished. U.S. Army Corps of Engineers.

1922—Another look at a 7-foot-deep channel; published as a U.S. House document. U.S. Army Corps of Engineers. HD 477, 68th Congress, Corp.

1924—Recommended dredging the river channel to 8 feet deep and lengthening
the jetty; published as a U.S. House document. U.S. Army Corps of Engineers. HD 477, 68th Congress, Corp.

1929—Broad-based Saco River survey of future uses and needs; published as a
U.S. House document. U.S. Army Corps of Engineers. HD 659, 71st Congress, Corp.

1930—Saco River study; published as a U.S. House document. U.S. Army Corps
of Engineers. HD 659, 71th Congress, Corp.

1934—Recommended jetty extension to Sharps Rocks; published as a U.S. House
document. U.S. Army Corps of Engineers. HD 11, 74th Congress.

1935—Recommended timber or concrete seawalls on adjacent eroded beaches;
report by Corps Beach Erosion Board jointly with state of Maine; unpublished. U.S. Beach Erosion Board and Maine Planning Board.

1939—Concluded that jetties were not responsible for erosion of adjacent
beaches; a review of reports. U.S. Army Corps of Engineers.

Table 8-1: *Continued*

1955—Concluded that jetties had not caused erosion at Camp Ellis. In future Corps reports and studies, this one is considered to be the most important; a Beach Erosion Control Report. U.S. Army Corps of Engineers.

1961—Noted subsidence of south jetty and possible connection of this jetty to the erosion of Hills Beach; a Beach Erosion Control Report.

1968—Estimated channel shoaling rate of 4,000 yards per year; a review of reports. U.S. Army Corps of Engineers.

1976—Assumed sand moves from north to south. Although more than twenty houses had been lost in Camp Ellis since 1951, this study concluded that benefits could not justify federal expenditures for a structure or beach replenishment to save buildings; a Beach Erosion Reconnaissance Report. U.S. Army Corps of Engineers.

1982—Dredging study; concluded dredge spoil should be put on beach. U.S. Army Corps of Engineers.

1987—Summarized recent history of Camp Ellis' Surf Street erosion problem, recommending concrete wall with rocks at the toe; it concluded that such a wall (which is contrary to Maine state law) would only "slightly alter existing physical conditions" (i.e., erosion rate and beach configuration). Also concluded that relocating Surf Street was "not only very expensive but socially unacceptable." An emergency report. U.S. Army Corps of Engineers.

1991—Assessment of coastal processes concluding that sand moves from north to south and that raising and tightening jetty in 1968–69 may have caused recent Camp Ellis erosion, but evidence is said to be unclear. "Lowering of the jetty is inconsistent with the objective of maintaining navigability of the entrance channel," it says, recommending additional engineering structures accompanied by sand nourishment. A Coastal Engineering Research Center study. Coastal Engineering Research Center, U.S. Army Corps of Engineers, Vicksburg, MS.

1992—Noted that erosion would be occurring even in the absence of the jetties. Recommended no action be taken beyond dredge-spoil disposal. The Corps' New England Division concluded that since the jetties are not causing the erosion, the Corps had no responsibility to mitigate the erosion problem at Camp Ellis. The Section 111 report. U.S. Army Corps of Engineers.

1994—Anticipated that 11,000 cubic yards of dredging per year would be needed regionally, including the Saco River. Done as a dredged-material management study for coastal Maine and New Hampshire. U.S. Army Corps of Engineers.

1994—An $850,000 physical model of the river mouth was used by the Coastal Engineering Research Center in Vicksburg, Mississippi, to evaluate the causes of erosion and the nature and impact of possible jetty alterations. Conclusion: build a shore-parallel offshore breakwater.

Table 8-2

Construction Projects by the Corps at Camp Ellis.

1827—Piers are built along the Saco River; channel dredging begins.

1867—A jetty is built along the north side of the inlet leading to Saco Bay. The top of the jetty is 10 feet wide and 10 feet above low-tide level.

1869–70—Dogleg is built at end of the jetty, extending its entire length to 4,315 feet.

1885–97—Jetty is incrementally raised (900-foot sections at a time, every two or three years, except for inshore portion) from 10 feet above low-tide level to 15 feet, with a 12-foot upper surface width to reduce channel infilling by sand washed over the jetty during storms.

1891–93—Jetty is constructed on the channel's south side to prevent sand from flowing into the channel from Hills Beach to the south; jetty is 4,500 feet long and 5 feet above the low-tide line.

1900—South jetty is lengthened at landward or inshore end to keep the jetty attached to the retreating shoreline at Hills Beach.

1910–12—South jetty is lengthened to 4,800 feet to reduce shoaling of the entrance channel.

1912—North jetty is lengthened at landward end to keep the jetty attached to the re-treating shoreline at Camp Ellis.

1912—A "spur" jetty is constructed (in effect an offshore breakwater attached at one end to the seaward end of the jetty) on the north jetty parallel to the shoreline to prevent fur-ther detachment of the jetty from the shore and probably also to preserve shorefront buildings in Camp Ellis.

1927–30—North jetty is lengthened to 5,800 feet to reduce shoaling of the entrance channel.

1935—Landward end of north jetty is lengthened and elevation raised to 15 feet above low tide to keep the jetty attached to the retreating land and to reduce sand flow over the jetties into the channel.

1936–37—North jetty is lengthened by 830 feet to extend to Sharps Rock to reduce shoaling at the entrance channel. Total north jetty length is now 6,630 feet.

1953—A 700-foot-long, 21-foot-high rock revetment, or seawall, is built to protect Surf Street. The revetment and a nearby timber bulkhead are seriously damaged in 1953 and 1954 storms.

1958—The north jetty is repaired and extended landward to keep the jetty attached to land.

1968—The landward 850 feet of the north jetty are raised to 17 feet above low-tide level to prevent sand from washing into the channel during storms. In addition, crevices in the rock are sealed and the surface smoothed to prevent sand from leaking through the struc-ture.

1969—Severe storms leave the shoreward ends of both the north and south jetties ex-posed. The gaps are repaired by building short rock revetments at the ends of both jet-ties, thus "permanently" attaching the jetties to land.

1970—The 1969 revetment at the end of the north jetty is rebuilt following storm damage.

1971—A 650-foot-long revetment is built on the beach at Hills Beach.

1994—The north jetty is 6,700 feet long and 17 feet above mean low water for the first 850 feet from land and 15 feet above mean low water for the remainder of its length. The south jetty is 4,850 feet long and 10 feet above mean low water for the first 800 feet and 6 feet above mean low water for the remainder.

Photo 8–2. Aerial view of Pine Point, where the sand from Camp Ellis has gone. Much of the land area shown here accreted after the Saco River jetties were built. Everything to the north of the parking lot (shown by the arrow) has accumulated since 1871. The large pine trees (dark area) behind the parking lot mark the old barrier island before jetties were built seven miles to the south at the mouth of the Saco River. (Photo by Joe Kelley)

disperse. The same phenomenon of tidal delta breakup and sand accretion on nearby beaches occurred on the South Carolina shore after the emplacement of the Charleston breakwaters.

By the turn of the century, the former tidal delta sand had washed ashore, adding 700 feet to the beach north of the jetty. Before long, however, starting in the years 1905 to 1910, the shoreline north of the jetty at Camp Ellis began to retreat. By 1934, it had retreated to its pre-jetty location. The 1968 smoothing of the landward portion of the north jetty was particularly damaging, greatly reducing its capacity to absorb the energy of breaking storm waves. Instead of dissipating their energy on the jetty, storm waves are reflected to Camp Ellis beach, accelerating the loss of beach sand. Erosion has continued unabated to the present day and has taken its toll in houses as well as beach sands (Photos 8–3 and 8–4).

Over the past sixty years more than thirty houses have been lost to

Photo 8–3. December 3, 1990. A high-tide view showing normal wave energy at Camp Ellis. Water from the waves crashing against the revetment in the fore-ground is absorbed in the interstices between revetment rocks so that backwash is reduced, reducing the amount of beach sand lost in turn. But during a storm this water absorption capability is overwhelmed, and massive beach erosion occurs as the revetment is destroyed. (Photo by Joe Kelley)

erosion at Camp Ellis. Many of the buildings currently at risk in the town were damaged in a large 1978 winter storm; four of those damaged in 1978 were destroyed in the 1991 Halloween storm (Photo 8–5). Sea-walls built by homeowners in 1961 were all destroyed during the storm of 1978. One owner who lost both a wall and a house in 1978 rebuilt, then lost both again in 1991.

A Change in Management

In the 1980s, the state of Maine acknowledged how precious its short sandy shoreline had become to the state's economy and quality of life. The state realized that its shores were not immune to Newjerseyization, and that if officials were not careful, Maine's few beaches would soon be replaced with seawalls, groins, and other attempts at shoreline stabilization.

The state geological survey hired a coastal geologist, and the Maine Department of Environmental Protection championed new laws in

Photo 8–4. December 5, 1990. A beachfront house shown in Photo 8-3 was destroyed in a storm that struck at high tide. (Photo by Joe Kelley)

Photo 8–5. A wooden bulkhead destroyed by the Halloween storm of 1991. This is one of several generations of walls at this location, each built after its predecessor was destroyed by storms. The cycle of destruction followed by rebuilding will continue into the future unless these buildings are moved. (Photo by Joe Kelley)

1983 prohibiting shoreline armoring. Seawalls and all other forms of shoreline armoring are illegal. High-rise buildings may be no more than 35 feet high and must be designed to be "readily movable." Once a building is at least 50 percent damaged, it must be removed from the beachfront at the owner's expense. Possibly the most environmentally sound in the nation, Maine's coastal management policies are supported by a broad political spectrum in the state. Although reversal of shoreline armoring is rare indeed on the American shoreline, consideration is now being given to removing jetties from the entrance to Wells Harbor, Maine.

The policies also brought an end to the unquestioning acceptance of Corps of Engineers pronouncements and management philosophy on Maine's coast. For more than a century, the Corps' New England Division (there are no district offices within this division) had provided the people of Maine with much needed navigation improvments and shoreline defenses. Few had questioned the inflow of federal dollars during that period; in fact, Maine's U.S. senators and representatives often were elected in part for their ability to gather Corps projects.

In 1987, the Corps recommended halting the shoreline retreat at Camp Ellis by building a seawall. The state rebuffed that proposal because it was clearly contrary to state laws. Maine's current solution of choice for Camp Ellis, consistent with its policy of strategic retreat to preserve beaches, is a buyout of property owners followed by reestablishment of a beach and dune system. In 1991, although the state chose retreat for Camp Ellis, the Corps' Coastal Engineering Research Center recommended more shoreline armoring, this time in the form of an offshore breakwater combined with beach replenishment. The breakwater, however, is also illegal by Maine state law.

The 1991 CERC report (Table 8–1) carefully documents the long series of unsuccessful alterations to the jetties, yet it ignores the apparent futility of such efforts and recommends more engineering in the form of the new rock offshore breakwater. State officials think a primary disadvantage of this recommendation is that the breakwater, while trapping sand and building up the beach in one location, will simply cause more erosion somewhere else. "Yet another engineering solution," declares Joe Kelley. "Failure after failure at Ellis Beach has taught the Corps nothing."

Kelley, a forty-five-year-old Maine native, is the state of Maine's coastal geologist. With a Ph.D. from Lehigh University, he spent a few years teaching at the University of New Orleans before returning to a land more comfortable for a man with his broad accent. Today, working for both the state's geological survey and the University of Maine, he seems to ably balance two different professional worlds: the politically restrictive one of state policy and the academic one of relative freedom.

A dedicated, dynamic individual incapable of standing still for long, Kelley was a major intellectual force behind Maine's current beach management policy. Although he possesses an extraordinary amount of political backbone for one who must face people whose houses are literally falling in, he acknowledges that a lot of invisible factors are responsible for Maine's successful beach policy. A survey of beachfront property owners a few years back revealed that only 5 percent vote in Maine, because most are residents of Massachusetts. Politicians are able to ignore pleas from nonvoters for seawalls and beach replenishment. Unlike most other coastal states, coastal residents who would like to dilute or overturn coastal management restrictions on development have little influence in the state legislature.

In his capacity as the state's coastal geologist since 1982, Kelley has dealt with the Corps of Engineers at all levels. He views the agency as a threat to the future of the state's coastal management policy and generally considers the Corps' efforts to manage Camp Ellis beach as lacking in scientific rigor. According to Kelley, "The army has known for more than fifty years that their earlier understanding of the bay shoreline was flawed, but they persist in coupling out-of-date geologic models with prehistoric engineering structures."

In Kelley's opinion, the large number of Corps studies conducted over the years on the ongoing erosion at the Saco River–Camp Ellis jetty is deceptive. According to him, "All of the Corps' studies paraphrase one another. There is seldom any original thinking, and *never* any field observations." The conclusion of the 1955 study—that the jetty was not the cause of the erosion problems at Camp Ellis—was based on the (unsupported) assumption that the dominant direction of sand transport is from north to south along the Saco Bay shore. But Kelley, along with Miles Hayes, Stewart Farrel, Duncan FitzGerald, and Dan Belknap—all respected coastal geologists familiar with this shoreline—strongly dispute the Corps' conclusion. Majority votes do not count in science, but the weight of field evidence is heavily on the scientists' side. The Maine scientists have found that the direction of sand transport is from the south to the north. If this is so, the jetties are certainly responsible for the downdrift Camp Ellis shoreline retreat.

Another ramification of this conclusion, according to Kelley, is that management of the Camp Ellis shoreline will eventually affect the supply of beach sand along all of the Saco Bay shoreline. For instance, he believes that the shoaling that began in 1950 in the next harbor to the north—at Pine Point, seven miles from Camp Ellis—is related to the erosion at Camp Ellis. Over a period of decades, sand released by the erosive action of the north jetty (where, as previously mentioned, six million cubic yards of sand were lost between 1859 and 1955) has slowly moved to the north and into the harbor at Pine Point. This sand has nourished beaches all along its path, including the local resort of Old Orchard Beach. Soon, however, the accretion trend will reverse as Camp Ellis runs out of sand to erode; Saco Bay shoreline erosion rates will increase dramatically. Kelley believes that it was this vast quantity of sand, eroded from Camp Ellis, that closed the Little River Inlet six miles to the north and so narrowed the Scarborough River Inlet as to require the Corps to construct a jetty there in 1956.

In a 1995 report, Kelley and Maine Geological Survey Director Walter Anderson noted: "In more than a century of working at Camp Ellis, never once has the Corps associated their activities at one end of the bay with their work at the other. Instead when the Maine Geological Survey suggested (repeatedly between 1990 and 1993) that sand from the planned dredge of Scarborough River be barged back to Camp Ellis, the Army cited cost as a prohibitive factor and instead insisted that the sand be put on Pine Point (which doesn't need it) or barged into deep water and dumped."

A second major point of disagreement between Maine coastal geologists and the Corps' New England Division is the source of the sand accumulating at the end of the Saco River jetties and in the Saco River channel. As discussed, the Corps assumes that the sand travels from a deposit of glacial material lying offshore and then is carried by longshore currents to the south into the channel. If this were the case, lengthening the jetties would have made sense. According to recent research observations by Kelley and colleagues, however, most of the supposed offshore sediment source is mud, not sand. Their research points to the Saco River, not the continental shelf, as the source of the channel-clogging sand. Based on water-current measurements and sediment studies, along with other evidence from the Saco River, Kelley has concluded that the Saco River supplies the sand that fills the channel and the anchorage and nourishes adjacent beaches. If this is accurate, extending the jetties makes no sense; they could be extended for miles and miles, and the channel would still clog with sand. By extending the jetties, the Corps also truncated the source of sand to Old Orchard Beach.

The results of the academic research in Saco Bay had no bearing on the New England Division's view of the nearshore oceanography. "They [the Corps] do not simply deny the evidence presented by the geologists, they . . . will not discuss the matter," says Kelley.

In 1994, the Corps' Coastal Engineering Research Center continued to argue that the dominant direction of sand movement is from north to south, disassociating the jetty from the erosion on adjacent beaches. The assumption of the Corps' research arm is not based on new data but is instead gleaned from the old reports. Department of Environmental Protection Commissioner Dean G. Marriott summed it up in a May 21, 1992, letter to Colonel Phillip R. Harris, commander of the New England Division:

> Data used in past reports was chosen for its availability, not for its applicability to Camp Ellis, or even Saco Bay. . . . The recent Corps reports [1987, 1991, 1992] present no new data. . . . Erroneous statements and conclusions made in earlier reports are just passed from one study to the next, despite the state's, the city's and residents' attempts to have the Corps reevaluate these conclusions. For example, the Corps insists that net transport of sand in the Camp Ellis area is to the south. . . . All our information leads us to conclude that net transport is to the north. We have been telling the Corps this for years as have the city and the residents, but Corps staff refuse to admit that the conclusion of one of their ancient reports might be in error.

In 1992, the Corps undertook a Section 111 report on Camp Ellis (Table 8–1). "Section 111" refers to a study to determine if a federally sponsored navigation project is responsible for shoreline degradation and, if so, to propose appropriate mitigation measures and estimate their cost. Maine officials believe the Corps' Section 111 Camp Ellis report had another goal. As Marriott states in his letter: "The intent of the Corps taking on the [Section] 111 study was not to find a solution to the problems, but to provide a means to justify the Corps walking away from the problem once and for all."

The dispute between the state and the Corps reached the highest levels. In a May 28, 1992, letter to Corps Lieutenant General Henry J. Hatch, conservative Republican Governor John McKernan Jr. wrote:

> Maine has some strong and progressive environmental regulations. . . . We have tried to work with the New England Division to find compromises that meet our standards and still

allow projects to go forward as the Corps would like to see
them done. However the Division has been of little help in
achieving these compromises. . . . The Corps staff has made
many statements to the municipalities, the press, legislators
and others that they want to help but the [state of Maine's] Department of Environmental Protection is preventing them
from doing so. I trust you can agree that it is not productive to
have one level of government criticizing and laying blame on
another. The end result of this discord is that little is being accomplished to deal with the troublesome issues Maine must
solve. . . . *I expect them [the Corps staff] to respect this State's
right to regulate its resources as it sees fit and to work with us
within the constraints of those laws* [emphasis added].

I must also take exception to the way in which the DEP was
informed of the final decision by the Corps to end work at
Camp Ellis. Department staff had requested a meeting with
the Federal Emergency Management Agency, the Corps, the
State of Maine and the City of Saco to discuss how all of our
agencies could work together to find a solution to the erosion
problem at Camp Ellis. Our feeling was that it was possible to
put a package together, involving participation and funding
from [all the parties involved] to bring to fruition the option of
a buyout and construction of a dune and beach system along
with any changes in the jetty that were determined to be appropriate as a result of the Section 111 study. This has been the
chosen option of the state and city for some time, and we have
communicated this to the Corps on numerous occasions. This
being the purpose of the meeting, state and city representatives were quite taken aback when, more than halfway through
the meeting, Corps staff announced . . . that the Corps was not
going to participate any further in finding a solution to the
Camp Ellis problem. . . . I think it is inappropriate for the
Corps to walk away from this problem, particularly in light of
the navigation project's impact on the adjacent shoreline.

Finally, the governor's letter questioned the Corps economic logic:
"With regard to the economics of doing a project at Camp Ellis, the benefit cost analysis is quite subjective. . . . I found it very interesting that in
1987, when the Corps was proposing to build a seawall, there was economic justification to do that work but in 1992 there is none."

The Corps did not walk away. The final stage of the Camp Ellis debate, at least from the Corps' viewpoint, depended on the results of a physical model study at the Coastal Engineering Research Center. The model at Vicksburg, Mississippi, was an $850,000 concrete imitation of the beach and nearshore zone off the mouth of the Saco River. Nearly the size of a football field, the physical model was a most impressive sight. Waves generated in the model presumably imitated natural waves in Saco Bay, albeit on a much reduced scale. The resulting water movement was observed and measured, and beach behavior was predicted.

Joe Kelley and Maine state geologist Walter Anderson, however, both urged the Corps to study sand transport at Camp Ellis rather than within a physical model in Mississippi. While designed to imitate nature, this display, like other physical and mathematical models, is based on a poor understanding of offshore topography, has no meaningful wave information from Saco Bay, and has no marine current measurements. According to Kelley and Anderson, "The cement model lacks a river to bring in sand, and no information on waves and storms in Saco Bay was used to develop it." "Basically," says Kelley, "[it is] a useless exercise to determine what should be determined in the field."

In April 1995, at a somewhat heated public meeting in Saco, the New England Division of the Corps presented its most recent conclusions about what should or could be done for Camp Ellis. At the meeting the results of the Corps' physical model study at CERC were presented. The model-indicated solution was predictable: a 3,000-foot-long, 15-foot-high, rock offshore breakwater in 10 feet of water parallel to the beach along Camp Ellis. Division representatives also announced that the cost-benefit ratio of this $14 million breakwater was 0.2 (that is, a twenty-cent return was expected for every dollar spent); therefore, the breakwater would not be built.

The CERC had come up with a solution that was prohibited by Maine's beach preservation law. Instead of working within the Maine system and evaluating the nourishment, jetty alteration, and building relocation alternatives that were within the law, the Corps' research center suggested additional armoring, a solution that had not worked previously at Camp Ellis and the *same* solution that CERC had suggested in its 1991 study before spending $850,000 on a physical model.

The Corps' New England Division relied entirely on the physical model results. Like CERC, it had not sought a solution within the context of Maine's coastal management program. Despite its public agreement to work with the state, the New England Division stepped aside after the breakwater solution had been presented at the public meeting and then thrown out because of the cost-benefit ratio. Camp Ellis was left with no solution in sight, at least none with federal participation.

"Is that it? Is that the end of the whole study?" queried a citizen from the back row. "That's about it," replied the New England Division representative.

NINE

Oregon Inlet, North Carolina

Northernmost inlet in North Carolina, Oregon Inlet is the essence of untamed, wild beauty (Photo 9–1). Waves crash in a white arc of surf against the myriad shifting shoals of the large ebb tidal delta at the ocean entrance of this "high-energy" inlet. To the commercial fishermen, primary users of the inlet, however, the shoals are a dangerous hindrance to navigation and make this inlet North Carolina's most treacherous. The natural beauty of these inlet shoals may largely be lost on a fishing captain wrestling the wheel of a pitching trawler in the Oregon Inlet channel.

During the last two centuries more than two dozen inlets have opened and closed along this northeastern North Carolina shoreline reach, a cycle that will continue into the future. Oregon Inlet, south of Nags Head in Dare County, North Carolina, was opened during a hurricane about three miles north of its present location. Calvin Midgett, a resident of the Outer Banks, witnessed the opening of the inlet on September 7, 1846. Midgett was a fisherman, farmer, and occasional employee of the U.S. Coast Survey, where he worked as a mapping assistant. On the fateful day, he was riding his pony along the beach to view the changes wrought by the storm that had been blowing for two days. Observing a change in the wind direction (from onshore to offshore) and intensity, he turned for home only to find his way blocked by a deepening sheet of water flowing from sound to sea across the island. Midgett and his pony rushed to the top of the highest nearby dune and spent five wet and windy hours there. Occasionally, as he prayed for his family's survival, breaks in the rainfall allowed him to see his house, now surrounded by swirling waters. He finally came home to a much damaged house, where he found his loved ones safe and sound. With the coming of dawn, the Midgetts saw the new inlet for the first time, not far from their house.

Midgett witnessed a phenomenon typical of most barrier island inlets. The new inlet channel formed when storm winds reversed, and water that had been pushed into Pamlico Sound by the storm's onshore winds was rushed seaward by offshore winds at the trailing edge of the storm. This storm-surge ebb blocked Midgett's path home and carved a waterway through a low, narrow point of the island. Named after the sidewheeler steamboat *Oregon*, the first vessel to navigate it, Oregon Inlet is currently the only barrier island inlet in the 120 miles between Cape Henry, Virginia, and Cape Hatteras, North Carolina.

Much as a storm will send the inlet into a rage of wave and spray, the political controversy that surrounds Oregon Inlet has been no less furious. Since 1970, when Congress authorized the construction of twin mile-long jetties there, debate has been fervent over whether they would bring environmental disaster or economic boon. The U.S. Army Corps of Engineers, fishermen, and the local Chamber of Commerce support the project as a way of taming the inlet and bringing prosperity to struggling coastal fishing communities. Corps officials assert that the jetties will be both environmentally and economically beneficial. Coastal scientists, environmentalists, and others oppose the project primarily because they believe that the Corps has not adequately examined the potential consequences of jetty construction.

The Oregon Inlet jetty controversy gained the attention of national conservation organizations, the U.S. Congress, and national news media before long. Throughout the 1980s, the proposed jetty construction may have been the most visible and contentious Corps of Engineers coastal project in the United States.

Because the jetties would be anchored on land, the Corps must first obtain agreement from the landowner, in this case the U.S. Department of the Interior: Bodie Island, to the north, is part of the Cape Hatteras National Seashore, managed by the National Park Service; Pea Island, to the south, is a National Wildlife Refuge managed by the U.S. Fish and Wildlife Service. Both are undeveloped except for an abandoned U.S. Coast Guard station, various park and wildlife refuge facilities on Pea Island, and a marina and defunct ferry landing on Bodie Island. The Department of the Interior has yet to agree to jetty construction, thus the jetties have not been built at the time of this writing.

Setting for Controversy

Three inlets—Oregon, Hatteras, and Ocracoke (from north to south)—afford access to Pamlico Sound (Figure 9–1). Hatteras and Ocracoke inlets are historically stable; although the channels within those inlets may move about, the inlets, in contrast to Oregon Inlet, have remained in more or less the same location for many years. Since opening, Oregon Inlet has moved, or migrated, southward at a rate of between 75 and 125 feet per year, causing Bodie Island to the north to lengthen

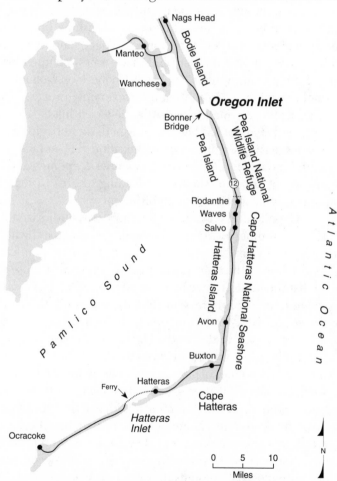

Figure 9–1. Index map of a portion of the North Carolina Outer Banks. The Cape Hatteras National Seashore begins just south of Nags Head, North Carolina, and extends to the south end of Ocracoke. Eight small towns exist within the seashore. Oregon Inlet is the northernmost inlet in North Carolina and the one closest to the fishing village of Wanchese.

and Pea Island to the south to retreat (Figure 9–2). Surf-zone transport
of beach sand in a predominantly southerly direction moves Oregon
Inlet southward as sand continually pours into the inlet from the north
side, forcing it to migrate south to keep from being choked with sand.
Migration of Oregon Inlet has claimed two lighthouses (built in 1814
and 1859) and the original life-saving station, all of which were built
south of the inlet. With the overwhelming evidence of southward migration of the inlet, the present Bodie Lighthouse was wisely constructed on the north shore in 1871, but it now stands about two miles
north of the inlet, too distant to be useful as a navigational aid.

During most of Oregon Inlet's history, small fishing boats navigated
its natural channel. In 1960 the Corps dredged and deepened the
channel for access "across the bar" and made a new channel leading to
the nearby fishing communities, such as Wanchese on Roanoke Island.
The channel dredging set in motion an irreversible process. As at numerous other artificially maintained Atlantic Coast inlets, once a navigable, maintained channel has been established, there begins a progres-
sion of ever increasing engineering stabilization that entails widening
and deepening and, eventually, jettying. Channel deepening and jettying
leads to erosion of adjacent shorelines, leading in turn to seawall construction or continual and costly replenishment.

When the Cape Hatteras National Seashore was authorized by Congress in 1937, a number of small fishing villages remained within park
boundaries. In the years that followed, North Carolina politicians and
developers envisioned the huge development potential of those villages.
Convinced that the limited capacity of the active car ferry across Oregon
Inlet was a hindrance to progress, in 1962 the state built the Herbert C.
Bonner Bridge, a fixed-span bridge with a high center that allowed
large-boat traffic to pass underneath. The bridge's construction did not
allow for inlet migration, however (Photo 9–2).

Lim Vallianos, then chief of coastal engineering for the Corps' Wilmington (North Carolina) District, said in later years that he warned state
engineers about the folly of constructing a bridge in the rapidly changing
Oregon Inlet environment. Nonetheless, construction began in late
1961. The folly soon became apparent. The 1962 Ash Wednesday storm,
a huge northeaster, brought three days of high winds accompanied by
spring tides, forcing great amounts of water into Pamlico Sound. As the
storm passed through the area, wind reversals caused a sudden seaward
rush of water that widened the inlet from a half mile to two miles, probably within twelve hours. The concrete bridge abutments on the north
side of the inlet were washed away, along with all kinds of construction

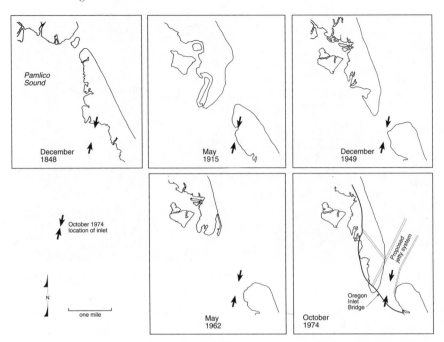

Figure 9–2. The history of Oregon Inlet is shown in these five map views taken from old charts. The inlet has migrated steadily and rapidly, averaging around 75 feet per year, since its formation in 1846. Migration has been caused by the strong flow of beach sand in a north-to-south direction, causing Bodie Island to lengthen, which forces the inlet to move south and shorten Pea Island. Migration was greatly slowed when the Bonner Bridge was constructed in 1962 and dredging was commenced to maintain a stable and fixed channel under the high span of the bridge. Inlet migration was halted by construction of the "little jetty" at the north end of Pea Island in 1992.

equipment. The inlet functioned exactly as inlets on the Outer Banks have always functioned; acting as a flexible, self-adjusting safety valve, the inlet virtually, according to marine geologist Stan Riggs of East Carolina University, popped its cork. The cross-sectional area of the inlet increased to let the water out of Pamlico Sound, keeping water from flowing across the islands and perhaps forming another inlet (as Oregon Inlet had formed almost 115 years before). Had another "permanent" inlet formed elsewhere, Oregon Inlet might have closed.

The North Carolina Department of Transportation (NCDOT) immediately re-initiated and quickly completed reconstruction of the bridge

Photo 9–1. Aerial view of Oregon Inlet looking out toward the Atlantic Ocean. The edge of the ebb tidal delta is clearly marked by a line of breaking waves. The sand shoals at the bottom of the photo are part of the flood tidal delta. (Photo by Mary Edna Fraser)

Photo 9–2. A view looking toward Pamlico Sound of the high center span of the Herbert C. Bonner Bridge crossing Oregon Inlet. The channel must be maintained under this center span, although the natural process of inlet migration would normally carry it southward with the inlet. Ultimately, the problems at Oregon Inlet began when over 120 years of inlet migration had to be stopped for this bridge, constructed in 1962.

in the same location. Fishing platforms were attached to the bridge at the north and south ends. During construction, the inlet, as inlets on the Outer Banks do after blowing their corks, quickly began to narrow and recover its pre-storm half–mile width but in a position slightly to the south. When the $3 million bridge was completed, the north-end fishing walkways extended over dry land.

Construction of the bridge forced a commitment to keep the inlet channel in one location under the high center span, rather than allowing it to move with the naturally migrating inlet. Once the inlet was forced to accommodate the bridge, its associated tidal deltas began to grow and clog the inlet. Inlet migration had to be replaced by an increasingly intensive dredging effort to keep the inlet channel open and in place.

The Oregon Inlet jetty project is known officially as the Manteo (Shallowbag) Bay Project (Figure 9–3). A minor plan component was dredging a channel to Manteo across Shallowbag Bay, hence the project's name. Principally, the plan called for two parallel rock jetties spaced 3,500 feet apart, extending over a mile seaward. The jetties, intended to stop sand from flowing into and clogging the inlet, would, according to plan, protect a 20-foot-deep, 400-foot-wide navigation channel. The plan would require the artificial movement (sand by-passing) of large amounts of sand past the jetties to simulate natural conditions and prevent the erosion of adjacent shorelines.

Cost estimates for construction of the jetties have varied between $80 and $120 million. In 1992 the jetties were projected to cost $94 million including design costs. Construction costs alone were $69 million. Amortized costs over a fifty-year period would be an estimated $13 million per year. The Corps estimates that sand-bypassing costs would be approximately $4 million per year compared to current dredging costs of $4 to $5 million per year. Combined channel dredging (between the jetties) and sand bypassing (moving the sand that has accumulated mainly on the north side of the jetties) is estimated to cost on the order of $500 million over fifty years.

The Inman Panel

In 1970, at the time of congressional authorization of the project, the Department of the Interior had raised questions concerning the physical and biological effects of the proposed project on adjacent Interior lands. In 1979, Interior impaneled several (four to eight at various times) coastal scientists and engineers to review the Corps' project documents

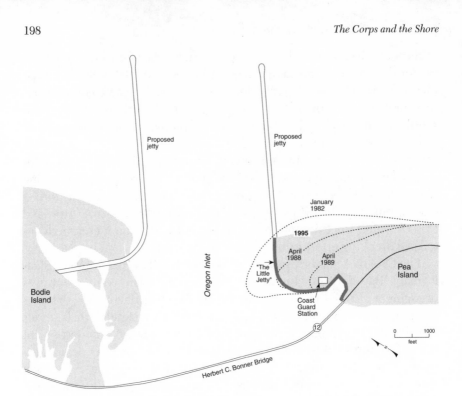

Figure 9–3. A map view of the proposed jetty project, including the existing "little jetty." The "little jetty" was built by the North Carolina Department of Transportation in 1989 to halt erosion at the northern tip of Pea Island. Shown here also are the position of the shoreline at the north end of Pea Island as shoreline erosion dramatically increased when the Corps began hopper dredging in 1983.

out of concern for the effect of the jetties on the Pea Island National Wildlife Refuge and the Cape Hatteras National Seashore. The Inman Panel as it became known, became a unique aspect of the Oregon Inlet saga and one that is probably responsible for much of its national visibility. All panel members have been coastal geologists, ecologists, or engineers from outside of North Carolina.

Douglas Inman, coastal oceanographer from Scripps Oceanographic Institution in La Jolla, California, was chair when the first two reports were written. When Inman retired from the Oregon Inlet scene, he was replaced as chair by Robert Dolan, professor of environmental science at the University of Virginia in Charlottesville and long-time coastal researcher on the Outer Banks. (Despite the change of chairs, the group, when convened, is still usually referred to as the Inman Panel.)

Members of the panel, along with virtually the entire marine science community of North Carolina, were not necessarily opposed to jetty construction. The panel has repeatedly evaluated many aspects of the project design and has produced four reports (in 1979, 1980, 1987, and 1991), all of which question the basic concepts behind the Corps' proposed plan for jetty construction. Their primary objection has been that the Corps never gave the public a fair basis for understanding and debating the potential consequences of jetty construction and never provided realistic cost projections.

We believe that the Inman Panel's review of the Corps' plans for the twin jetties has been the primary reason that they have yet to be built. Because the Department of the Interior, as landowner, has so far based its decision on whether to grant permission for construction on the panel's recommendations, the Corps has been, in effect, forced to respond to their criticisms and questions. The Corps has yet to do so to the department's satisfaction.

The Players

In 1988, the one and only meeting of representatives of all involved North Carolina parties, proponents and opponents, took place in Nags Head, North Carolina. It was a meeting sponsored by the North Carolina Coastal Federation and chaired by the organization's director, Todd Miller. At the head table, Miller brandished a sledge hammer for a gavel, a humorous symbol of the great divergence of opinions around the table. The meeting involved fishermen, state and federal government officials, and the local marine science community. Participants left with their views unchanged.

At the meeting, the six scientists (from four different universities) spoke first, all questioning the Corps' conclusions and assertions. Tom Jarrett, who had replaced Lim Vallianos as the Wilmington District's chief of coastal engineering, spoke next. He began by saying, "I have heard a lot of should, could, possibly, might. When the Corps has to design a project, we have to say can and would." The local fishermen and others who were looking for a permanent solution were more than ready to accept such a statement, aimed at scientists who seemed never to have solid answers. As discussed in chapter 3, engineers are generally comfortable speaking in absolutes; scientists, however, particularly those aware of the unpredictability of the dynamic coastal environment, speak in probabilities and likelihoods.

Economics are the primary factor driving support for the jetties. The northeastern corner of North Carolina—Dare, Currituck, and Hyde counties—is generally economically depressed. Much of the employment is seasonal, related to fishing, construction, and tourism. Since World War II, local and state politicians have contended that the key to a successful local economy is a stable and deep Oregon Inlet channel. In Dare County, however, where the inlet is located, commercial fishing had been of decreasing significance in the local economy in recent years relative to booming tourist and construction industries. Nonetheless, in the late 1980s, even the Hardees fast-food hamburger chain expressed support for building the jetties. In a high-profile foray into controversial politics, Hardees produced a bumper sticker saying: SUPPORT OREGON INLET JETTIES—HARDEES DOES!

Among local interests, the most effective supporters have been the offshore fishermen of Wanchese. For fishermen, Oregon Inlet is a hazard that must be navigated before reaching their fishing grounds in the Atlantic. Promises of safer passage through the inlet, translating into more time for fishing and better access to fish, make the jetties very attractive. Ownership of most of the facilities and vessels in Wanchese resides in three families: the Tillets, the Ethridges, and the Daniels. Weatherbeaten and speaking with a Down East accent, a sort of Outer Banks form of Elizabethan English, the patriarchs of these families have been much sought after by the media for the "human face" they give the debate.

Allied with the fishermen was the small but vocal business community that formed a local pro-jetty group known as the Oregon Inlet Commission. At one point they were funded by the state to promote and lobby for the jetties. The commission hired public relations experts, lobbyists, and engineering consultants. They skillfully orchestrated media events, devised legislative strategies, and kept state politicians in line. But they could not refute the conclusions of Interior's Inman Panel.

The jetty project had virtually no political opposition of consequence in the state. The late U.S. Representative Walter B. Jones of North Carolina, powerful chairman of the House Merchant Marine and Fisheries Committee, whose congressional district included the Outer Banks, was a strong supporter of the jetties. In the 1980s, both of North Carolina's U.S. senators, Terry Sanford and Jesse Helms, could be counted on to argue that the jetties were critical for the state fishing industry. Visitors to Senator Helms' office, whether for or against the jetties, were given a polite reception, a carton of cigarettes, and thanked for smoking if they lit up. Sanford's predecessor, John East, a conservative Republican U.S. senator from North Carolina, was less diplomatic. Jetty opponents were shown the door before they could make their case. During the late 1980s and the early 1990s, former North Carolina Governor Jim Martin made numerous visits to Interior secretaries James Watt, William Clark, Donald Hodd, and Manuel Lujan, Jr., pleading the case for the jetties.

Twice the jetties have been "awarded" to politicians to help their election campaigns. In 1990, with less than two weeks to go before election, Senator Jesse Helms announced that the jetties were as good as built. Only one additional report was needed, and then construction would begin. Senator Helms was reelected, although it is doubtful that he needed the help to defeat his opponent; he failed, however, to carry Dare County, where Oregon Inlet is located. In 1992, the Republican gubernatorial candidate, Jim Gardner, was presented with the jetties by outgoing Republican governor Jim Martin as a pre-election present, again with the understanding that only one more report needed to be finished before construction began. In both cases the hoped-for report with positive environmental findings never materialized.

In 1988, the fiscally conservative Reagan administration had rebuffed pleas from Governor Martin and staunchly opposed the jetties on economic grounds. Governor Martin returned to Washington, D.C., during the Bush administration and made better progress with Interior Secretary Lujan, who, over strong objections by agency science and legal staff, issued a tentative special-use permit to allow jetty construction. It was soon rescinded by his successor, Bruce Babbitt.

Jim Hunt, two-term Democratic governor until 1980, and reelected to a third term in 1992, was the architect of the state's innovative coastal management program. Under the auspices of the program, for the first time in any state, hard engineering structures were prohibited on open-ocean shorelines. The reason: preservation of beaches for future generations. Despite this far-sighted policy stance, Hunt supported the jetties (which are indeed hard structures but were not to be located on state land) and, late in 1993, visited Interior Secretary Bruce Babbitt to further the jetty cause. In 1994 Governor Hunt promised to visit personally with President Clinton to convince him of the need for the jetties, provided the Oregon Inlet Commission furnished new economic and scientific information favoring the structures.

Rather than serving as objective technical advisors in the process, the Corps' Wilmington District staff has been a constant supporter and public promoter of the jetties. Wilmington District coastal engineer Lim Vallianos traveled throughout North Carolina's lower coastal plain presenting the jetty plan and its benefits before civic clubs and the like. Larry Saunders, long-time economist and spokesman for the District, was ever ready with calming statements for the press in response to the latest blasts from critics. We are not aware of any instance in which the Corps publicly acknowledged anything except absolute certainty that the jetties would perform as planned, despite overwhelming contrary scientific, engineering, and economic evidence, discussed below.

A number of national groups joined in opposition to the jetties, each with a different viewpoint. At various times throughout the project's history, opponents joined forces to take the Corps and/or the state to court. Essentially every major environmental group opposed the jetties, including the Sierra Club, National Wildlife Federation, National Audubon Society, Wilderness Society, Coast Alliance, and National Parks and Conservation Association. Several very effective state groups, such as the North Carolina Coastal Federation and the North Carolina Wildlife Federation, distanced themselves from the fray; they were allied in other environmental battles with fishermen who favored the jetties. Virtually all of the major daily newspapers of North Carolina opposed the jetties. With each development along the political path of the jetties, a flurry of editorials would appear, most critical of the Wilmington District.

Taxpayer interests were represented by the National Taxpayers Union. The opposition of sports fishermen was expressed by several organizations including the Sport Fishing Institute, *Salt Water Sportsman*, and the North Carolina Beach Buggy Association (NCBBA). Under the seemingly tireless leadership of retiree George Deems, the NCBBA carried out a sophisticated anti-jetty campaign based on the concern over potential coastal land loss and degradation of fisheries, as well as the limited vehicle access that jetty construction and sand-bypassing operations would impose. Deems was the only vocal opponent of the jetties who actually lived on the Outer Banks.

In 1981, the North Carolina Academy of Science issued a position paper protesting the District's poor understanding of the natural processes at inlets. The letter provoked an eleven-page response from the District colonel that, in the academy's view, was little more than specious rhetoric, calling the paper "the product of a misinformed and perhaps misled group."

Initially, the most visible critic within North Carolina's marine science community was Stan Riggs, a marine geology professor from East Carolina University. A 55-year old with a University of Montana doctoral degree and thirty years of study along North Carolina's coast, Riggs has advised governments and geological surveys all over the world about exploration for phosphate rock. An adventurous sort, he once owned and operated a large wooden sailing schooner, formerly a Baltic Sea freighter that he unsuccessfully tried to turn into a research vessel. He became acquainted with the Outer Banks in the late 1960s and early 1970s and spent five years with undergraduates exploring the coastal waters. Blessed with an insatiable curiosity about the geologic and biologic environment, he has spent years diving, coring, sampling, and making seismic surveys and observing the dynamics of the continental shelf, barrier island, and adjacent estuarine systems of North Carolina. He found the Wilmington District's plans to jetty the inlet ill conceived and personally offensive.

One of Riggs's major research discoveries on the Outer Banks was that the shoreface, the surface extending seaward from the shoreline to a depth of 30 feet or so, is much more complex than just the smooth pile of sand assumed by coastal engineers. He found very thin layers of sand overlying mud and rocks at many shoreface locations, as well as occasional outcrops of mud and rock. He knew from his research that the shoreface in the vicinity of Oregon Inlet that the thick mud was originally deposited in Pamlico Sound and then overrun by the barrier island sands during its migration. After perusing the jetty design documents, Riggs concluded that the mud deposits had not been considered in the design process of either the jetties or the bridge. He informed the Corps' Wilmington District through official channels that a jetty design assuming a sand substrate might be very wrong, offering his data and samples from the area as evidence available for examination. The foundation characteristics of a sandy substrate versus a muddy one, which could shift or flow more easily than sand, would make a real difference in jetty design.

Instead of welcoming Riggs's information, the district at first ignored it. When he finally got the district's attention, after much effort, the Corps was at the inlet within months, using helicopters, boats, and land-surveying crews to obtain the information already obtained by Stan Riggs and his graduate students using a small skiff.

During much of the 1980s, Riggs was deeply involved in his other research and took a more advisory role on the Oregon Inlet jetty scene. Coming to the fore among jetty opponents was Ken Hunter, a tough, sharp-tongued, talented writer and self-employed consultant from California. For most of the 1980s, Hunter moved through the Washington,

D.C., scene from one borrowed office to another, sometimes temporarily employed, sometimes working out of his Harper's Ferry, West Virginia, home. He knew all the players, was intimidated by no one, and knew how to read the ponderous and intimidating documents produced by the Corps. He flooded the anti-jetty activists with information. Like a general orchestrating a battle, he would ask one person to call someone and get certain information and ask another person to please write an opinion piece for the newspaper, while, of course, furnishing a first draft himself.

Ken Hunter's major discovery was a critical flaw in the fishery economics assumptions of the Corps' 1976 cost-benefit ratio. When he revealed the economic problem to the Corps' Wilmington district colonel, he received much the same treatment as Stan Riggs had with his scientific revelations. The colonel, while admitting a problem might exist, replied that there was no requirement for them to restudy project economics. Hunter persisted and talked about his discovery to, among others, newspaper reporters. Before too many days had passed, Corps headquarters in Washington, D.C., announced publicly that a "critical error" had been discovered in its cost-benefit analysis.

Ken Hunter's major discovery was a critical flaw in the fishery economics assumptions of the Corps' 1976 cost-benefit ratio, dubbed the "case of the missing fish" by one local editorial writer. Hunter revealed that the Corps had attributed 70 percent of the total "with jetties" benefits to the increased harvest of "nontraditional" fish (sometimes referred to as "trash fish"), which includes squid, hake, mackerel, sea herring, and butterfish. Although foreign fleets harvest these species, American consumers show little interest in them. The American market has long preferred the "traditional" fish, such as flounder, croaker, gray trout, and bluefish. Besides the fact that such a trash fishery does not exist in this country, Hunter pointed out that if a trash fishery were to be successful, it would more likely be off New England and Long Island, where those species exist in significantly greater numbers than near Oregon Inlet. Overall, Hunter estimated that the Corps had overestimated the projected increased catch of nontraditional species 17-fold.

Correcting for the Corps' error, Hunter determined that, rather than the 1 to 1.4 cost-benefit ratio reported by the Corps, a more accurate ratio would be 1 to 0.34. That would mean that federal taxpayers would pay about $3 for every $1 of benefits attributable to the jetties.

One of the reasons that the Corps' 1976 economic analysis relied on the harvest of nontraditional species has to do with "net" benefits versus "transfer" benefits. In order for a project to be eligible for federal funding, it must provide a net gain to the national economy. In the case of the proposed jetties, if fishing boats with their traditional harvest were to switch from other U.S. ports, such as Norfolk, Virginia, to Oregon Inlet and Wanchese, the only net benefit would be for Wanchese. The benefit to the national economy would not change; the result would simply be a transfer in benefits. The Corps had to find something unique about the Oregon Inlet–Wanchese fishery to argue economic justification for jetty construction.

The Wilmington District was directed by Corps' headquarters in Washington, D.C. to redo the 1976 analysis because of the "critical error." The re-analysis was completed in 1984, and, in spite of the loss of its major trash-fishery benefit, the District again determined a positive cost-benefit ratio by including $906,000 for annual "land loss" benefits. It reasoned that since the jetties would stop the inlet from migrating, the monetary value of the land that would otherwise be eroded was a benefit. The Corps did not take into account, however, that land gained on one side of a migrating inlet is lost on the other side. Doubts about the 1984 analysis prompted the federal Office of Management and Budget to request that the jetty project undergo another cost-benefit analysis, this time to be done by an independent contractor. Hunter's discovery had led to the first and only cost-benefit study of the Oregon Inlet jetties by an independent consultant, a study that showed that project costs outweighed project benefits.

The Kearney/Centaur company completed its analysis in 1988 and concluded that the cost of the jetties, assuming that the Corps' estimates of construction, maintenance, and sand bypassing were accurate, outweighed the benefits by a 0.81 to 0.93 ratio. The Kearney analysis caught the criticism of economists, especially David Campbell, a resource economist then with the National Wildlife Federation in Washington, D.C. According to Campbell, the Kearney/Centaur analysis, as had previous Corps analyses, failed to take into account the fall in wholesale fish prices inevitable with the assumed large increase in fish catches. Furthermore, Campbell revealed that the Kearney/Centaur report assumed that the jetties would reduce dredging costs in the harbor, miles away from the inlet. Had these factors been taken into the accounting project, costs would have outweighted the benefits by an even greater ratio than that calculated by Kearney/Centaur.

The negative 1988 analysis made no difference. The Corps proclaimed a new benefit, namely that the jetties were needed to save State Highway 12 south of the inlet from erosion, which by the Corps' admission had been caused by its own hopper dredging.

In 1990, the Corps undertook yet another economic analysis. The construction by the state of North Carolina of a "terminal groin and revetment" (see the discussion of the "little jetty" at the end of this chapter) at Oregon Inlet altered jetty construction requirements, changing the cost side of the jetty economic equation. The groin would provide the first 2,000 feet of the mile-and-a-half long south jetty. As a result, the estimated cost of jetty construction (not counting dredging costs) dropped from $100 million to $87 million, with an average annual operation and maintenance cost of $5 million. The 1996 estimate is $100 million including dredging costs.

In the 1990 analysis, the Corps continued to assume an increased harvest of nontraditional species, but 50 percent of the overall project benefits were attributed to increased income of commercial fishermen from the harvest of traditional species. According to fishery biologists at North Carolina State University and with the National Marine Fisheries Service (NMFS), however, the fisheries were already severely depleted from overfishing and habitat degradation and would only continue to decline if the jetties were built. In 1995, NMFS considered anglerfish, bluefish, butterfish, croaker, shark, striped bass, weakfish, flounder, scup, black seabass, and sea scallops, all species found in North Carolina waters, to be overfished and in a declining state. Jetties would give more boats access to an already overused resource, while at the same time decreasing the likelihood that fish populations could recover to sustainable levels. The Corps did not consider these possibilities in their 1990 economic analysis.

By 1994, the North Carolina shelf fishery was undeniably in trouble. Overfishing and lack of state-regulated protections had taken their toll. The North Carolina Division of Marine Fisheries, an agency known for long-standing support of the jetty project, continued to promote the project. In a November 1994 report to Governor Hunt, the Division attributed reductions in fishery landings in recent years to "two factors. . . : problems with navigational safety for vessels using [Oregon Inlet], and severe declines in availability of important species harvested by vessels using the inlet." The review concludes that Fishery Management Plans will restore fish stocks to healthy levels. The division predicted that once the jetties were built, the landings would nearly double over the average 1978–93 landings. All this supported the division's argument that the jetties would be a strong economic boon to local fisheries.

Comments submitted to the Wilmington District in February 1995 by the National Marine Fisheries Service's (NMFS) Southeast Regional Office on fishery landing projections contradict those optimistic claims. According to NMFS, "The main reason for decreasing commercial harvests in North Carolina and along the Atlantic coast is due primarily to overfishing and a reduced resource base. It is unrealistic to assume that conservation efforts will be able to restore fishery resources prior to completion of the [Oregon Inlet jetty] project. The assumption that even a modest increase in landings will be realized as a result of the project is unrealistic, based on the present condition of fisheries and the need to reduce harvests for a considerable period of time to rebuild depleted fishery stocks."

As in past cost-benefit analyses by the Corps in which the benefits side of the cost-benefit equation has been based on increased fish landings through Oregon Inlet, the NMFS comments reveal that these would be transferred rather than net benefits. According to NMFS, "Although it may be true that stabilizing Oregon Inlet will increase catches landed in Dare County, North Carolina, it does not follow that these increased landings represent new landings over and above those currently being landed. . . . Thus virtually every projected increase in landings attributed to improving the Oregon Inlet harbor facilities will be at the direct expense of other ports, particularly those located in North Carolina, Florida, and the mid-Atlantic."

Project proponents and opponents alike found the basis for their disagreements in the economic and environmental questions surrounding the proposed jetties. The Corps kept its fellow project proponents happy with seemingly solid information. Opponents, however, found ever more flaws in the fabric of the Corps' arguments.

The Corps Defends Its Jetty Plan

Corps argument #1: **The dredging alternative won't work, hence the jetties are needed.**

Although economists and dredging experts have countered at various times throughout the history of the jetty debate that dredging is a cost-effective approach in the changeable inlet, commercial fishermen and local officials soon became convinced that jetties were the only viable solutions. Dredging was viewed by the Corps as too costly and impermanent to suffice at Oregon Inlet. In all the years since the jetties were authorized by Congress in 1970, commercial and sport fishermen have navigated Oregon Inlet.

The Inman Panel convened a subpanel of dredging experts in 1992 that concluded that the dredging-only alternative was feasible, determining that "a navigational channel through Oregon Inlet could be maintained by dredging and sand bypassing [of the dredge spoil] to the adjacent barrier islands." Costs should be "competitive with those of the [Corps'] jetty and sand management plan."

Showing considerable skepticism of the Corps' motives, the Inman Panel noted in its 1991 report, "Unless the dredging only alternative is fully supported by the Corps of Engineers it is unlikely that it will work to expectations." A dredging company representative made the claim to us in 1994 that he believed that the Corps "rigs" its Oregon Inlet contracts to make the dredging alternative for channel maintenance look insufficient. The timing of contract awards forces dredging to be carried out in the fall rather than in the late spring, when calmer weather would allow perhaps a more lasting job of channel maintenance.

Ken Hunter, in his review of the cost-benefit analyses, noted with even more skepticism than the Inman Panel that the Corps had requested $1.5 million in congressional appropriations for channel dredging. Yet, at the same time, the Corps was making the public claim that $14 million per year would be necessary to maintain the channel, arguing that dredging was too expensive and impermanent to be considered as an alternative. Hunter voiced suspicion: "Is the Corps implicitly confirming the dark inferences some have drawn about the present level of its dredging and buoying operations? A hazardous channel would be the strongest argument for a permanent, structural solution."

Corps argument #2: **Sand-bypassing will take care of the downdrift erosion caused by the jetty.**

One of the major economic sticking points on the cost side of the cost-benefit ledger has been the uncertainties of sand-bypassing at the inlet. How much sand would it take to prevent jetty-induced land loss to both the north and the south? How much would it all cost? These questions have never found adequate answers.

When the Corps released its initial design plan, available sand-bypassing equipment was not adequate for Oregon Inlet's high waves. The initial sand-bypassing plan consisted of using a dragline bucket suspended by a cable between two large towers. Sand would be scooped up on the updrift side of the jetties and deposited on the beach on the downdrift side. The National Park Service objected to this as too intrusive for a national seashore, where recreational access is of utmost importance. In another early sand-bypassing idea, the Corps suggested sinking old liberty ships offshore to shelter the dredges that would move sand across the inlet.

Finally the Corps decided to use a floating breakwater (sloping-front breakwater, or SFB) that would be hauled out to sea during every sand-bypassing operation. The proposed design consisted of two barge-like components attached and filled with water to tilt them skyward. The "barges" would bob up and down, banging on the bottom in the nearshore waves, all the while protecting the sand-bypassing dredge.

Unfortunately, no such breakwater exists except on paper, and wave-tank tests of a model breakwater, at last report, have proven unsuccessful. Sometime in the late 1980s, the floating breakwater disappeared from the plan, and opponents were assured that it had been an unnecessary appendage of the jetty design. Nonetheless, in 1992, the floating breakwater was once again part of the jetty plan.

Even if the offshore breakwater were to work to shelter the dredges, it could not withstand storms. The required demobilization time of one week (when the equipment is taken back to port after use or upon word of an approaching storm) was far greater than the time needed for the local formation and movement of northeasters that commonly develop off Cape Hatteras. The dredges would not operate when most natural sand movement was occurring. Sand movement during storms would take sand offshore, out of the littoral drift system, to form the massive pile of sediment typically found underwater at the seaward end of jetties. To complicate the situation further, it is likely that the jetties would cause shoreline erosion in two directions. Although most of the sand carried along shore moves to the south, sand moves to both the north and the south across the inlet, changing direction and strength with season and weather. If sand were bypassed only to the south, the erosion rate would increase on shorelines to the north. Although the Corps stated that it would bypass sand in two directions if need be, the idea did not go beyond informal discussion.

In the 1990s, in response to the concerns expressed about the sand-bypassing system by the Inman Panel and others, the Wilmington District promised to maintain the beaches, in perpetuity, for six miles to the south and six miles to the north, no matter the cause of the erosion. This, we believe, is a promise that the Corps cannot legally make. Funding to mitigate jetty-caused erosion (estimated by the Wilmington District to cost $7 to $10 million annually) would depend on congressional appropriation. How long would Congress support the pumping of sand onto undeveloped national seashore or wildlife refuge beaches when cities up and down the coast are clamoring for the same beach replenishment money?

The Corps' commitment will also always depend on having a readily available source of sand along the Outer Banks, south of Oregon Inlet. Coastal sand supplies are a finite resource, limited both naturally and by the amount of funding available for finding and mining fill sources. We foresee a day when the Corps can no longer fulfill its obligation because funding has become insufficient to reasonably find and emplace sand along the 12-mile shoreline stretch to either side of the Oregon Inlet channel.

Familiar though the Wilmington District is with the congressional appropriations process and the likely scarcity of sand sources (especially given its earlier work based on Stan Riggs's research), its proposed plan did not include these uncertainties. As a result, there was a perception among some observers that with the promise to perpetually maintain the beaches, the scientific objections had been met or were resolved. On the contrary, an entire set of new concerns was raised.

Corps argument #3: We have spent over $1.5 million on sophisticated studies and models, so we know how the inlet operates and what effect the jetties would have.

Where, the District engineers asked, were the jetty opponents' models? Although local scientists and the Inman Panel were able to independently discredit the models, the District's assertions that it had spent a large amount on sophisticated studies and that scientists were basically guessing were very effective in the local (Dare County) media.

The Coastal Engineering Research Center was contracted by the Wilmington District to study and model the inlet. The CERC is routinely requested to make studies of various aspects of many Corps coastal projects, but the value of this seemingly valid routine is undermined in practice because CERC depends on the Corps districts for its funding. Local districts fund the studies, formulate the questions to be answered by the studies, and present the results as they see fit to the public. (See the final chapter for further discussion of this process and our recommendations to seek a remedy.)

Corps argument #4: The Oregon Inlet jetties are needed to make the Wanchese Seafood Park a success.

Much of the staunch support of the jetties from the fishing community lay in another state-federal venture: the Wanchese Seafood Industrial

Park. Construction of the seafood park, long discussed and finally partly financed by the federal government with funds intended to support economically distressed areas, was completed in 1980. The $8 million facility ($4 million federal) was supposed to include seafood-processing plants along with boat construction and maintenance facilities. By the time the industrial park was completed, it was already clearly a failure. The blame was put on jetty opponents. "If we had the jetties, we'd have the fish!" was the common theme of local political speeches.

In conjunction with the development of the seafood park, local fishermen, whose families had for generations navigated Oregon Inlet with boats suited to the protean inlet channel, were given low-interest loans by the federal and state governments to purchase large, high-volume fishing vessels of 12- to 14-foot drafts that require a 20-foot-deep channel. Such a channel would be difficult to maintain without jetties unless dredging was increased.

In the early stages of planning for the facility, the growing opposition to the jetties argued that the Wanchese Seafood Park would be used as the economic justification for the jetties. Some were opposed to the seafood park because they assumed that it would be used to justify construction of the jetties. To defuse opposition to the park, the Wilmington District and the state promised that it would not be used as justification. In the March 1977 Final Environmental Impact Statement for the Wanchese project, the Wilmington District declared, "The harbor and associated facilities will not be used to justify stabilization of Oregon Inlet." The report added: "The State of North Carolina has made the determination that development of Wanchese Harbor is economically viable without stabilization of Oregon Inlet." Within a year the seafood park was the only justification for the jetties.

Corps argument #5: Jetties work. They make navigation safer and channel maintenance less costly. Conditions at Oregon Inlet have caused a number of drownings, and the jetties will reduce this serious hazard.

The Corps and the Oregon Inlet Commission have long sought public support and sympathy for the project by citing eight deaths in the 1960s and 1970s in four inlet-related incidents. Jetty proponents have attributed the deaths to problems with the inlet channel, insisting that those dangerous conditions would be alleviated once the jetties were built.

Eric Olson, working for the Wilderness Society, decided to investigate the actual causes of death in the incidents cited by the Corps and the local media by scanning the files of the *Coastland Times*. He found that the eight deaths had little directly to do with problems of the channel. Rather, each death could be attributed to poor judgment or negligence.

- 1971. A boat captain unfamiliar with Oregon Inlet tried to enter the inlet at night by following another boat, but his floodlight was not working, leaving him unable to see adequately. His boat went aground on the inlet shoals, and three people died.

- Christmas Day, 1978. In clear weather and on a calm day, three men, all of whom had been drinking, decided to go for a joy ride in a 56-foot fishing trawler on which one of the three was a crew member—without permission from the trawler's captain. They ran aground. One of the three drowned when he tried to swim ashore. The other two, who stayed with the boat and waited for high tide, returned to shore unharmed with the boat undamaged.

- April 1979. A boat with a history of radio and engine problems dropped anchor during bad weather outside of the inlet to wait for better conditions before attempting passage through the inlet. Several hours after it had anchored, other boats called it in as being aground and foundering, but no one was seen aboard. The bodies of the three crew members were found later. The Coast Guard conjectured that they may have tried to get through the channel during a brief respite in the bad weather.

- A "freak wave" in the inlet swept a young boy, one of thirty-six passengers on a moonlight cruise, off the deck of a 58-foot tour boat. The boy drowned. The captain of the boat lost his master mariner's license permanently after being judged negligent not only for failing to require that passengers wear life jackets, but also for not even announcing where the jackets were stored.

Tragic as the deaths may be, they should not have been attributed to channel conditions. In every case there was a significant element of human error or incompetence. After dark, without lights, during storm conditions, or in the hands of drunken skippers, there is no such thing as an easy-to-navigate inlet. The Corps continues to cite inlet-related deaths as "due to Oregon Inlet conditions." In its 1990 economic analysis, the Corps claimed that "27 vessels and 27 lives will be lost during the next 50 years *due to the present inlet conditions*" (emphasis added).

In a 1980 letter to the Corps, the Interior Department questioned whether the Corps had adequately taken into account ways in which jetties could make the inlet *more* hazardous under some conditions, rather than less. Interior noted that the jetties could alter tidal and stormwater flow through the inlet, making navigation more perilous. If a ship were to go aground on a jetty rock in a jettied inlet, it would be in a great deal more trouble than if it were to go aground on sand in a natural inlet. In a number of instances, perhaps at most jettied inlets, the navigation channel moves until it is right up against the rocks. Such channel meander at Barnegat Inlet, New Jersey, brought a large number of vessels to their end, hard aground on a large boulder wall. Closer to the Outer Banks, Masonboro Inlet, North Carolina, and Little River Inlet, South Carolina, have jettied navigation channels that occasionally have wandered up against the rocks. In addition, waves diffract at the seaward end of jetties and produce localized conditions where vessels must navigate larger and trickier waves at the entrance to the jetties than are present in the open ocean away from the entrance.

The formal decision of whether or not to build the jetties, however, has not rested on the danger of the inlet. Economic and environmental issues have formed the legal basis of decision making thus far, and the safety problem has remained largely an issue used by proponents to gain public support for the project.

Corps argument #6: The jetties will not do significant harm to marine fauna and flora.

Ironically, the jetties would probably have a deleterious effect on the very industry they are meant to assist, although the Inman Panel points out that the degree of damage is difficult to quantify. Len Pietrafesa, a physical oceanographer, and John Miller, a zoologist, both of North Carolina State University, have established that the presence of the jetties would likely damage populations of valuable commercial fish species.

Unlike many estuaries, Albemarle Sound, connected to the sea only by Oregon Inlet, is essentially limited in its fish production capacity to the number of juvenile fish that successfully pass through the inlet. Passage through the inlet is a critical part of many fish and plankton life cycles. Several species of finfish and shellfish of commercial and recreational importance are born at sea, then travel into the Albemarle-Pamlico Sound, where they find food and shelter until they return to the open ocean as adults. These include shrimp, spot, croaker, menhaden, flounder, spotted seatrout, gray trout, and channel bass. Other species, such as the blue crab, travel into the protection of the sounds as adults to mate and give birth; some female crabs release their eggs offshore in the vicinity of inlets, to be swept into the backbarrier estuaries. Some plankton species, an all-important source of food for fish, also depend on safe passage through the inlet in their life cycles.

The movement of estuarine-dependent planktonic organisms through ocean inlets is precarious at best. Although some species are able to position themselves and locate desirable currents, getting through the inlet to the estuarine nursery grounds is largely a matter of fate. At natural inlets, with wide entrances and an array of currents, the opportunity for planktonic organisms to be carried into the estuary is moderate. About half of organisms moving past an inlet are pulled inside, following the path of the flood tides in shallow water along the margins of the inlet. At jettied inlets this number may be dramatically lower since planktonic organisms moving past the inlet along the shoreline would encounter a narrower opening in deeper water with more predators, well offshore with fewer eddies and side currents that can carry them into growth and maturation areas.

In a July 19, 1991, letter to the Wilmington District, Andrew Kemmerer, regional director of the National Marine Fisheries Service, wrote, "If the Oregon Inlet jetties significantly reduce fish recruitment in Albemarle and Pamlico Sounds, the navigation project could possibly cause more harm than good with respect to ecological and commercial and recreational fisheries related values." According to Kemmerer, although "serious concerns . . . were raised as early as 1980, . . . the Wilmington District has made no substantive interim evaluation effort." Kemmerer concludes, "Available information and the views of our science staff indicate that long-standing fishery related concerns over jetty construction at Oregon Inlet may be well-founded."

Apparently the Corps' only scientific response to the assertions about biological passage problems with the jetties was based on a Texas study by B.J. Copeland, now with the North Carolina Sea Grant Program. The Texas study, however, concluded only that plankton can pass through a jettied inlet and did not address the problem of relative numbers.

The Inman Panel's Criticisms

In countering the Corps' arguments, jetty opponents came to depend on the findings of the Inman Panel, which found critical shortcomings in the Corps' plan and defending arguments. Consistently, in each of its three reports, the Inman Panel has questioned specific aspects of the proposed jetty project. Just as consistently, the Corps has failed to address the criticisms effectively. Some of the panel's criticisms are as follows:

1. *The Corps' plan is a "moving target."* Details of the jetty plan, such as the sand-bypassing plan, the floating breakwaters, jetty spacing and orientation, have varied considerably with time. The panel's 1987 report noted that what the Corps viewed as its "flexibility in engineering design" was actually necessitated by the "inaccuracies in the Corps' understanding of environmental forces operative at Oregon Inlet." The panel argued that this so-called flexibility "precludes a definitive assessment of environmental impact or a realistic cost/benefit analysis."

2. *The Corps used questionable methods to estimate the inlet's sediment budget, possibly throwing the results off by more than 50 percent.* The sediment budget in this case is an estimation of the amount of sand moving through and around the inlet; it is a critical piece of information in determining the amount of sand bypassing needed to offset erosion of adjacent beaches. The accuracy of sediment budget calculation, therefore, is also very important in determining both project costs and environmental impact.

3. *The Corps seems to expect that by "freezing" the inlet in place, the adjacent islands would also stay in place.* The Corps claims that "once the jetties are completed and the sand bypassing program initiated, the position of the barrier islands, both north and south of the inlet, will be stable." The reality is that the islands adjacent to Oregon Inlet, like the inlet itself, are constantly changing. The overall trend of the islands is landward migration. One of the potential consequences of jetty construction feared by the panel and many of its members' professional colleagues is that if the jetties were built, the islands would continue to migrate and move away from the jetties, in a few decades leaving behind a new cape.

4. *The Corps minimizes the effects of sea level rise on barrier islands and does not consider the strong likelihood of increased rates of sea level rise as a result of potential global warming.* The ultimate cause of barrier island migration is accepted by most scientists to be sea level rise. One estimate is that on the Outer Banks a 1-foot rise in sea level translates to approximately 1,000 to 5,000 feet of shoreline retreat. The Corps concludes that a sea level rise of 1 foot per century

(believed to be the current rate of sea level rise in North Carolina) would "only cause an average of one foot of shoreline [retreat] per year."

5. *The Corps has argued that dredging alone is insufficient, and that only with jetties can the inlet remain passable.* The Inman Panel, however, found that the Corps had dismissed the dredging-only alternative too handily after failing to give it a "fair and unbiased assessment." For instance, the Corps ruled out as prohibitively expensive a sand-pumping method that would use a pumping station and onshore pipeline as part of a dredging operation, yet made it part of the jetty operation (with very little difference in design or technique).

6. *The Corps' reliance on a sloping-float breakwater in the proposed sand-bypassing system is questionable.* The panel found that the SFB has never been used successfully anywhere in the world, and that experience with other types of floating breakwaters, all in wave climates milder than that of Oregon Inlet, have proven them to be "high maintenance installations, with frequent failure due to fatigue of mooring and connectors." The Corps has not done any field testing in the high-wave-energy Oregon Inlet environment; therefore, if it were used, the SFB would be experimental. Although the panel believed the SFB to be "conceptually promising," it concluded that it was "an unproved critical component" of the Corps' Oregon Inlet plan.

7. *The alignment of the jetties is such that waves from the east-northeast would simply be funneled into the channel, intensifying wave action and increasing the navigation hazard, especially for small boats.*

The panel concluded: "Many believe if the final decision on the jetty plan had been based on the project's scientific, engineering and economic merits alone, it would have been deauthorized years ago."

In our view, among the many talented, knowledgeable people and organizations that have urged caution before Oregon Inlet is irreversibly harnessed, the real "hero" of the Oregon Inlet jetty saga is the Inman Panel. The panel did not take a stand for or against the jetties; such was not its place. More important, it provided a scientific buttress for scrutiny of a Corps plan on behalf of the public interest such as no Corps plan has received before or since. Although the panel could not overcome the politics that continue to keep the Oregon Inlet jetty project active, it provided an important, objective, scientific basis for public debate. We suggest that similar panels could provide scientific and engineering scrutiny of Corps coastal projects and discuss this recommendation further in our concluding chapter.

The Little Jetty

Until 1983, most dredging was done in Oregon Inlet by sidecasters, dredges that place dredged sand a few yards to the side of the channel. The advantage of the sidecasting dredge is that it keeps sand in the system and is less disruptive of the sand supply to adjacent shorelines. Unfortunately, much of the sand simply flows back into the channel, and thus more frequent dredging is required by this than by other dredging techniques.

In 1982, over a lot of protests and expressions of concern from local scientists, environmental groups, and the National Park Service, the Corps began hopper dredging at Oregon Inlet. Hopper dredging is the least expensive way to dredge a channel, but it impinges greatly on the sand supply of local beaches. Sand is sucked up into the hold of a dredge and is dumped at sea, taking it out of the coastal system. The Park Service, well aware of the erosion damage done on many shorelines around the world by hopper dredging, at first refused to agree to the change in dredging method. The Corps acquiesced by promising to dump the dredged sand off Pea Island in water more shallow than 17 feet, where at least some of the sand could be expected to come back ashore naturally. In practice, it dumped the dredged sand in much deeper water, thus essentially assuring that shoreline erosion would occur. Later, at a public meeting, Wilmington District engineer Tom Jarrett said it was not reasonable to expect dredge crews to risk life and limb in shallow water.

Less than a year after the Corps started its hopper dredge operation, the north end of Pea Island began to erode at rates ranging up to 300 feet per year. This resulted from the removal of 750,000 cubic yards of inlet sand annually. The Corps admitted that was the cause of the sudden erosion problem but stated repeatedly that pumping sand onto the eroding end of Pea Island would be too costly.

The Pea Island erosion threatened both the southern land connection of the Bonner Bridge and the U.S. Coast Guard Station. Spectacular displays of crashing storm waves could be seen near the southern bridge abutment. Although the bridge was nearing the end of its design life and

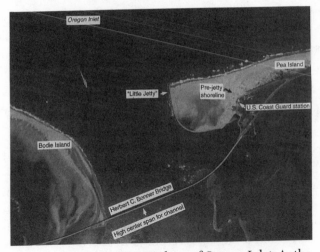

Photo 9–3. A summer 1995 photo of Oregon Inlet. As the inlet migrates, or as Bodie Island lengthens, more and more of the Bonner Bridge is over land. The open ocean is at the top of the photo, Pamlico Sound at the bottom. (Photo courtesy of N.C. Department of Transportation)

had been declared in need of replacement by the NCDOT, it became the new main focus of the jetty debate.

In the late 1980s, the state of North Carolina asked the Corps' Wilmington District to devise a plan to save the bridge, and the engineers recommended construction of a 3,000-foot "terminal groin" to solve the problem (that hopper dredging had caused), arguing that the soft solution (pumping sand) was too costly and impermanent. The terminal groin neither replaces the proposed twin jetties, nor, according to the Corps and the state, is it a part of the jetty project. We find the Corps and state assertions difficult to accept given that the terminal groin has the same cross-sectional dimension and is in the same location as the proposed south jetty. It seems, in effect, a start for the larger structure.

The little jetty was built in 1989–90 at a total cost of around $16 million (Photo 9–3). It is 3,150 feet long, starting from a revetment at the southern abutment of the bridge and snaking around the old U.S. Coast Guard station harbor, whence it extends along the inlet's southern shore into the open ocean. The little jetty is a far larger structure than was needed to protect the highway abutments, akin to shooting a fly with an elephant gun. The highway could have been easily and economically preserved by building the revetment next to it or, better yet, by stopping the hopper-dredge–induced erosion by pumping dredged sand from the channel to the north end of Pea Island.

The "terminal groin" is neither: First, it does not function as a groin, which is a sand-trapping structure. Second, the designation "terminal" refers to a structure placed at the end of a sand transport system where downdrift erosion and environmental damage would be minimized. A true terminal groin should cause little damage to adjacent beaches, in contrast to in-system groins and jetties, which are very damaging. On the Outer Banks, a structure placed at the tip of Cape Hatteras, where the north-south sand flow ceases, would indeed be a terminal groin. Rock headlands on the California coast act as natural terminal groins, trapping sand between them. The Oregon Inlet terminal groin is placed squarely in the middle of a long north-to-south sand transport system ending at Cape Hatteras, 50 miles to the south. The little jetty (according to the Corps' definition, a jetty is built in an inlet and designed to keep the inlet from migrating), as it is more appropriately called, will sooner or later accelerate shoreline retreat to the south.

In addition to designing the little jetty for the NCDOT, the Corps' Wilmington District also wrote the environmental assessment and "finding of no significant impact." Because the highway was decreed to be in an emergency state, the NCDOT was able to obtain an exemption from North Carolina's Coastal Area Management Act for building a hard stabilization structure on the North Carolina coast. The declared emergency status allowed the Corps, for the first time, to bypass the scientific criticisms of the Inman Panel.

Acquiescence of the U.S. Fish and Wildlife Service made construction of the little jetty possible. The structure is anchored on the Pea Island National Wildlife Refuge. The National Park Service never wavered in its opposition to the little jetty but had very little say because the national seashore was not directly affected. The Fish and Wildlife Service, however, could not counter the political pressure. More than fifteen years of holding off hard stabilization at the inlet, in a state where hard stabilization is illegal, were lost, almost in an instant.

Robert Dolan, then chairman of the Inman Panel, described the Corps' plan for the terminal groin as "the most overstated, verging on dishonest, statement that I've seen in a professional document." He went on to express the frustration that many scientists have felt in dealing with the Corps engineers, who are not subject to peer scrutiny as scientists are:

If a scientist made such a statement based on the inadequate data that the Corps has used in this plan, and used the "cookbook" designs they have used, he or she would be discredited for life. However, in this case, as in dozens of others, when it turns out that this "terminal groin" does not work as claimed, no one in the Corps of Engineers will be discredited. . . . It will all be forgotten and another cycle of "corrections" will be instituted.

As soon as construction began, the Corps began pumping sand from the inlet to the downdrift beaches of Pea Island. Yet the Corps' refusal to pump sand to Pea Island was the reason the structure had to be built. Sand pumping was "too costly" to do before the little jetty was built but was not so after construction.

March 1996: The North Carolina DOT announced that it was hastening plans for a new bridge across the inlet. The unstated reason was that the inlet had become more narrow than ever. The little jetty had reduced the flexibility of the inlet so that, as sand poured into the inlet from Bodie Island to the north, the inlet was being squeezed into a narrow configuration. Strong currents through the inlet threatened to undermine the bridge.

TEN

Politics, Science, and Engineering

Currently, the future of our beaches rests primarily in one agency: the U.S. Army Corps of Engineers. As discussed in chapter 1, other federal agencies, including the National Oceanic and Atmospheric Administration (NOAA), the Federal Emergency Management Agency (FEMA), and the Department of the Interior, and the coastal states have some coastal management authority, but it is the Corps that replenishes eroded beaches, builds seawalls and the like, and serves as a technical advisor to the other agencies. It is a daunting responsibility. Increasingly, the Corps must balance different interests as it never has before. When beaches are threatened, ongoing development and the protection of beachfront buildings conflict with tourism-based economies and environmental quality. In an era of shrinking budgets and beaches, with our society rapidly approaching a time when we may ill afford to have beaches and buildings too, is an organization of engineers the best coastal manager?

The Corps' original mission at the beach was military fortification. As more people moved closer to the sea's edge, the Corps was called on to bring its expertise to the design and building of structures, such as seawalls, groins, and jetties, which then seemed the sensible response to beach erosion. Before long, however, people recognized that those protective structures damage beaches and increase shoreline erosion on adjacent beaches.

As knowledge of coastal dynamics and shoreline erosion has grown, approaches to coastal management have changed. NOAA, through the Coastal Zone Management Act, now bases its policies on a philosophy of siting buildings away from eroding shores. Similarly, the National Park Service has adopted a policy against any coastal engineering, hard or soft, at national seashores. Nevertheless, the Corps continues to recommend the use of seawalls, breakwaters, groins, and jetties, often over

Photo 10–1. Is this the future of America's beaches? Here the rocks in front of the Folly Beach seawall provide the only place for one's beach towel. (Photo by Gered Lennon)

Figure 10–1. The location of the Kissimmee River in Florida, showing Lake Okeechobee and the Everglades. Returning the river to its natural meandering state is viewed by many as an example of the "greening" of the Corps.

viable, less environmentally damaging alternatives and often in contradiction to state and sister agency policies (Photo 10–1).

We believe that the Corps' current structure—its modes of decision making, project design, and implementation—are no longer suited, and perhaps never have been, for American coastal management. Further, the Corps is not providing the American people with technically competent advice on how best to preserve beaches for future generations. How should the Corps change to meet the changing demands? President Clinton's 1995 budget proposals call for severely curtailing the Corps' activities on beaches. It would limit the agency to projects of "national interest." Is this the best approach? One must look to the Corps' past efforts to judge whether or not it can change; if it cannot, we see restructuring of the organization or removal of its coastal management responsibilities as the only alternatives.

Corps defenders point to the "greening" of the Corps as a measure of its flexible response to the American public's increasing environmental awareness. The Corps' duty of supervising the nation's "navigable waters" includes supervision of many types of wetlands, and in some parts of the country, particularly Alaska, the Corps is credited as a defender of wetlands preservation. Elsewhere, particularly in New England and the Southeast, the Corps' reputation is different. In North Carolina, the Corps' Wilmington District has sent letters to landowners detailing ways to avoid the Corps' own wetlands dredge and fill permit requirements by filling wetland areas incrementally rather than all at once.

Frequently cited as the premier example of its changing attitudes is the Corps' effort to reestablish the meanders of the Kissimmee River in Florida (Figure 10-1). The winding Kissimmee (a Calusa Indian word meaning "long river") had been channelized, that is "straightened," by the Corps in the 1960s. The Kissimmee River and its floodplain are an integral part of a 9,000-square-mile watershed system, including Lake Okeechobee, that extends from Orlando, Florida, to the Everglades. After a wet season and a series of hurricanes in 1947 caused extensive flooding, public outcry spurred Congress to approve a Corps-designed flood-control plan in 1954. In the 1960s, work started on "Canal 38," or "the ditch," as it is known to many.

The channelization of the Kissimmee is another instance in which the negative consequences of a Corps plan were well understood when alternatives were still being considered. Loss of wetlands and water-quality problems were anticipated, but the project went ahead anyway. It took $32 million and ten years to straighten the river, which turned the 103-mile Kissimmee into a 52-mile, 200-foot-wide, 30-foot deep canal. Construction was completed in 1970, and almost immediately the drainage of 200,000 acres of floodplain wetlands caused a decline in water quality and the loss of waterbirds and commercially valuable fish species. Flooding increased, as water that would have been absorbed by the river floodplain was sent downstream.

One year after the canal's completion, the state of Florida was calling for the Kissimmee's restoration. In 1991, under a congressional mandate, the Corps began restoring about one-third of Canal 38, which will cost nearly $400 million, more than ten times as much as the entire original project. While restoration of the river is a worthwhile effort, planning for foreseeable consequences would have been true evidence of greening.

In reference to the Corps' river management, the Sport Fishing Institute wrote in its May 1992 newsletter, "It has not been until very recently that the Corps has begun to acknowledge civilian pressure to reevaluate its long-standing resource management policies to fulfill the demands of a stressed environment and the present day American economy." Another 1992 article, appearing in *American Forests*, is more generous, saying, "Being practical . . . , the army engineers recognize that today's clients are less likely to request flood control and navigation improvements than they are to seek environmental restoration."

What about the beaches? At the national level, the Corps may have refocused its emphasis from seawalls to beach replenishment as the environmentally preferable erosion response. However, we have seen little evidence of greening at the district level in coastal projects. As our case studies establish, the structural "solution" is the one proposed more often than not by Corps district engineers, and the potential for beach degradation associated with erosion-control structures is consistently understated. We have reached the conclusion that, while the greening process is perhaps under way at Corps headquarters in Washington, D.C., and in a few district offices, most coastal district offices are still working to fortify the nation's beaches. Concern for buildings is much greater than for beaches.

The greening of the Corps at the shore depends upon adopting the long view, taking into account global warming and rising sea level, and recognizing the profound value of the beach to society as a whole. The Corps argues that it has recognized the societal value of beaches by, beginning in the 1980s, putting replenishment before seawalls and other structures as the preferred response to erosion. But beach replenishment has proven to be costly, temporary, and unpredictable. The next step in greening would be for the Corps to make careful and objective analyses of the building relocation, or retreat, alternative to shoreline erosion problems. The Corps has gone from seawalls to beaches; once the Corps takes the next step and begins relocation of buildings in appropriate communities, its greening will be complete.

In states that have adopted the retreat philosophy in their coastal management policies, local Corps division and district officials have proposed plans that are illegal, as we have seen. At Camp Ellis, Maine, the Corps recommended construction of a breakwater despite Maine law and over the state's plan to move the community.

In North Carolina, the Wilmington District has proposed building a 1,000-foot groin in conjunction with a beach replenishment project on the south end of Topsail Island. The district assumes that the groin would increase the durability of the replenished beach, which is probably true, and that the structure would not affect the sand supply to islands to the south, which similar experiences suggest is false (see chapter 2). In 1989, Tom Jarrett, a Wilmington District engineer, told the state's Coastal Resources Commission that North Carolina's prohibitions against groins, seawalls, and other hard structures on ocean beaches limited the district's shoreline activities and could turn district engineers into "paper pushers." In 1991 the Wilmington District offered to advise the town of Topsail Beach in its push for Coastal Resources Commission permission for a hard structure.

Although "arrogance" is a term normally ascribed to individuals rather than organizations, there seems no better term for the Corps' district-level approach to beaches. As long ago as 1830 Alden Partridge, a former West Point superintendent, characterized the Corps as a "privileged order of the very worst class." Today, The Wilmington District's and the New England Division's apparent indifference toward North Carolina's and Maine's respective coastal management goals is, in our opinion, arrogant. Another example, we believe, is the installation of reverse turbines on the Savannah River's Richard B. Russell Dam, at the Georgia–South Carolina border. Dam construction was started in January 1976 and was completed in December 1984. The dam has eight turbines: four that carry water from the reservoir and four reverse turbines that push water back into the reservoir during off-peak power hours to artificially maintain the water level in the reservoir. The total cost as of December 1994 was $576 million, of which $93 million had been spent on the reverse turbines. Unfortunately, the reverse turbines do not just move water, they also suck in fish and anything else within their pull.

In 1982, prior to construction of the reverse turbines on the Russell Dam, the Corps found that two thousand pounds of fish were killed within 2.5 hours on a trial run of the reverse turbines at the Truman Dam in Missouri. A similar episode occurred at the Ludington Pump-Storage Plant on Lake Michigan. Several rounds of experimentation over two years resulted in no solution to Truman Dam's fish loss problem, and the use of the reverse turbines was curtailed pending a solution. In an article in the *Missouri Conservationist*, planner William Dieffenbach wrote that tests done in 1984 at the Truman Dam "created a stir from Missouri to Washington, D.C. People began to really understand that large pumps could be fish-eating machines."

Although the Savannah District had not awarded the contracts to a construction company for the Russell Dam's reverse turbine construction, as the dramatic events at the Truman Dam unfolded, the Corps proceeded as planned. According to a history of the Savannah District, the Corps declared that the Russell Dam would not cause any problems for fish populations because the Savannah District had used "different construction techniques [than in Missouri] and because of [its] . . . commitment to provide screening devices" to keep the fish safe. In 1992, the Corps started up the $93 million Russell Dam reverse turbines and pump-storage facility. Thousands of herring were immediately killed, the state brought suit against the Corps (the case is unsettled at the time of writing), and the turbines have not operated since.

District Economics

The cost-benefit ratio is a critical determination in the course of a project; only projects with favorable ratios are funded by Congress. For Corps districts, which receive funding based on the cost of their projects, the cost-benefit analysis is essentially a survival mechanism. For coastal projects, we have found the analyses rarely, if ever, accurately capture the long-term costs in a dynamic natural system. Among the inherent flaws in the Corps' calculation methods is its assumption that the design costs are inflexible; thus, no margin of error is incorporated to make allowances for storms or design errors. For instance, the estimated fifty-year costs and sand needs can (and usually do) suddenly and dramatically increase with a single storm (see chapter 4 for more detailed discussion). A particularly misleading analysis of benefits was made by the Wilmington District concerning the Oregon Inlet jetties and the North Carolina fishery as discussed in chapter 9. Among the Corps' assumed benefits from the jetties is an increase in fish landings, but in reality the jetties could harm the fishery. Among coastal projects, as previously discussed, we argue that actual costs usually are much higher than cost estimates. Among inland projects, the Tennessee-Tombigbee Waterway (Figure 10–2) is infamous among Corps watchers for its selective public reporting of changes in the cost-benefit ratio with new information and unforeseen events. It has also been described as "engineering arrogance in a class all its own."

Built to create a shortcut to the Gulf of Mexico allowing ships to bypass long stretches of the Mississippi River, the Tennessee-Tombigbee Waterway technically shortened the route from the heartland to the sea by as much as 550 miles. Because of twelve locks and dams and a narrow channel, however, the canal did not reduce ship travel time, and it made

Figure 10–2. The dotted line shows the approximate path of the Tennessee-Tombigbee Waterway connecting the Tennessee River with the Gulf of Mexico. This is perhaps the most commonly cited example of cost-benefit analysis gone awry.

shipping more costly. The largest civil works project completed by the Corps was dubbed the "very epitome of pork barrel" by the *Miami Herald*. It cost nearly $2 billion (compared to an originally estimated $323 million) by the time it was completed in January 1985. .

Even before the waterway construction was finished, independent shipping projections, the benefits side of the equation, were far below Corps estimates. Cost estimates rose dramatically before the project began and continued their ascent once construction was under way. According to Jeffrey Stine's book about the waterway, *Mixing the Waters*, within one year the estimated project cost increased by over half a billion dollars, from $815 million to $1.4 billion. Economist Joseph Carroll wrote that "transport savings on whatever traffic does develop may not cover the annual operation and maintenance costs . . . the nation will be fortunate indeed to capture as much as 20 cents for every dollar invested in the Tombigbee Canal. The Corps' navigation benefit estimates appear to be overstated by a factor of ten or so because of the phantom freight in the traffic base and because of the faulty criteria used to calculate benefits."

Economist Carroll's words proved prophetic. A brochure declaring the virtues of the new waterway issued by the Corps in June 1985 projected that shipments would "gradually build up to some 40 million tons annually." Nearly ten years later, in 1993, shipments were less than eight million tons, 20 percent of projected levels.

Science As Practiced by the Corps Districts

Science requires balancing nature's known complexities and coming to the most reasonable, defensible conclusions possible with the available information. Scientific research must include recognition and acceptance of and preparation for the inherent uncertainties that are an integral part of all coastal environments. At the local level, however, we find no evidence that the Corps understands this critically important approach to science. Instead, we see three strategically modified practices of science that we label client science, dogmatic science, and politicized science.

Client science entails sorting through evidence, facts, and theories and reporting only those items that support the hoped-for conclusion. It is attributed to private consulting companies that find for the client and ignore evidence that could damage a client's interests. This type of science is tolerated because a fact or accepted theory, sometimes with a prominent scientist's name attached, can be used to give credence to a certain set of conclusions. Unfortunately, relatively few people would recognize that such conclusions either represent only a part of the picture or come with hidden consequences. An example of Corps client science comes from Oregon Inlet (chapter 9). A study of marine larval transport through a jettied inlet in Texas was used to support conclusions about jetties' potential impacts on larvae at Oregon Inlet. But the questions answered in the Texas study were not the questions asked at Oregon Inlet.

Dogmatic science—or "hard and fast" science—states conclusions without accounting for natural uncertainties in the studied system. Conclusions are stated as immutable facts, without the caution that is the trademark of good science. For instance, the passage of a big storm is referred to as "unusual" or "unexpected," even though sound science recognizes that storms of any magnitude can be expected. Similarly, dogmatic science treats all shorelines equally, skirting the accepted premise that beaches have inherently unique behaviors and wide variability.

To some degree, what we see as the Corps' fallacious practice of dogmatic science is part of the age-old conflict between the scientific and the engineering approach to problems. Engineers, who must make a final decision about some design or other, often find themselves at odds with and frustrated by the caution demanded by science. Scientists recognize the probabilistic nature of predictions about the likelihood or the magnitude of natural events that might affect some engineering design. Pilkey saw this difference early on. His father, a civil engineer involved in the design of nuclear reactors at Washington's Hanford plant, complained repeatedly about geologists' unwillingness to predict the absolute highest probability magnitude of earthquake possible in the area.

Politicized science, in which political expediency determines the outcome of scientific research and engineering design, is perhaps the greatest weakness of Corps district-level science. We distinguish, however, between politicized science and politics, as in public scrutiny of a project. The public should be given ample opportunity to participate in the decision-making process surrounding Corps projects. But, in order to do so, the public needs accurate and understandable scientific and engineering findings. Scientific data that has been influenced by political considerations is not only worthless, it is also potentially dangerous. Political and societal debate should be based on sound science and engineering, not the other way around.

Even when sound science and engineering support a project, politics can alter the outcome. An example is the Westhampton Beach groin project in a barrier island community on the South Shore of Long Island, New York (Figure 10-3). Although the project's initial science and engineering plans were not politicized, the application of science and engineering in the project construction were directly altered by politics. After the 1962 Ash Wednesday storm, the Corps' New York District undertook the construction of twenty-one groins (completed in 1977), each about 480 feet long. Groins are shore-perpendicular structures that inevitably cause erosion because they interrupt the flow of sand in the longshore current. And the Westhampton groins have been especially destructive. Along this east-west trending shoreline, natural sand movement, or drift, is from east to west. To reduce the groins' destructive effect, the Corps should have built the groins in a continuous west-to-east sequence, starting from the jetties at Moriches Inlet at the west end of the island. Instead, the Corps built the groins in an east-to-west sequence and left a three-mile gap between the last groin and the Moriches jetty. Newspaper accounts credit the Corps with warning that construction should have begun at the far west end of the beach, but, according to a 1983 *New York Times* account, wealthy property owners on

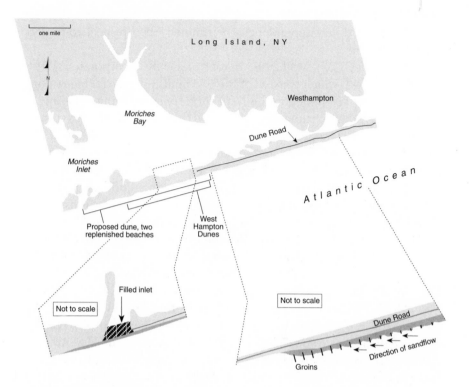

Figure 10–3. The groins at Westhampton, New York, completed in 1977, should have started at Moriches Inlet to the east; instead, a 3-mile gap between the westernmost groin and the inlet was allowed to remain. Severe erosion ensued as a result, culminating with formation of a new inlet across the much narrowed island in 1993.

the east end of the island "used their political influence . . . and the county told the Corps of Engineers that it would not pay its local share unless the project was changed to go from east to west."

Rapid erosion ensued in the three-mile gap between the last groin and the jetty, a number of beach cottages were abandoned or destroyed, and a new inlet formed across the erosion-narrowed island. The cost to taxpayers in repair and replenishment and seawall construction so far: $120 million.

Although the Corps deserves credit for publicly advising that construction should begin at the west end of the beach—the downdrift end—we believe that there is no excuse for the knowing misapplication of basic design principles because of political pressure. What motivates the Corps to abandon these principles to politics? We suspect the current Corps districts' dependence for funding on a project-to-project basis is to blame.

In an aside, Gary Vegliante, mayor of newly incorporated Westhampton Dunes (which consists of the two hundred or so cottages along the 3-mile strip) is quoted in the *New York Times* as saying, "[Federally funded beach replenishment] is a solution that could be applied in similar disputes all along the East Coast and California." Although the mayor's enthusiasm is perhaps understandable, a "solution" that will spend approximately $200 million every few decades for every 3 miles of shoreline is an unrealistic and unaffordable national erosion response.

Affordable or not, the nearby community of Fire Island was listening. Fire Island property owners hired the West Hampton Dunes' attorney and filed a $70 million lawsuit against the Corps for alleged erosion damages caused by the Westhampton groin field. We believe that, if Fire Island succeeds in their suit against the Corps, a precedent could be set that would be a boon for beachfront property owners and their attorneys but extremely costly for taxpayers. Would this precedent make the Corps liable for every instance in which an erosion control structure caused downdrift erosion? That would include much of the U.S. Atlantic and Gulf of Mexico shoreline! Ironically, however, many of the structures in question, including those at Westhampton, have been built at the behest of beachfront property owners.

Politicized science also played a role in the implementation of the Seabright project, discussed in chapter 4. Sand was first pumped at Monmouth Beach in the middle of the project area. Steve Keehn, manager of a private consulting company working for the Corps, told *The New York Times* (August 15, 1995) that "it would have been preferable from an engineering perspective to start the project from its northern end and work southward to minimize loss of sand by erosion. But a political component to the project determined the starting point."

The Districts and the Coastal Engineering Research Center

The Coastal Engineering Research Center has contributed valuable insights into some aspects of the behavior of coastal systems. The Center's research pier at Duck, North Carolina, has a deservedly good reputation for its scientific and engineering research. Qualified engineering researchers are engaged in objective studies at the Center's main laboratory in Vicksburg, Mississippi. But, for all intents and purposes, the Coastal Engineering Research Center is a research laboratory run by and for engineers without a lot of input from coastal geologists or oceanographers. We believe that, compared to the Center's engineering effort, CERC's science is weak. Much of the excellent basic research concerning the nature of waves and sediment transport gathered at Duck has yet to permeate the principles of beach design used at the district level; so long as research and its application are divorced, change in the Corps' response to coastal erosion will be slow indeed.

The limited output or application of CERC's discerning science is attributable to its dependent relationship with the districts. The research funding for CERC comes primarily from the individual Corps districts. The districts do not, however, have to give contracts to CERC; they are free to choose civilian contractors for studies, which they often do, leaving CERC in the position of a competing consulting group. CERC's economic reliance on the districts virtually assures that it will not become an internal voice of critical evaluation.

As a result of the research limitations that arise from having to compete for funding, little of the research at CERC directly addresses the everyday principles used in the design of coastal engineering projects. While there is a great deal of looking ahead in the hope of formulating new principles and approaches, such as the mathematical models discussed in chapter 3, there is inadequate hindsight review and evaluation of currently applied design principles.

We believe that CERC could infuse good science and fresh ideas into the Corps system but is effectively prevented from doing so by the CERC-district relationship. Specifically, this relationship hampers CERC's effectiveness in several ways:

- *The districts fund a large proportion of CERC's research activities.*

- *The districts ask CERC project-specific questions only.* As previously indicated for several projects, notably Presque Isle, Pennsylvania, Camp Ellis, Maine, and Oregon Inlet, North Carolina, CERC is contracted by the districts to research very specific questions. The center is not asked to evaluate questions raised by the Corps' critics, such as the veracity of replenished beach durability predictions, the likely success of sand-bypassing systems at jettied inlets, and the scientific validity of cost-benefit ratios.

 For CERC to contribute to the understanding of coastal

processes and to improve the quality of coastal engineering, its research must systematically evaluate key issues critical to the engineering of beaches and the management of erosion-control projects,
including: erosion caused by jetties; the ecological impact of jetties
(specifically larval and plankton passage through jettied inlets); the
biological impact of dredging; the economic and environmental effectiveness of beach replenishment; oceanographic processes on replenished beaches; and geologic controls of shoreline erosion.

- *The districts present CERC research results to the public.* The results of research performed at CERC are introduced for public debate by district engineers, not by the scientists and engineers who
performed the studies. Although CERC research results are presented in the Corps' literature, because of their technical nature
they are essentially inaccessible to the public. Important in the
public arena are those statements made to the media, or in public
hearings and the like, which are made at the district level, usually
with a pro-project slant. Experiences in Presque Isle, Pennsylvania
(chapter 7), and Oregon Inlet, North Carolina (chapter 9), provide
examples of this dilemma.

- *The districts use the cost, magnitude, and sophistication of CERC
studies to defuse project criticism.* Corps districts often respond to
scientific criticisms of a project by citing the existence of a very
costly study performed by CERC. As noted in chapter 9, during the
public debate over jetty construction at Oregon Inlet, North Carolina, the Corps' Wilmington District declared that it had spent over
$1 million on CERC studies and that project "opponents" had
nothing comparable to offer. But, the high cost of a study does not
prove that all of the right questions have been asked, nor does it
guarantee the efficacy of the answers.

What Is To Be Done?

If the Corps is to continue to be at the forefront of coastal management,
the agency needs political and structural reform. The following are several suggestions that we believe, from a scientist's perspective, would
improve the Corps' overall proficiency as coastal manager, its contribution to coastal research through CERC, the effectiveness of its district
activities, and the interaction among districts and coastal communities.

Recommendations for Improvements
in the Corps' Practice of Coastal Science

- *Coastal engineering should be updated to reflect current under-standing of nearshore oceanographic processes.* Coastal engineering design should be based on the very latest understanding of coastal processes. Currently, little organized effort is made to update design parameters apace with research. In the design of replenished beaches, for instance, the principle used to estimate how much sand will be lost from the beach because of replenishment sand-grain size dates to the 1950s; it is one that is now recognized by geologists as invalid.

  The many assumptions made in design and modeling, such as in the GENESIS model discussed in chapter 3, should be reassessed. The concept of the equilibrium profile of the shoreface used to esti-mate the required volume of replenishment sand has come under strong geologic and oceanographic criticism. Sediment transport studies at CERC's Duck, North Carolina, research pier show that large volumes of sediment are transported from the beach to the continental shelf. But Corps district engineering designs continue to assume that closure depth (a sort of sand fence discussed in chapter 3) occurs near the base of the shoreface.

- *All projects should be monitored.* Without the performance evalua-tion afforded by monitoring, one cannot objectively evaluate the success of design methods or the accuracy of the various models cur-rently depended on for predicting project success. Monitoring should be considered an integral part of all projects, but the Corps has only recently undertaken any monitoring of replenished beaches. It has yet to monitor the performance of hard structures, such as the offshore breakwaters at Presque Isle, Pennsylvania, in a systematic fashion. In a 1994 letter from the Corps to the Office of Management and Budget, the Corps concedes that "monitoring of beach nourishment projects . . . has not been as good as it should have been."

  Unfortunately, even the limited monitoring that has been con-ducted at replenished beaches has been, in our view, inadequate. CERC began monitoring the Ocean City, Maryland, project immedi-ately after its emplacement but stopped after three years. After sev-eral storms and significant loss of the dry beach, the district reported that 90 percent of the sand was just offshore, still providing storm pro-tection for the community. We dispute the "offshore sand" argument, but only through monitoring will the question be resolved.

The New York District carried out a multimillion-dollar monitoring project on Rockaway Beach, New York, so poorly that very little useful information was gained. Among other failings, the monitoring study matched offshore topographic profiles with onshore profiles taken months apart. This is not valid practice in a rapidly changing beach environment.

Virtually the only replenished beach monitoring efforts that have successfully tracked the movements of artificially emplaced sand have been conducted by academic geologists and engineers. The requisite organizational flexibility to go to the beach and take topographic profiles immediately after a storm, for example, does not exist in most Corps districts. Gail Ashley and Susan Halsey, New Jersey coastal geologists, monitored the rapid disappearance of one of the many Ocean City, New Jersey, nourishments, determining the rates and pathways of beach loss with considerable accuracy. Paul Gayes, a geologist from the Coastal Carolina College, has been contracted by the Corps to track the movement of replenishment sand at Folly Beach, South Carolina. According to Gayes, replenishment sand is being swept offshore, beyond closure depth, via shoreface gullies. Work done by Duke University researcher Rob Thieler shows similar offshore sand movement down shoreface gullies at Wrightsville Beach, North Carolina. District engineers, however, both at Folly and at Wrightsville Beach, claim that the sand is just offshore, providing storm protection for the community.

The difference in these scientists' approach to monitoring and the Corps' approach lies in the questions asked and the time devoted to finding answers. The Corps limits beach profiles to a predesignated study area; if the replenishment sand leaves the area, the engineers do not go in search of it (as Ashley and Halsey did in New Jersey). All Corps monitoring accepts the assumed limits of sand transport; study areas stop short of closure depth, so do not test whether sand is traveling beyond it (as Thieler has found off Wrightsville Beach). The Corps limits the study period, as at Ocean City, Maryland, gathering only short-term, relatively useless, information.

All this begs the question, however, of who should be doing the monitoring? We do not believe that the districts should be responsible. Were it freed from its financial dependence on the districts, CERC would be a candidate. One of the reasons that monitoring has not been done more regularly is the high cost that districts have attached to it. The Baltimore District estimated that monitoring the Ocean City, Maryland, project would cost 5 to 10 percent of the total project cost. That would mean that monitoring would cost more than $6 million. In our experience, a carefully designed monitoring project can produce useful information for a tenth of that money. In our view, the Corps consistently exaggerates monitoring costs, but in any case, expenditures on monitoring will pay off in improvements to the design of future projects, knowledge gained about coastal dynamics, and insights into the Corps' project performance.

Monitoring is important during projects as well, if the Corps is to avoid the charges of incompetence that some have leveled. An example comes from just off the New Jersey–New York coast. In late November 1993, 6 miles off Sandy Hook, New Jersey, and 2 miles from the channels leading into the New York and New Jersey harbors, the Corps dredge *McFarland* ran aground in approximately 12 feet of water on a rock mountain of the Corps' dredgers own making.

Why was an area of 70-foot waters transformed into "Mt. Spike," as the rock mound was dubbed by local environmentalist Cindy Zipf? Mt. Spike formed as, day after day, the Corps dredge took its loads of unwanted rocks to a designated offshore disposal site and dropped them at a marking buoy. By dumping at the buoy, the dredgers were sure that they were hitting the proper quadrant of the dump site. Rather than moving the buoy within the quadrant to spread the rocks around, the dredgers kept dumping their rock loads on precisely the same spot, until they had created a rock mountain nearly 60 feet high. Mt. Spike went unnoticed until the *McFarland* ran into it. Subsequently, the Corps requested $1.5 million from Congress to dismantle the underwater mountain. In late 1994, it remained untouched, left to settle on its own.

- *Corps coastal engineering must incorporate coastal system uncertainties.* The greatest uncertainty in the coastal system is storms. Yet coastal engineers still regard storms as unexpected or characterize them as unusually severe. The Corps needs to better incorporate the uncertainties of storm occurrence in estimating costs, sand-volume requirements, and project durability, as well as in its environmental impact statements. Currently, all estimates are reported as single-figure predictions with no indication that the next big storm's time of arrival or magnitude is an uncertainty. For instance, the nourishment interval of the Folly Beach replenishment was given as eight years when a more accurate figure, based on hindsight, would have been eight plus or minus seven years. The sand volume required to

keep a beach at Ocean City, Maryland, intact for fifty years was estimated at 15 million cubic yards, while actual volume requirements
now appear to be 15 million plus or minus 25 million cubic yards.
Corps representatives' repeated assertion that the U.S. Congress
demands certainty does not justify nonprobabilistic science on the
shoreline. Scientists and engineers should make only those estima-
tions that are within their capabilities.

- *The Corps should do more to observe and learn from how nature
  works at the beach.* As discussed in chapter 3, the engineering design of beach replenishment and other coastal projects in the United
  States is increasingly based on mathematical models. Given our current, at best, rudimentary knowledge of the oceanographic
  processes of the nearshore zone, engineering reliance on these
  models is premature. We have much to learn from Dutch and Australian engineers, who observe the natural behavior of a beach as a
  guide to replenishing it.

Recommendations for Improvements in the Corps' Coastal Engineering Research

- *Remove the Coastal Engineering Research Center from its financial
  dependence on the districts.* Currently, except for some administrative funding provided directly through congressional appropriation,
  all of the Coastal Engineering Research Center's funding comes
  from "reimbursable work," that is, research done for Corps districts
  or other agencies. Thus, CERC is directly dependent on the districts
  for most of their funding. We believe that CERC should receive all
  funding directly from Congress rather than through the districts.
  This would remove CERC from its role as a "consulting group" for
  the districts and remove the incentive for engaging in "client
  science."

- *Improve the quality of basic scientific research at CERC.* Although
  CERC has contributed to our scientific understanding of beaches,
  its oceanographic and geologic efforts are weak. To improve project
  design and the mathematical models on which designs are based,
  more oceanographic realism should be employed and fewer assumptions made. As currently structured, we do not believe that
  CERC is capable of providing basic scientific grounding. Although it
  exists at all levels in the Corps, the need to overcome the gap be-

tween the scientific and engineering approaches is the most desperate at CERC.

- *Allow CERC more direct interaction with coastal communities and the public.* Currently, CERC communicates with district engineers, who, in turn, relate CERC research results to local project sponsors (the community) and the public. The districts frame the results in a way that supports their preferred project alternative. Were it to be removed from its financially dependent relationship with the districts, CERC would presumably be more detached from state and local politics and, thus, better able to provide objective reports to the public. At the same time, if CERC were in direct contact with community leaders, researchers would gain a better picture of the performance of various Corps beach endeavors.

- *Replace the Coastal Engineering Research Board with an outside advisory board.* The Coastal Engineering Research Board (CERB), through periodic meetings, oversees the Corps' coastal research efforts at all levels. Although the board has outside members who are engineers or scientists, it is run by U.S. Army generals. A CERB dominated by independent scientists could enhance Corps science. Research always works best in an environment where the exchange of views is encouraged and where criticism is solicited and expected. In our view, the primary motivation of both CERB and CERC seems to be protecting the institution rather than promoting the very best in scientific and engineering research.

Recommendations for Changes at the District Level

- *Reform the system by which districts receive their funding.* Currently, each district is funded solely on the basis of its approved projects or on the work it does for other federal, state, and local agencies. Congress does not provide districts with annual budgets as it does most government agencies. No project, no funding, no district. An annual struggle to justify funding is not a good way to promote the best science and engineering.

  We believe that the current system of funding encourages greater expenditures than necessary. For instance, in general, a replenished beach is designed at a cost of 15 percent of construction costs. Coastal engineering consultants tell us privately that they design replenished beaches for about 7 percent of construction costs.

Topsail Island, North Carolina, provided another example of wasteful spending. In 1995 at the southern end of Topsail Island a small Corps sidecasting dredge created a new channel to the sea straight through the center of New Topsail Inlet. The natural channel was nowhere near the Corps' channel. It was up against the south end of Topsail Island, whence it wandered its crooked way seaward by heading north along the front of the island for a few hundred yards. In this inlet, used primarily by small recreational boats and maintained only irregularly by the Corps, nature provides a fine but ever-changing channel that wends its way through inlet shoals.

According to a former town councilman who witnessed the dredging, past experience demonstrated that the new channel would not last and that nature would simply revert to the natural channel. In his view, the new Corps channel "would last fifteen minutes." His assumption was that the district "had to spend some year end funds." Although it lasted longer than fifteen minutes, the new channel quickly shoaled and disappeared, while boaters continued to use the natural channel.

A similar dredging procedure produces another "fifteen minute" channel at Bogue Inlet, North Carolina, five inlets to the north of New Topsail Inlet. Dredging in such diverse places as San Francisco Harbor, California; Grays Harbor, Washington; and Pamlico Sound, North Carolina, suggests that the districts, at times at least, are able to maintain funding through unnecessary dredging operations.

- *Require districts to coordinate with state coastal zone management programs and management policies of other federal agencies.* As discussed in several chapters, Corps division and district level engineers have proposed plans contrary to the laws and regulations of coastal states and to the adopted policies of sister agencies. In those states—and on federal lands, for example, where the use of hard structures is prohibited—the Corps should seek alternative ways to solve the local problem.

- *Relieve districts of their current project design responsibilities and replace them with a central design group.* The primary responsibilities of Corps districts should be issuing permits, overseeing construction, and maintaining already constructed projects. In project design district engineers should serve only as a source of local knowledge not as the primary or sole designer as they do currently. District engineers and scientists are, at present, too vulnerable to practice the types of science discussed above: client, dogmatic, and politicized. Removing this responsibility from districts could lead to the formation of a central design group, much as CERC is a central research organization. Besides improving the design effort, a central design group would be more distant from the influence of local politics than districts are at present.

Recommendations to Improve the Interaction among Districts and Coastal Communities

- *Coastal communities must be active partners with the Corps districts in federally funded projects.* In many instances, some described in the preceding chapters, we have seen frustration and dissatisfaction arise between communities and their local Corps district as a direct result of lack of communication. In those situations, communities have generally relied too heavily on district engineers to communicate timely and comprehensive information. District engineers too often do not realize that community leaders and the public do not understand the Corps' jargon and approaches. What are terms of economic convenience for the Corps are actual numbers for most citizens. For instance, the term "fifty-year beach" is understood within the Corps to mean the span of the agency's economic commitment to a replenishment project; to a community, it means how long the beach that was built by the Corps along its shoreline will last.

  In response to our questions during a meeting with Charleston District engineers, the Folly Beach city administrator was shocked to learn for the first time that, because low-cost sand was potentially no longer available, the Corps might have to abandon the project as too costly. Yet this was a possibility that the district had been aware of before the beach was emplaced. If the state of Maine had maintained a close and publicly visible liaison with the Corps' New England Division, acrimony and misunderstanding could perhaps have been avoided. Instead, an angry letter from the state's governor to the Corps' commanding general decried a lack of cooperation.

  Communities should not passively accept Corps project designs, estimates of long-term project costs, or estimates of replenished beach durability. North Myrtle Beach, South Carolina, city officials might well ask the Charleston District why it assumes the nourishment interval of the city beach to be ten years when the eight-year estimated interval at Folly Beach, South Carolina, has proven to be far too long.

Local and state officials should take the initiative and require that Corps officials meet with them regularly and frequently. When possible, communities should hire a qualified independent outside consultant as a liaison with the district.

- *The community perspective must be considered when evaluating the success of a Corps coastal project.* The startlingly different views by the Corps' Charleston District and the Folly Beach city administrator on the success of that community's replenished beach are highly instructive. Folly Beach considers the beach a failure; the Corps considers it a success. Certainly, a fair evaluation of the success of any replenished beach cannot be exclusively an internal federal government affair. It must take community opinion into account.

Recommendations to "Outside" Groups or Agencies Concerned with Scrutiny of the Corps

- *Hindsight of Corps of Engineers coastal management activities must not be done by the Corps.* We recommend that agencies concerned with the quality of Corps science and engineering secure the aid of independent panels of outside experts. Among the many examples of the need for more expert oversight is the recent and egregious "purple book." In 1992, the Office of Management and Budget responded to criticism by asking the Corps to report on its record of success in predicting the costs of replenished beaches. The result was Document IWR report 94-PS-1, entitled Shoreline Protection and Beach Erosion Control Study. We found the 115-page document, sandwiched between striking purple paper covers, to be an outstanding example of the reason the fox should not guard the chicken coop.

  In the report, for reasons that are not at all clear to us, the Corps chooses to underplay the importance of replenishment on the national scene. In determining that only 0.3 percent of the U.S. shoreline has been replenished, the Corps used a lower-forty-eight total shoreline mileage of 37,000 miles and added in the 47,000+ miles of Alaska shore (none of which has been replenished). This shoreline mileage total includes every nook and cranny of the nation's many bays and estuaries, even though, with the exception of the Corpus Christi, Texas, and Harrison County, Mississippi, beaches, replenishment is basically an open-ocean shoreline-stabilization technique. Thus, 0.3

percent is an extremely low percentage, not representative of the actual amount of U.S. artificially replenished shoreline. If one considers only the beachfront mileage along developed shorelines, replenishment becomes a major form of shoreline management. For example, 50 percent of the developed shoreline of east Florida, south of Cape Canaveral, has been replenished or soon will be.

Using data from more than a hundred replenished beaches, the report concludes that the Corps' cost performance has been nothing short of spectacular: "Considering the program as a whole, the actual and estimated costs for those projects . . . are $1,340,900,000 and $1,403,000,000 respectively." Similar success is claimed for the Corps' prediction of required sand volumes: ". . . there has been an actual placement of 72.5 million cubic yards of sand fill compared to an estimated 64.7 million cubic yards."

For both sand volume and costs, the Corps stated that actual and predicted totals fall within 5 percent of one another, but such an optimistic view is unjustified for two reasons:

1. The purple study used misleading predictions. For any Corps project, a whole stream of predictions, estimates, and projections are produced during the course of planning, design, and construction. However, the estimates that should count for hindsighting the Corps' accuracy of predictions, quality of engineering, are those agreed to early on by Congress, the state, and community, and that are used to calculate the cost-benefit analysis that determines which alternative will be taken. These are not the estimates used in the purple report.

2. The purple report fails to take into account whether or not the beach was maintained. For example, the Corps notes correctly that the 1976 Tybee Beach, Georgia, project was under budget in terms of both dollars and sand but fails to note that the beach disappeared within a year and that for ten years (1977–1987) Tybee had no beach. Thus the assertion that Tybee Beach sand-volume and dollar estimates were accurate is meaningless.

The purple report and its shortcomings demonstrate the need for outside review of the Corps' work at every level of project design and subsequent outside evaluation of its performance. Outside review panels should also serve to arbitrate in disagreements between the Corps and its critics. For instance, the Corps produced a fourteen-page, single-spaced, line-by-line response contradicting a two-page letter sent to the OMB criticizing the purple report. What is the OMB to conclude without an independent expert evaluation to discern the veracity of the two viewpoints?

- *Independent scrutiny of individual district projects should be handled by panels of distinguished scientists and engineers.* Every case study in this book, and each of the illustrative examples given in this chapter, indicates an overall need for greater oversight of Corps activities on beaches. We believe that our recommendation to free CERC of its dependent funding relationship with the districts and this final recommendation to provide qualified oversight are particularly critical to the improvement of Corps science and engineering.

  The panels we recommend should comprise scientists and engineers who are respected in their fields of expertise, should be independent of any relationship to the Corps district or the project to be reviewed, and should be familiar (through research or similar experience) with the project area. The costs incurred for such panels should be built into the project costs. The panels should be given a clear directive to evaluate the project's science and the engineering aspects and the validity of the design, not necessarily to make recommendations as to whether the project should be undertaken. Such panels could also be called upon to arbitrate and evaluate criticisms of the Corps' work.

  By far the most successful example of evaluation of a Corps project becoming an integral part of the public debate was the Inman Panel's review of the Oregon Inlet jetty proposal. Although it is still possible at this writing that the jetties will be built, the Inman Panel achieved an unprecedented degree of success. We believe that the Inman Panel was able to engage the district, which local scientists could not, for several reasons: the impanelment by a sister federal agency, which owned the land on which the jetties would be built; the distinguished background of the panel members in their respective fields of expertise; and the fact that all panel members were from out of state (lending an air of objectivity), even though most had some local oceanographic knowledge.

  Another evaluative panel that succeeded in helping the public better understand and consider a Corps district proposal was the National Academy of Science's panel convened to examine alternative methods for saving the Cape Hatteras lighthouse in North Carolina. The 208-foot lighthouse, virtually a symbol of the state of

North Carolina and focal point of the Cape Hatteras National Seashore, is the tallest brick lighthouse in the United States. It was originally built in 1870, 1,500 feet back from the shoreline. Shoreline retreat has since eaten away steadily at the beach fronting it, so that the lighthouse now stands close to destruction.

In 1982 a large storm nearly took the lighthouse. It was saved only by the quick thinking of National Park Service (NPS) personnel, who tore up a parking lot in the middle of the storm and threw it into the sea in front of the structure. The close call precipitated a debate in North Carolina over how to save this landmark.

The alternatives considered were: let the lighthouse fall in; build a seawall; replenish the beach fronting the lighthouse; and move the lighthouse. Replenishment was not considered a viable option because previous replenishment efforts had failed. The Park Service asked the Corps to design and estimate the costs of building a seawall. The Corps' Wilmington District's idea was to surround the lighthouse with a wall and let it go to sea where it would become an offshore island as shoreline retreat continued. In 1985 the construction cost of the seawall was estimated to be $5 million. In public, the Corps reported the low cost of the seawall but failed to mention the extreme costs (buried deep in its report, far from the conclusion and summary sections) of maintaining an island offshore in the highest wave-energy coastal reach on the Atlantic Coast. While NPS estimates for the fifty-year costs maintenance of the seawall as an offshore island ranged from $50 to $100 million, estimates of the costs associated with moving the lighthouse in the late 1980s ranged from $2 to $5 million, with no associated long-term maintenance costs (apart from regular lighthouse maintenance).

In the mid-1980s the National Academy of Sciences and the National Academy of Engineering convened a panel of scientists and engineers, which concluded that if the lighthouse were to be saved, it should be moved. According to Park Service officials, the Corps lobbied for the seawall option, stating repeatedly that the lighthouse would fall apart if moved. The panel's structural engineering experts assured the Park Service that the structure could easily withstand the move.

In November 1995, the Park Service announced a two-step plan to save the lighthouse: move it 100 feet landward and build a large new groin to hold the shoreland in place. Unfortunately, this is only a short-term solution. Whatever the structure's eventual fate, the public gained a better understanding of the alternatives and the consequences of each as a result of the objective analysis provided by the joint National Academy of Sciences and National Academy of Engineering panel.

The panel that we recommend to watchdog specific Corps projects could also be formed under the auspices of the National Academy of Sciences. Or a panel could be congressionally appointed through the Office of Management and Budget or the General Accounting Office. Until the appropriate agency and the mechanisms for convening panels have been established, we recommend that private, nonprofit organizations (such as conservation groups and academic scientific societies) or state or local governments form these panels from among qualified local scientists.

A federal presence on beaches may be important, if only to withstand the pressure from beachfront property owners to build seawalls on beaches when erosion threatens private property. Should the Corps provide that federal presence? Only if reforms are made swiftly. There is an immediate need for greater oversight, better cooperation among federal agencies with coastal management responsibilities, and increased respect for state-level beach preservation policies. We are a society that loves the seashore; we need to be certain that our beaches are receiving the best, most capable management possible.

Glossary

Accretion—The seaward growth of land; opposite of *shoreline erosion* or *shoreline retreat*.

Backwash—The seaward return of a wave in the intertidal zone. Backwash carries sand in a seaward direction.

Barrier Island—An elongate island of sand bounded by *inlets* at either end and separated from the mainland by a *lagoon*. Barrier islands front most of the U.S. coast from Long Island, New York, to the Mexican border.

Barrier Island Migration—A process of island movement caused by rising sea level and/or insufficient sediment supply, in which a barrier island rolls over itself like the tread on a bulldozer. Simultaneous *shoreline retreat* of the open-ocean beach and increase of the land area by *overwash* on the *lagoon* side of the island results in island migration.

Beach—A strip of unconsolidated sand or gravel found at the seaward margin of the coast and accumulated in the zone affected by wave action along the *shoreline* of a body of water.

Beach Replenishment (Beach Nourishment)—The replacement of sand on an eroded beach from an outside source such as an offshore sand deposit, an inlet tidal delta, or an upland sand quarry. One of the responses to *shoreline retreat*.

Berm—A term used by coastal engineers to describe the artificial dune built on the landward side of a replenished beach for the purpose of reducing storm damage to a community.

Borrow Area (Borrow Site)—The source of *beach replenishment* sand. In the early days of replenishment, lagoonal areas behind islands were commonly used as borrow areas. Today, the preferred borrow areas are inlets or offshore sand deposits.

Bulkhead—Relatively low and small seawalls designed not to protect buildings from waves, but to keep land from eroding from behind them.

Closure Depth—The water depth beyond which, it is assumed, little beach sand will be transported in a seaward direction. Typically assumed by coastal engineers (on the U.S. Atlantic and Gulf coasts) to be somewhere between 12 and 30 feet.

Coast—Biologically, the zone where land, ocean, and air interact, extending inland to the limit of tidal or sea spray influence. Politically, the inland limit of the coastal zone varies by state, sometimes defined as the band of counties that border the sea.

Continental Shelf—The section of sea floor between the beach and the point at which the sea floor begins to slope steeply (the upper continental slope). Typically, ocean depth at the edge of the shelf is 300 to 400 feet.

Downdrift—The direction of *net longshore transport* of sand on an annual basis. Analogous to downstream in a river.

Dredge Spoil—Material dredged from channels and harbors.

Dune—A sand hill, landward of the high-tide line formed by the deposition of windblown sand. In coastal areas, dune sand is almost always derived from the beach.

Dynamic Equilibrium—The four major controls that govern a beach: (1) wave and tidal energy; (2) quality and quantity of sediment supply; (3) beach shape and location; and (4) relative sea level. As any of these four factors change, the others adjust accordingly.

Ebb Tidal Delta—The body of sand in a *lagoon* pushed seaward by the outgoing (ebb) tide. The ebb tidal delta is the location of most shipwrecks in inlets.

Estuary—A coastal water body that is connected to the sea so that fresh and salt water mix. Commonly, estuaries occupy former river valleys flooded by the sea during sea level rise.

Flood Tidal Delta—A body of sand that extends into the *lagoon* formed by sand carried by the incoming (flood) tide. Flood tidal deltas add to barrier island width when the inlet migrates or opens somewhere else. The delta is usually colonized by salt marshes or mangroves.

Groin—A wall built perpendicular to the shoreline intended to trap sand traveling laterally in the *surf zone*. It can be built of almost anything and is often successful in building up a beach in place, but, in so doing, it causes a sand deficit and erosion *downdrift*.

Inlet—The waterway that separates *barrier islands* and allows passage between the open ocean and an inland harbor. Inlets generally form during storms, usually when *storm surge ebb* cuts a channel through an island.

Jetty—A shore-perpendicular wall, usually much longer than a *groin*, built at an inlet to stabilize a navigation channel. Usually severely interrupts the longshore transport of sand.

Lagoon—Coastal water body separated from the sea by a low-lying strip of land, often a *barrier island*. Commonly, the term *lagoon* is used interchangeably with *bay estuary* and *sound*.

Littoral Drift—See *longshore current*.

Longshore Current—Longshore currents are *surf zone* currents formed as breaking waves strike the shoreline at an oblique angle, forcing some of the surf zone water to move laterally along the beach. Also called *littoral drift*.

Mathematical Shoreline Model—Mathematical equations intended to describe beach processes that are combined to predict beach behavior.

Nearshore—The innermost continental shelf, comprised of the *surf zone* and the *shoreface*.

Net Direction of Longshore Transport—The direction along a shoreline toward which the *longshore current* carries more sand on an annual basis. Corresponds to *downdrift* direction. Also called the dominant direction.

Newjerseyization—The process of stemming *shoreline retreat* at the price of the beach through *shoreline armoring*. The result is loss of the recreational beach and a completely armored shoreline.

Nourishment Interval—The predicted length of time between necessary additions of sand to a replenished beach, usually based on the assumption that one-third to one-half of the beach will be lost during this time.

Offshore Breakwater—A coastal engineering structure built offshore and parallel to the shore to reduce wave energy and slow *net longshore transport* by forming a *wave shadow* on the beach. Sediment is deposited in the lee of breakwaters such that a *tombolo* may form.

Overwash—The process of waves washing over an island during a storm. Overwash produces deposits of sand called overwash fans that increase island elevation.

Relocation—The practice of moving buildings or infrastructure back from retreating shores, one of the responses to *shoreline retreat*. Includes actually picking up and moving buildings intact, demolishing and rebuilding elsewhere, and rebuilding storm-destroyed buildings elsewhere.

Revetment—A common type of *seawall* built directly on a surface such as the seaward slope of a *dune*. They are frequently constructed of boulders; the large rocks provide ample interstitial cavities that absorb some of the water from a breaking wave, reducing sand-removing *wave reflection* and *backwash*.

Scarp—A small bluff, in the unconsolidated material of a beach, usually parallel to the *shoreline*.

Seawall—A coastal engineering structure built on the beach, parallel to the *shoreline*, intended to protect buildings from wave action.

Shoreface—The *nearshore* zone extending from the low-tide line to a typical water depth of approximately 30 feet.

Shoreline—The wet/dry boundary of the beach, which naturally moves up and down with the tide. For mapping purposes, the shoreline's location is determined by some mean position such as the mid-tide line or mean sea level.

Shoreline Armor—Fixed structures, such as *seawalls*, *groins*, and *offshore breakwaters*, built on the beach and designed to hold the shoreline in place, i.e., to stabilize it. Another term for *stabilization*.

Shoreline Erosion—Land loss caused by wave or wind action. Commonly shoreline erosion is used interchangeably with *shoreline retreat*. The latter is the scientifically preferred term.

Shoreline Retreat—The landward movement of a beach.

Stabilization—One of the human responses to *shoreline retreat*, in which attempts are made to hold the shoreline in place. Stabilization may be "hard" (armoring the shoreline with erosion-control structures) or "soft" (beach replenishment).

Storm Surge—The temporary rise in local sea level caused by a storm.

Storm Surge Ebb—The seaward return flow of storm waters that were forced onto the upland or into the *lagoon*. Usually the ebb starts when winds reverse direction as the storm moves ashore.

Surf Zone—The linear zone adjacent to the beach where waves break. The size of the surf zone varies, widening from several yards in calm weather to hundreds of yards during storms.

Tidal Delta—A body of sand formed at an inlet by tidal currents (see *flood* and *ebb tidal deltas*).

Tombolo—A seaward bulge of the beach connecting the land with an offshore island or to a human-built *offshore breakwater*.

Updrift—The opposite direction from the *net direction of longshore transport* of sand on a beach. Analogous to upstream in a river.

Wave Shadow—A shoreline reach along which waves are blocked or their energy reduced by a natural or human-built obstruction.

Notes

Most of the material directly quoted is referenced below. Additional references can be found in the "Suggested Readings."

page xii: Baker, V. R. "Geomorphological Understanding of Floods." *Geomorphology* 10: 139–156, 1994.

page 2: Platt, R., H. C. Miller, T. Beatley, J. Melville, and B. G. Mathenia, *Coastal Erosion: Has Retreat Sounded?* Boulder: Institute of Behavioral Sciences, University of Colorado, 1992.

page 9: Williams, Lt. Gen. A. E. "Corps of Engineers: Relying on Research to Save Dollars." *Sea Technology* (January 1994): 34–35.

page 10–11: U.S. Army Corps of Engineers. *Six Steps to a Civil Works Project.* Brochure #EP1105-2-10, May 1990.

page 45: Basco, D. R. "Boundary Conditions and Long-Term Shoreline Changes Rates for the Southern Virginia Ocean Coastline." *Shore and Beach* 59: 8–13, 1991.

page 48: Tait, J. F., and G. B. Griggs. "Beach Response to the Presence of a Seawall: A Comparison of Field Observations." *Shore and Beach* 58: 11–28, 1990.

page 68: Thieler, E. R., A. L. Brill, W. J. Cleary, C. H. Hobbs III, and R. A. Gammisch. "Geology of the Wrightsville Beach, North Carolina Shoreface: Implications for the Concept of the Shoreface Profile of Equilibrium." *Marine Geology* 126: 271–287, 1995.

page 69: Moore, B. "Beach Profile Evolution in Response to Changes in Water Level and Wave Height." M.S. Thesis, Department of Ocean Engineering, University of Delaware, Newark, 1982.

page 69: Hayes, M. O. "Hurricanes as Geologic Agents: Case Studies of Hurricanes Carla, 1961, and Cindy, 1963." *University of Texas Bureau of Economic Geology,* Rept. Inv. No 61, 1967.

page 70: Gayes, P. T. "Post-Hurricane Hugo Nearshore Side Scan Sonar Survey; Myrtle Beach to Folly Beach, South Carolina." *Journal of Coastal Research* SI#8: 95–111, 1991.

page 70: Wright, L. D. *Morphodynamics of Inner Continental Shelves.* Boca Raton: CRC Press, 1995.

page 72: Smith, A.W.S. "The Coastal Engineering Literature and the Field Engineer." *Journal of Coastal Research* 10: iii–viii, 1994.

page 73: Baker, V. R. "Geomorphological Understanding of Floods." *Geomorphology* 10: 139–156, 1994.

page 77: "Was Miami Beach Worth Saving?" *Florida Trend,* September 1985.

page 85: Michael Stephens, consulting engineer, personal communication, 1994.

page 93: Komar, P. D. *Beach Processes and Sedimentation.* Englewood Cliffs, N. J.: Prentice-Hall, 1976.

page 94: The Honorable Mike Synar, U.S. House of Representatives, personal communication, 1989.

page 96–97: Nordheimer, J. "Beach Project to Pump Sand and Money." *The New York Times,* March 12, 1994.

page 98: Figdore, S. "Sea Devouring Tons of Sand." *Asbury Park Free Press,* July 1995.

page 98: Sharkey, J. "A Town Draws Lines in the Shifting Sand." *The New York Times,* July 16, 1995.

page 98: Nordheimer, J. "Despite Costly Efforts by Army Engineers, a Beach in New Jersey Continues to Erode." *The New York Times,* August 15, 1995.

page 98: Johnson, T. "Surf Calmer as Debate Swells." *Newark Star Ledger,* August 21, 1995.

page 99: Daniel, J. "Dance of Denial: Threats to Salmon in the Columbia River Basin." *Sierra* 78: 64–75, 1993.

page 106: "Beach Erosion at Folly Beach, S.C." Letter from the Secretary of War, Douglas MacArthur. House Document 156, 74th Congress, 1st Session, Washington, D.C., April 1935. (The MacArthur Report)

page 109: Stringer-Robinson, G. *Time and Tide on Folly Beach, South Carolina.* Folly Beach, S. C: Gretchen Stringer-Robinson, 1989.

pages 113, 115, 118: Vicki Zick, City of Folly Beach, S. C. personal communication, 1994.

page 121: Paul Gayes, Coastal Carolina College, personal communication, 1994.

page 123: Vicki Zick, City of Folly Beach, S. C., personal communication, 1992.

page 132: Alperin, L. M. *History of the Gulf Intracoastal Waterway.* Navigation History NWS–83–9, National Waterways Study, U.S. Army Engineer Water Resources Support Center, Institute for Water Resources, Washington, D.C., 1983.

page 133: Robert Morton, University of Texas, personal communication, 1994.

page 136: Spear, M. J., Regional Director, U.S. Fish and Wildlife Service, 1991. Unpublished letter to Lt. Colonel James E. Arenz, U.S. Army Corps of Engineers Galveston District, Galveston, Tex., June 14, 1991.

page 140: Reid, W. V., and M. C. Trexler. *Drowning the National Heritage: Climate Change and U.S. Coastal Biodiversity.* Washington, D.C.: World Resources Institute, 1991.

page 140–141: Robert Morton, University of Texas, personal communication, 1993.

page 142: Ohman, J. P., The Coalition to Save the Gulf Intracoastal Waterway. Unpublished letter to Dr. Robert Morton, Bureau of Economic Geology, Austin, Tex., November 2, 1992.

page 147: National Park Service. *National Natural Landmarks Program.* Federal Register, Vol. 52, No. 35, 36 CFR Ch 1 (7 - 1 - 85 version), §62.1 – § 62.9. Washington, D.C., Monday, February 23, 1987.

page 147: Miller, J. R., Associate Regional Director, Management and Operations, National Park Service, Department of the Interior. Statement before the U.S. House of Representatives Committee on Interior and Insular Affairs, Subcommittee on Oversight and Investigations. Washington, D.C., June 22, 1990.

page 148: Stull, J. Directer, Presque Isle Audobon Society. Testimony before the U.S. House of Representatives Committee on Interior and Insular Affairs, Subcommittee on Oversight and Investigation. Washington, D.C., June 22, 1990.

page 148: Bissell, J. K., Curator of Botany, The Cleveland Museum of Natural History. Unpublished letter to Arthur A. Davis, Secretary, Department of Environmental Resources, Harrisburg, Pa., February 22, 1989.

page 156: McKinney, B. "Army Corps Certain Breakwall Idea Sound." *The Times-News Weekender,* Erie, Pa., Saturday, February 18, 1989.

page 156: "Breakwalls Protect Beaches." *Erie Daily Times,* Erie, Pa., Thursday, February 23, 1989.

page 159: Haurwitz, R. "Erie Beach Project Weathers Criticism." *The Pittsburgh Press,* Sunday, April 30, 1989.

page 163: "Breakwalls Protect Beaches." *Erie Daily Times,* Erie, Pa., Thursday, February 23, 1989.

page 163: McKinney, B. "Army Corps Certain Breakwall Idea Sound." *The Times-News Weekender,* Erie, Pa., Saturday, February 18, 1989.

page 164: Bissell, J. K., Curator of Botany, The Cleveland Museum of Natural History. Unpublished letter to Arthur A. Davis, Secretary, Department of Environmental Resources, Harrisburg, Pa., February 22, 1989.

page 164: Haurwitz, R. "Erie Beach Project Weathers Criticism." *The Pittsburgh Press,* Sunday, April 30, 1989.

page 164: National Park Service. *National Natural Landmark Status Report, Part II. Information on Threat or Damage Reported.* Reports to the National Park Service filed by E. C. Masteller, Landmark Patron. Washington, D.C., June 4, 1986 and June 15, 1988.

page 165: Kostmayer, Rep. P. H. *Presque Isle: Protecting a National Natural Landmark.* Opening Statement before the U.S. House of Representatives Committee on Interior and Insular Affairs, Subcommittee on Oversight and Investigations, Washington, D.C., June 22, 1990.

page 165: Kershner, B., Field Coordinator, Great Lakes United. Testimony before the U.S. House of Representatives Committee on Interior and Insular Affairs, Subcommittee on Oversight and Investigations, Washington, D.C., June 22, 1990.

page 165: Stull, J., Director, Presque Isle Audubon Society. Testimony before the U.S. House of Representatives Committee on Interior and Insular Affairs, Subcommittee on Oversight and Investigations. Washington, D.C., June 22, 1990.

page 165: Andrezeski, Senator A. *Presque Isle: Protecting a National Natural Landmark.* Statement before the U.S. House of Representatives Committee on Interior and Insular Affairs, Subcommittee on Oversight and Investigations. Washington, D.C., June 22, 1990.

page 166: Daly, W. R., and J. Pope. *Detached Breakwaters for Shore Protection: Final Report.* Coastal Engineering Research Center, U.S. Army Corps of Engineers Waterways Experiment Station, Vicksburg, Miss., 1986.

page 168: National Society of Professional Engineers. *Shoreline Erosion Control on Presque Isle Peninsula Named Outstanding Engineering Achievement.* National Society of Professional Engineers, Alexandria, Va., January 12, 1994.

page 169: C. Dean, *The New York Times,* personal communication, 1993.

page 169: Kinal, B. "Army Corps Earns Praise for Peninsula Breakwaters." *Erie Daily Times,* Erie, Pa., December 28, 1993.

page 170: Kinal, B. "Army Corps Earns Praise for Peninsula Breakwaters." *Erie Daily Times,* Erie, Pa., December 28, 1993.

page 170: Plerzynski, J. "Are the Peninsula Breakwalls Working? Presque Isle Superintendent gives them Thumbs Up for Now." *Millcreek Sun,* week of August 7, 1994.

page 184: J. Kelley, University of Maine, personal communication, 1993.

page 185: J. Kelley, University of Maine, personal communication, 1993.

page 186: Kelley, J. T., and W. A. Anderson. "The Maine Shore and the Army Corps: A Tale of Two Harbors, Wells and Saco, Maine." *Maine Policy Review,* in review.

page 187: J. Kelley, University of Maine, personal communication, 1993.

page 187: Marriott, D. C., State of Maine, Department of Environmental Protection, Augusta, Maine. Unpublished letter to Col. Phillip R. Harris, U.S. Army Corps of Engineers, New England Division. May 21, 1992.

page 187–188: McKernan, Jr., Governor J. R. Unpublished letter to Lt. General Henry J. Hatch, Chief of Engineers, U.S. Army Corps of Engineers. Augusta, Maine, May 28, 1992.

page 189: Miller, B. P., U.S. Army Corps of Engineers, New England Division. Unpublished letter to Robert Blakesley, State Planning Office, State of Maine. With: Modified Scope of Work and Time and Cost Estimates to Perform a Physical Model Study of Camp Ellis Beach, Saco Bay, Maine. Waltham, Mass., 1993.

page 189: Kelley, J. T., and W. A. Anderson. "The Maine Shore and the Army Corps: A Tale of Two Harbors, Wells and Saco, Maine." *Maine Policy Review,* in review.

page 189: J. Kelley, University of Maine, personal communication, 1993.

page 190: Kelley, J. T., and W. A. Anderson. "The Maine Shore and the Army Corps: A Tale of Two Harbors, Wells and Saco, Maine." *Maine Policy Review,* in review.

page 191: Benton, S. "Calvin Midgett's Long Day." *Carolina Notebook,* Vol. 7, No. 4. Division of Conservation Education, North Carolina Wildlife Resources Commission, Raleigh, N. C., February 1988.

page 198: North Carolina Coastal Federation. "Summary of Proceedings" from a forum on the proposed jetties for Oregon Inlet held in Kill Devil Hills, N. C. Swansboro, N. C., July 8, 1988.

page 200: Babington, C.. "Reagan rejects Martin's appeal for Oregon Inlet jetties." *The News and Observer,* Raleigh, N. C., Tuesday, September 13, 1988.

page 201: Environmental Defense Fund, Environmental Policy Institute, Friends of the Earth, Isaak Walton League of America, National Audubon Society, National Parks and Conservation Association, National Recreation and Park Association, National Wildlife Federation, Sierra Club, and The Wilderness Society. *Oregon Inlet Jetties will Harm National Seashore and Wildlife Refuge.* Joint statement and fact sheet with cover letter to members of the U.S. House of Representatives, Washington, D.C., 1984.

page 201: North Carolina Beach Buggy Association. "Jetties—What the Dare Press Didn't Tell." *The Coastland Times,* Manteo, N. C., May 23, 1985.

page 201: Jenner, M., Executive Secretary, N. C. Academy of Science, Inc., Raleigh, N. C. Letter to Col. R. K. Hughes, U.S. Army Corps of Engineers, Wilmington District, Wilmington, N. C. May 6, 1981.

page 201: Hughes, R. K., Colonel, U.S. Army Corps of Engineers, Wilmington District, Wilmington, N. C., Letter to Dr. Martha G. Jenner, Executive Secretary, North Carolina Academy of Science, Inc., Raleigh, N.C. March 19, 1981.

page 203: Hunter, K. *Big "Fish Story" in Corps' Plans for Jetties at Oregon Inlet: Basic Errors Alleged in Economic Analysis.* Press Release, Washington, D.C.

page 205: Kearney/Centaur Company. *A Reassessment of the Economic Feasibility of the Oregon Inlet Project.* DACW 54-87-C-0029. Prepared for The Institute for Water Resources, U.S. Army Corps of Engineers. A.T. Kearney, Inc., Raleigh, N. C., 1987.

page 205: Campbell, D. C. *The Economics of Environmental Policy with Respect to the Oregon Inlet Jetties.* American Water Resources Association Symposium on Coastal Water Resources. Wilmington, N. C., May 22–25, 1988.

page 205: Kemmerer, A. J., Regional Director, Southeast Region, National Marine Fisheries Service, St. Petersburg, Florida. Letter to Frank Reynolds, Chief, Planning Division, Wilmington District, U.S. Army Corps of Engineers, Wilmington, N. C., June 2, 1995.

page 206: North Carolina Division of Marine Fisheries. *Review of Commercial Fisheries Landings Projections and Status of Fishery Management Plans for the Oregon Inlet, North Carolina Area.* Division of Marine Fisheries, North Carolina Department of Environment, Health, and Natural Resources, Morehead City, N. C., December 1994.

page 206: National Marine Fisheries Service. *Comments on Oregon Inlet Project* (unpublished report). Southeast Regional Office, National Marine Fisheries Service, National Oceanic and Atmospheric Administration, St. Petersburg, Fla., 1995.

page 207: "Dredging Won't Do Job At Inlet, Say Engineers." *The Coastland Times,* Kill Devil Hills, N. C., Tuesday, January 18, 1983.

page 207: Oregon Inlet Technical Observation Committee. *The Dredging Only Alternative for Oregon Inlet.* U.S. Department of the Interior, Washington, D.C., April 26, 1992.

page 207: Hunter, K. *New Errors Riddle Corps' New Economic 'Justification' for Building Jetties on North Carolina's Coast.* Unpublished white paper, Washington, D.C., September 25, 1984.

page 209: U.S. Army Corps of Engineers. *Manteo (Shallowbag) Bay, North Carolina: Feature Design Memorandum; Sand Bypassing (Management).* Wilmington District, U.S. Army Corps of Engineers, Wilmington, N. C., 1994.

page 212: Pietrafesa, L. J., and G. S. Janowitz. "Physical Oceanographic Processes Affecting Larval Transport around and through North Carolina Inlets." Pages 34–50 in *American Fisheries Society Symposium 3.* Bethesda, Md: American Fisheries Society, 1988.

page 213: Kemmerer, A. J., Regional Director, National Marine Fisheries Service, Southeast Region, St. Petersburg, Florida. Response to letter of June 4, 1991 from L. W. Saunders, Chief, Planning Division, U.S. Army Corps of Engineers, Wilmington District, Wilmington, N. C., July 19, 1991.

page 217: North Carolina Department of Transportation. *Environmental Assessment and Finding of No Significant Impact for Construction of a Terminal Groin and Revetment at Pea Island, Dare County, N.C.* North Carolina Department of Transportation, Raleigh, N. C., 1989.

page 218: U.S. Fish and Wildlife Service. *Right of Way Permit to Provide Protection of Bonner Bridge and North Carolina Highway 12, Dare County, North Carolina.* Environmental Assessment, U.S. Fish and Wildlife Service, Southeast Region, Department of the Interior, Atlanta, Ga., June 1989.

page 218: Dolan, R. Unpublished comments on the proposed construction of a terminal groin at Oregon Inlet, 1989.

page 220: Carter, L. J. *The Florida Experience: Land and water policy in a growth state.* Baltimore: Johns Hopkins University Press, 1974.

page 220: Cullimore, D. "Restoration of a River." *Sierra* 70: 18–23, 1985.

page 220: Hamilton, J. "Hard Corps Revival on the Kissimmee: Can the Army's Engineers March to Nature's Drummer?." *Sierra* 77: 71–74, 1992.

page 220: Toner, M. "Fixing a Broken River." *National Wildlife* 29: 18, 1991.

page 222: Sport Fishing Institute. "The Greening of the Corps?" *SFI Bulletin,* 434, Washington, D.C., May 1992.

page 222: Davis, N. D. "The Greening of the Corps." *American Forests.* (July/August 1992): 13–16.

page 223: T. Jarrett, U.S. Army Corps of Engineers, Wilmington District, unpublished presentation before the North Carolina Coastal Resources Commission, 1989.

page 223: Dieffenbach, W. H. "War and Peace on Truman Dam." *Missouri Conservationist,* (June 1991): 9–13.

page 224: Barber, H. E. and A. R. Gann. *A History of the Savannah District U.S. Army Corps of Engineers.* Savannah District, U.S. Army Corps of Engineers, Savannah, Ga., 1989.

page 224: Moser, D. "Dig They Must, the Army Engineers, Securing Allies and Acquiring Enemies." *Smithsonian* 7: 40–51, 1976.

page 224: Chang, S. "Tenn-Tom versus the Mississippi River." *Transportation Journal* 25: 47–48, 1986.

page 224: Stine, J. K. "Environmental Politics in the American South: the Fight over the Tennessee-Tombigbee Waterway." *Environmental History Review* 15: 1–24., 1991

page 225: Stine, J. K. *Mixing the Waters: Environment, Politics, and the Building of the Tennessee-Tombigbee Waterway.* Akron, Ohio: The University of Akron Press, 1993.

page 225: Carroll, J. L. "Tennessee-Tombigbee Waterway Revisited." *Transportation Journal* 22: 5–20, 1982.

page 227: McCormick, L. R., O. H. Pilkey, Jr., W. J. Neal, and O. H. Pilkey Sr. *Living with Long Island's South Shore.* Durham, N.C.: Duke University Press, 1984.

page 227–228: Winerap, M. "Beach Erosion: Nature vs. Shortsighted Man." *The New York Times,* June 12, 1993.

page 228: "U.S. to Spend $80 Million to Restore a Barrier Island." *The New York Times,* November 1, 1994.

page 229: McQuiston, J. T. "Erosion Pact Could Help Other Beaches Around U.S." *The New York Times,* 1995.

page 229: Norheimer, J. "Despite Costly Efforts, a New Jersey Beach Erodes." *The New York Times,* August 15, 1995.

page 232: U.S. Army Corps of Engineers. "Line-by-Line Critique of Professor Orrin Pilkey. Letter dated June 3, 1994 to Mr. Bruce Long, Office of Management and Budget," unpublished memorandum (no date).

page 233: Ashley, G. M., and S. D. Halsey. "Littoral Sediment Dispersal of Materials Dredged from Barnegat Inlet used as Beach Nourishment on the Northern End of Long Beach Island, NJ." *New Jersey Marine Science Consortium Abstracts, 1980–81.* New Jersey Marine Science Consortium, 1981.

page 233: P. Gayes, Coastal Carolina College, personal communication, 1994.

page 233: E. Robert Thieler, Duke University Department of Geology, personal communication, 1995.

page 239: U.S. Army Corps of Engineers. *Shoreline Protection and Beach Erosion Control Study; Phase I: Cost Comparison of Shoreline Protection Projects of the U.S. Army Corps of Engineers,* IWR Report 94–PS–1. Shoreline Protection and Beach Erosion Control Task Force, U.S. Army Corps of Engineers, Alexandria, Va., 1994. (The "purple report").

page 242: U.S. Army Corps of Engineers. *Seawall and Revetment Design for Long-Term Protection of Cape Hatteras Lighthouse, North Carolina.* Prepared for the National Park Service, Cape Hatteras National Seashore, by the Wilmington District, U.S. Army Corps of Engineers, Wilmington, N. C., November 1985.

Suggested Readings

Chapter 1. America and the Beach

Baker, V. R. "Geomorphological Understanding of Floods." *Geomorphology* 10: 139–156, 1994.

Davis Jr., R. A. *Coasts*. Upper Saddle River, N. J.: Prentice-Hall, 1996.

———. *The Evolving Coast*. New York: Scientific American Library, 1994.

Kaufman, W., and O. H. Pilkey, Jr. *The Beaches are Moving: The Drowning of America's Shoreline*. Durham: Duke University Press, 1983.

Moore, J. W., and D. P. Moore. "The Corps of Engineers and Beach Erosion Control 1930–1982." *Shore and Beach* 51: 13–17, 1983.

———. *The Army Corps of Engineers and the Evolution of Federal Flood Plain Management Policy*. Boulder: Institute of Behavioral Sciences, University of Colorado, 1989.

National Strategy for Beach Preservation: Second Skidaway of Oceanography Conference on America's Eroding Shoreline, J. D. Howard, W. Kaufman, and O. H. Pilkey, conference convenors, Savannah, Ga., June 1985.

Parkman, A. *Army Engineers in New England: The Military and Civil Work of the Corps of Engineers in New England 1775–1975*. Waltham, Mass.: New England Division, U.S. Army Corps of Engineers, 1978.

Platt, R., H. C. Miller, T. Beatley, J. Melville, B. G. Mathenia. *Coastal Erosion: Has Retreat Sounded?* Boulder: Institute of Behavioral Sciences, University of Colorado, 1992.

Chapter 2. Coastal Processes and What to Do about Them

Carter, R. W. G. *Coastal Environments: An Introduction to the Physical, Ecological and Cultural Systems of Coastlines*. London: Academic Press, 1988.

Carter, R. W. G., and C. D. Woodroffe, ed. *Coastal Evolution: Late Quaternary Shoreline Morphodynamics*. Cambridge: Cambridge University Press, 1994.

Fox, W. T. *At the Sea's Edge: An Introduction to Coastal Oceanography for the Amateur Naturalist*. New York: Prentice-Hall Press, 1983.

Hall, M. J., and O. H. Pilkey. "Effects of Hard Stabilization on Dry Beach Width for New Jersey." *Journal of Coastal Research* 7: 771–785, 1991.

King, C. A. M. *Beaches and Coasts*. New York: St. Martin's Press, 1972.

Leatherman, S. *Barrier Island Handbook*. College Park: Laboratory for Coastal Research, University of Maryland, 1988.

Niederoda, A. W., D. J. P. Swift, A. G. Figueiredo, and G. L. Freeland. "Barrier

Island Evolution, Middle Atlantic Shelf, USA." *Marine Geology* 63: 363–396, 1985.

Pilkey, O. H. "Coastal Erosion" *Episodes* 14: 46–51, 1991.

Pilkey, O. H., and E. R. Thieler. "Erosion of the United States Shoreline." Pages 3–7 in *Quarternary Coasts of the United States: Marine and Lacustrine Systems*, eds. C. H. Fletcher III and J. F. Wehmiller. Society for Sedimentary Geology, Special Publication 48. Tulsa, Okla: Society for Sedimentary Geology, 1992.

Pilkey, O. H., and H. L. Wright III. "Seawalls Versus Beaches." *Journal of Coastal Research* SI: 41–64, 1988.

Reid, W. V., and M. C. Trexler. *Drowning the National Heritage: Climate Change and U.S. Coastal Biodiversity*. Washington, D.C.: World Resources Institute, 1991.

Swift, D. J. P. "Continental Shelf Sedimentation." Pages 311–350 in *Marine Sediment Transport and Environmental Management*, eds. D. J. Stanley and D. J. P. Swift. New York: Wiley, 1976.

Tait, J. F., and G. B. Griggs. "Beach Response to the Presence of a Seawall: A Comparison of Field Observations." *Shore and Beach* 58: 11–28, 1990.

Thieler, E. R., R. S. Young, and O. H. Pilkey, Jr. "Discussion of: 'Boundary Conditions and Long-Term Shoreline Changes Rates for the Southern Virginia Ocean Coastline." *Shore and Beach* 60: 29–30, 1992.

Wright, L. D. *Morphodynamics of Inner Continental Shelves*. Boca Raton: CRC Press, 1995.

Wright, L. D., J. D. Boon, S. C. Kim, and J. H. List. "Modes of Cross-Shore Sediment Transport on the Shoreface of the Middle Atlantic Bight." *Marine Geology* 96: 19–51, 1991.

Chapter 3. Beaches by the Numbers

Dean, R. G. "Equilibrium Beach Profiles: Characteristics and Applications." *Journal of Coastal Research* 7: 53–84, 1991.

Hanson, H., and N. C. Kraus. "GENESIS: Generalized Model for Simulating Shoreline Change." Technical Report CERC–89–19. Coastal Engineering Research Center, U.S. Army Corps of Engineers Waterways Experiment Station, Vicksburg, Miss., 1989.

Larson, M., and N. C. Kraus. "SBEACH: Numerical Model for Simulating Storm-Induced Beach Change." Technical Report CERC–89–9. Coastal Engineering Research Center, U.S. Army Corps of Engineers Waterways Experiment Station, Vicksburg, Miss., 1989.

Morton, R. A. "Formation of Storm Deposits by Wind-Forced Currents in the Gulf of Mexico and the North Sea." Pages 385–396 in *Holocene Marine Sedimentation in the North Sea Basin*, ed. S. D. Nio. International Association of Sedimentologists, Special Publication No. 5. Copenhagen: International Association of Sedimentologists, 1981.

Pilkey, Jr., O. H. "Mathematical Modeling of Beach Behavior Doesn't Work." *Journal of Geological Education* 42: 358–361, 1994.

Pilkey, O. H., R. S. Young, D. M. Bush, and E. R. Thieler. "Predicting the Behavior of Beaches: Alternatives to Models." Pages 53–60 in *Littoral 94: Proceedings of the Second International Symposium of the European Coastal Zone Association for Science and Technology,* eds. S. de Carvalho and V. Gomes. Instituto de Hidráulica e Recursos Hídricos, Faculdade de Engenharia da Universidade do Porto, Portugal, 1994.

Pilkey, O. H., R. S. Young, S. R. Riggs, A. W. S. Smith, W. Huiyan, and W. D. Pilkey, "The Concept of Shoreface Profile of Equilibrium: A Critical Review" *Journal of Coastal Research* 9: 255–278, 1993.

Thieler, E. R., A. L. Brill, W. J. Cleary, C. H. Hobbs III, and R. A. Gammisch, "Geology of the Wrightsville Beach, North Carolina Shoreface: Implications for the Concept of the Shoreface Profile of Equilibrium." *Marine Geology* 126: 271–287, 1995.

Titus, J. G., and V. K. Narayanan. *The Probability of Sea Level Rise.* EPA 230-R-95-008, U.S. Environmental Protection Agency, Washington, D.C., 1995.

Young, R. S., O. H. Pilkey, D. M. Bush, and E. R. Thieler. "A Discussion of the Generalized Model for Simulating Shoreline Change (GENESIS)." *Journal of Coastal Research* 11: 875–886, 1995.

Chapter 4. Beach Replenishment

Clayton, T. D. "Beach Replenishment Activities on U.S Continental Pacific Coast." *Journal of Coastal Research* 7: 1195–1210, 1991.

Dixon, K. L., and O. H. Pilkey, Jr. "Beach Replenishment along the U.S. Coast of the Gulf of Mexico." Pages 2007–2020 in *Coastal Zone '89: Proceedings of the Sixth Symposium on Coastal and Ocean Management,* eds. O. T. Magoon, H. Converse, D. Miner, L. T. Tobin, and D. Clark. New York: American Society of Civil Engineers, 1989.

———. "Summary of Beach Replenishment on the U.S. Gulf of Mexico Shoreline." *Journal of Coastal Research* 7: 249–256, 1991.

Houston, J. R. "Beachfill Performance." *Shore and Beach* 59: 15–24, 1991.

Leonard, L., T. D. Clayton, K. Dixon, and O. H. Pilkey, "U.S. Beach Replenishment Experience: A Comparison of the Atlantic, Pacific, and Gulf Coasts." Pages 1994–2006 in *Coastal Zone '89: Proceedings of the Sixth Symposium on Coastal and Ocean Management,* eds. O. T. Magoon, H. Converse, D. Miner, L. T. Tobin, and D. Clark. New York: American Society of Civil Engineers, 1989.

Leonard, L., T. Clayton, and O. H. Pilkey. "An Analysis of Replenished Beach Design Parameters on U.S. East Coast Barrier Islands." *Journal of Coastal Research* 6: 15–36, 1990.

Leonard, L., K. L. Dixon, and O. H. Pilkey. "A Comparison of Beach Replenishment on the U.S. Atlantic, Pacific, and Gulf Coasts." *Journal of Coastal Research* SI: 127–140, 1990.

Pilkey, O. H. "A 'Thumbnail Method' for Beach Communities: Estimation of Long–Term Beach Replenishment Requirements." *Shore and Beach* 56: 23–31, 1988.

———. "The Engineering of Sand." *Journal of Geological Education* 37: 308–311, 1989.

———. "Another View of Beachfill Performance." *Shore and Beach* 60: 20–25, 1992.

Pilkey, O. H., and T. D. Clayton. "Beach Replenishment: The National Solution?" Pages 1408–1419 in *Coastal Zone '87: Proceedings of the Fifth Symposium on Coastal and Ocean Management*, eds. O. T. Magoon, H. Converse, D. Miner, L. T. Tobin, D. Clark, and G. Domurat. New York: American Society of Civil Engineers, 1987.

——— "Summary of Beach Replenishment Experience on U.S. East Coast Barrier Islands" *Journal of Coastal Research* 5: 147–159, 1989.

Pilkey, O. H., and K. Dixon. Testimony of Orrin H. Pilkey, Jr., before the Environment, Energy, and Natural Resources Subcommittee of the House Committee on Government Operations, Washington, D.C., April 28, 1989.

U.S. Army Corps of Engineers. *Shore Protection Manual, Volumes I and II.* Coastal Engineering Research Center, U.S. Army Corps of Engineers Waterways Experiment Station, Vicksburg, Miss., 1984.

Chapter 5. Folly Beach: Reclaimed Heyday?

Hales, L. Z., M. R. Byrnes, and P. J. Neilans. "Evaluation of Beach Fill Response to Storm Induced and Long-Term Erosional Forces, Folly Beach, S.C." Technical Report, CERC-91. Coastal Engineering Research Center, U.S. Army Corps of Engineers Waterways Experiment Station, Vicksburg, Miss., 1991.

Neal, W. J., W. C. Blakeney, O. H. Pilkey, Jr., and O. H. Pilkey, Sr. *Living with the South Carolina Shore.* Durham: Duke University Press, 1984.

Stringer-Robinson, G. *Time and Tide on Folly Beach, South Carolina.* Folly Beach, S. C.: Gretchen Stringer-Robinson, 1989.

U.S. Army Corps of Engineers. "Folly Beach General Design Memorandum," Charleston District, U.S. Army Corps of Engineers, Charleston, S.C., 1991.

Chapter 6. Sargent Beach, Texas

Alperin, L. M. *Custodians of the Coast: History of the United States Army Engineers at Galveston.* Galveston, Tex.: U.S. Army Corps of Engineers, 1977.

————. *History of the Gulf Intracoastal Waterway.* Navigation History NWS–83–9, National Waterways Study, U.S. Army Engineer Water Resources Support Center, Institute for Water Resources, Washington, D.C., 1983.

Carver, R. D., W. J. Dubose, J. M. Heggins, and B. J. Wright. "Revetment Stability Tests for Sargent Beach, Texas." Technical Report CERC-93-14. Prepared for U.S. Army Engineer District, Galveston. Coastal Engineering Research Center, U.S. Army Corps of Engineers Waterways Experiment Station, Vicksburg, Miss., 1993.

King, B. D., and R. Bisbee. "Planning Aid Report on the Section 216 Study, Gulf Intracoastal Waterway—Texas Section Sabine Lake to Matagorda Bay." U.S. Fish and Wildlife Service, Department of the Interior, Galveston, Tex., 1989.

Morton, R. A., O. H. Pilkey Jr., O. H. Pilkey Sr., and W. J. Neal. *Living with the Texas Shore.* Durham: Duke University Press, 1983.

U.S. Army Corps of Engineers, Galveston District. "Gulf Intracoastal Waterway, Section 216 Study, Sargent Beach, Texas; Feasibility Report and Final Environmental Impact Study." Southwestern Division, U.S. Army Corps of Engineers, Galveston, Tex., February 1992.

Chapter 7. Presque Isle: The End of a Beach

Bissell, J. K. "Rare Plants and Rare Plant Communities of Presque Isle." *Bartonia* 57: 2–8, 1993.

"Breakwall Hopes." *The Meadville Tribune.* Meadville, Pa., Friday, February 3, 1989.

Bureau of Resources Programming and Bureau of State Parks. *Presque Isle "Yesterday," "Today," "Tomorrow".* Department of Environmental Resources, Commonwealth of Pennsylvania, Harrisburg, Pa., 1979.

Carter, C. H., W. J. Neal, W. S. Haras, and O. H. Pilkey Jr. *Living with the Lake Erie Shore.* Durham: Duke University Press, 1987.

Daly, W. R., and J. Pope. *Detached Breakwaters for Shore Protection: Final Report.* Coastal Engineering Research Center, U.S. Army Corps of Engineers Waterways Experiment Station, Vicksburg, Miss., 1986.

Drescher, N. M. *Engineers for the Public Good: A History of the Buffalo District U.S. Army Corps of Engineers.* Buffalo, N. Y.: Buffalo District, U.S. Army Corps of Engineers, 1982.

Johnson, D. "Corps Protects Eroding Lake Erie Shore." *Engineer Update,* Vol. 17, January 1993.

Knuth, P. "Alternative Strategies for Beach Nourishment: Presque Isle Peninsula." Unpublished report to the Presque Isle State Park Advisory Committee. Erie, Pa., 1987.

Moffat & Nichol Engineers. "Evaluation of Segmented Offshore Breakwaters for Beach Stabilization at Presque Isle State Park, Erie, Pennsylvania." Report presented to Commonwealth of Pennsylvania, Department of Environmental Resources. Moffat & Nichol Engineers, Raleigh, N. C., 1988.

Office of Resources Management, Bureau of State Parks. *Recreational Guide for Presque Isle State Park.* Bureau of State Parks, Department of Environmental Resources, Commonwealth of Pennsylvania, Harrisburg, Pa., 1990.

Pennsylvania Geological Survey. "Pennsylvania Trail of Geology: Presque Isle State Park, Erie County; A Dynamic Interface of Water and Land." Park Guide 21. Bureau of Topographic and Geologic Survey and Bureau of State Parks, Department of Environmental Resources, Commonwealth of Pennsylvania, Harrisburg, Pa., 1991.

U.S. Army Corps of Engineers. *Shoreline Erosion Control Project, Phase II, General Design Memorandum, Detailed Project Design, Presque Isle Peninsula, Erie, Pennsylvania.* Buffalo District, U.S. Army Corps of Engineers, Buffalo, N. Y., April 1986.

————. *Addendum: Shoreline Erosion Control Project at Presque Isle Peninsula, Erie, Pennsylvania.* Buffalo District, U.S. Army Corps of Engineers, Buffalo, N. Y., July 1986.

Chapter 8. Camp Ellis, Maine

Coastal Engineering Research Center. "Assessment of Coastal Processes in Saco Bay, Maine, with Emphasis on Camp Ellis Beach." Coastal Engineering Research Center, U.S. Army Corps of Engineers Waterways Experiment Station, Vicksburg, Miss., December 1991.

Farrell, S. C. "Present Coastal Processes, Recorded Changes, and the Post-Pleistocene Geologic Record of Saco Bay, Maine." Unpublished Ph.D. thesis. University of Massachusetts, 1972.

Farrell, S. C. "Sediment Distribution and Hydrodynamics, Saco River and Scarboro Estuaries, Maine." Contribution #6, University of Massachusetts, 1972.

Kelley, J. A., D. F. Belknap, D. M. FitzGerald, L. K. Fink, S. M. Dickson, D. C. Barber, S. Van Heteren, and P. A. Manthorp. "A Sand Budget for Saco Bay, Maine." Report to Maine–New Hampshire Sea Grant College Program and Maine Geological Survey, Open-File Report in press.

Kelley, J. T., and W. A. Anderson. "The Maine Shore and the Army Corps: A Tale of Two Harbors, Wells and Saco, Maine." *Maine Policy Review*, in review.

Kelley, J. T., A. R. Kelley, and O. H. Pilkey, Sr. *Living with the Coast of Maine.* Durham: Duke University Press, 1989.

Kelley, J. T., R. C. Shipp, and D. F. Belknap, "Geomorphology and Late Quaternary Evolution of the Saco Bay Region." Pages 47–66 in *Studies in Maine Geology*, eds. R. D. Tucker and R. G. Marvinney. Maine Geological Survey, Vol. 5, 1989.

Maine State Planning Office. "A Study of Beach Processes and Management Alternatives for Saco Bay." Maine State Planning Office, Augusta, Maine, 1979.

Chapter 9. Oregon Inlet, North Carolina

Horizon Planning Group. "An Assessment of the Regional Economic Benefits of the Oregon Inlet Stabilization Project." Northeastern North Carolina Regional Economic Development Commission, 1995.

North Carolina Department of Transportation. "Transportation Impacts of Corps of Engineers Stabilization Project at Oregon Inlet." North Carolina Department of Transportation, Raleigh, N. C., March 1988.

Pilkey, Jr., O. H., W. J. Neal, O. H. Pilkey, Sr., and S. R. Riggs. *From Currituck to Calabash: Living with North Carolina's Barrier Islands*. Durham, N.C.: Duke University Press, 1978.

U.S. Army Corps of Engineers. "Final Environmental Impact Statement, Wanchese Harbor Development Project." Wilmington District, U.S. Army Corps of Engineers, Wilmington, N. C., 1977.

———. "Manteo (Shallowbag) Bay, N.C., General Design Memorandum—Phase 1 Plan Formulation (Design Memorandum 1)." Wilmington District, U.S. Army Corps of Engineers, Wilmington, N. C., 1977.

———. "Final Supplement to the Final Environmental Impact Statement: Manteo (Shallowbag) Bay Project, Dare County, North Carolina". Wilmington District, U.S. Army Corps of Engineers, Wilmington, N. C., August 1980.

———. "1990 Update of 1984 Economic Analysis: Manteo (Shallowbag) Bay Project, North Carolina". Wilmington District, U.S. Army Corps of Engineers, Wilmington, N. C., 1990.

———. "Environmental Assessment and Finding of No Significant Impact, Discharge of Dredged Material on Pea Island National Wildlife Refuge and Advanced Maintenance of the Oregon Inlet Channel, Manteo (Shallowbag) Bay Project, Dare County, North Carolina." Wilmington District, U.S. Army Corps of Engineers, Wilmington, N. C., July 1990.

———. "Manteo (Shallowbag) Bay, North Carolina: Feature Design Memorandum; Sand Bypassing (Management)." Wilmington District, U.S. Army Corps of Engineers, Wilmington, N. C., 1994.

U.S. Department of the Interior. "The U.S. Army Corps of Engineers 'Manteo (Shallowbag) Bay Project'—A Departmental Objection to the Construction of Jetties on Pea Island National Wildlife Refuge and Cape Hatteras

National Seashore at Oregon Inlet, Dare County, North Carolina." Washington, D.C., unpublished memorandum.

The "Inman Panel" Reports (listed chronologically):

Kraft, J. C., D. L. Inman, R. A. Dalrymple, R. Dolan, and W. Odum. (National Park Service Coastal Advisory Committee). "Report on the Potential Effects of the Proposed Oregon Inlet Jetties on Shore Processes along the Outer Banks of North Carolina." Report to the U.S. Department of the Interior, Manteo, N. C., 1979.

Inman, D. L., J. C. Kraft, R. A. Dalrymple, and R. Dolan. (National Park Service Coastal Advisory Committee). "Report Number Two (7 August 1980) on the Potential Effects on the Proposed Oregon Inlet Jetties on Shore Processes along the Outer Banks of North Carolina." Report to the U.S. Department of the Interior, Washington, D. C., 1980.

U.S. Department of the Interior. "The Oregon Inlet Shallowbag Bay Project: Executive Summary Reports from the Department of the Interior's Inman Committee." U.S. Department of the Interior, Washington, D. C., January 1986.

Inman, D. L., J. C. Kraft, R. A. Dalrymple, and R. Dolan. (National Park Service Coastal Advisory Committee). "Discussion of the U.S. Army Corps of Engineers Proposed Manteo (Shallowbag) Bay Project: The Stabilization of Oregon Inlet, North Carolina." Cape Hatteras National Seashore, National Park Service, U.S. Department of the Interior, Manteo, N. C., December 1987.

Dolan R., D. Aubrey, R. Dean, D. Inman, J. Miller, and J. Teal. "Review of the Corps of Engineers Plan for the Stabilization of Oregon Inlet, North Carolina." Draft Report to the Department of the Interior. Contract No. 14-16-004-91-070, Washington, D. C., December 1991.

Chapter 10. Politics, Science, and Engineering

McPhee, J. *The Control of Nature.* New York: The Noonday Press, 1989.

Shallat, T. *Structures in the Stream: Water, Science, and the Rise of the U.S. Army Corps of Engineers.* Austin: University of Texas Press, 1994.

Stick, D. *The Outer Banks of North Carolina.* Chapel Hill: The University of North Carolina Press, 1958.

Stine, J. K. *Mixing the Waters: Environment, Politics, and the Building of the Tennessee-Tombigbee Waterway.* Akron, Ohio: The University of Akron Press, 1993.

Index

About the Authors

Orrin H. Pilkey is the James B. Duke professor of geology at Duke University where he has taught and carried out marine geology research for 30 years. Prior to coming to Duke he spent three years at the University of Georgia Marine Institute on Sapelo Island, Georgia, which is where he first became interested in beaches. The first 20 years of his career Pilkey studied sediments on the continental shelves, continental rises, and Abyssal plains on the deep sea floor. The destruction of his parents home in Waveland, Mississippi, by Hurricane Camille in 1969 was the first event leading him back into shallow water and to the specialty of coastal geology.

In 1979 he co-authored with Wallace Kaufman, *The Beaches are Moving* (Doubleday and Duke-Press), a widely acclaimed book sounding the alarm about beach loss in America. This was followed by the 18-volume *Living with the Shore* series (published by Duke-Press), state–specific books about the hazards and problems of coastal development, edited, and sometimes co-authored by Pilkey, his father of the same name, and William J. Neal, a professor of geology at Grand Valley State University in Michigan. In recent years his often controversial research has centered on the impact of seawalls on beaches, the national beach replenishment experience, the viability of the retreat option and the validity of engineering models and design procedures on the beaches. He has received a number of awards including the Francis Shepard Medal for excellence in marine and coastal geology and recognition of his public service efforts from the American Geological Institute, the National Association of Geology Teaches, and the American Association of Petroleum Geologists. His work has been featured in a number of magazines including *The New York Times Magazine* and *Smithsonian* magazine.

Katharine L. Dixon's love of the coasts and bays of the mid-Atlantic comes from a childhood spent sailing with her parents and brother in the Chesapeake Bay and its tributaries. After graduating from the College of William and Mary, she worked as a naturalist and environmental educator for the Virginia Coast Reserve of The Nature Conservancy. Helping students and adults understand the delicate balance of the undeveloped barrier island system off Virginia's coast led her to realize how unplanned development can threaten beaches and barrier islands.

An interest in bridging the gap between coastal science and coastal management led Dixon to graduate work with Orrin Pilkey at Duke. There, Dixon gained her first real exposure to the Corps' workings on the shore through study of beach replenishment along the Gulf of Mexico.

She then worked as the coastal issues specialist for the National Wildlife Federation in Washington, D.C., where she led that organization's campaign for expansion of the Coastal Barrier Resources System and reform of federal coastal policies, particularly the National Flood Insurance Program. She returned to North Carolina out of interest in closer involvement with coastal management and environmental protection issues at the state and local level.